T0312460

Perfect Bound

Perfect Bound

A memoir of trauma, heartbreak
and the words that saved me

Lindsay Nicholson

MUDLARK

Mudlark
HarperCollins*Publishers*
1 London Bridge Street
London SE1 9GF

www.harpercollins.co.uk

HarperCollins*Publishers*
Macken House, 39/40 Mayor Street Upper
Dublin 1, D01 C9W8, Ireland

First published by Mudlark 2024

1 3 5 7 9 10 8 6 4 2

© Lindsay Nicholson 2024

Lindsay Nicholson asserts the moral right to
be identified as the author of this work

A catalogue record of this book is
available from the British Library

ISBN 978-0-00-868527-0

Printed and bound in the UK using 100%
renewable electricity at CPI Group (UK) Ltd

MIX
Paper | Supporting
responsible forestry
FSC
www.fsc.org
FSC™ C007454

This book contains FSC™ certified paper and other controlled
sources to ensure responsible forest management.

For more information visit: www.harpercollins.co.uk/green

For Cora Eleanor Potter

The more perfect a person is on the outside, the more demons they have on the inside.

Sigmund Freud

n: perfect binding: a way of making a magazine in which the pages are stuck together with glue rather than sewn or stapled together, generally used for more upmarket titles. Also known as square-backed.
adj: perfect bound

Even if they are a crowd of sorrows, who violently sweep your house empty of its furniture, still, treat each guest honourably. He may be clearing you out for some new delight.

Rumi

Contents

PROLOGUE: Standfirst

PART I: Raw Copy

PART II: Unbound

PART III: Small Achievable Promises

EPILOGUE: Proof Marks

PROLOGUE

Standfirst

A Letter from the Editor

2 January 2017 – The Lake District

The side of the HGV rears up like an iceberg. Crashing is inevitable. I will be blown apart by the force of impact, shattering into a thousand pieces. Even if I survive, I will never be the same person again. But I know I will not survive. I don't even want to. Why should I be saved when I haven't been able to save those I love?

My right foot jerks, stamping uselessly on the brake. I fling forward hard as if restrained by a seat belt, followed by a ricochet back against the headboard of my bed.

A deafening bang, the ear-splitting screech of metal on metal, then terrifying silence. There is a man lying in the road who I assume is dead. I open my eyes, sit up in bed, snapping on the lights; he is still there in my peripheral vision, on the floor of my hotel room. If I was asleep before – and I don't think I was – I am wide awake now. But the living nightmare spools on. I smell petrol, mingling with the damp grass on the central reservation of the dual carriageway, and burning rubber as the cars behind me skid to a halt. Although some part of me understands that none of this is real, that knowledge alone is not enough to halt the hallucinations, a dystopian vision of carnage invading this country house hotel. I shrink back in horror as the roses on the wallpaper melt, red gore dripping down the walls.

I hear screams, heart-rending cries of pain and despair, even more shocking when I realise they are coming from me. I can't seem to silence them, so I bury my face in the pillow trying not to disturb the other hotel guests.

My heart bangs in my chest; I struggle to breathe. The harder I try to resist the ghosts of my past life crowding around me, the more insistent they become, begging me to pay attention to them. I brace my body against their onslaught only to feel the bed bucking and rocking underneath me as if in the grip of demonic possession. I cling on tight to stop myself being flung to the floor.

And, this is how, crouching in a kneeling position, both hands clamped onto the headboard, my face buried in the pillows, I pass the endless hours until morning.

Daylight mercifully chases away the terrors. It doesn't occur to me to call for help – or even tell anyone what I have gone through. This is not the first time I have spent such a night, although I don't usually experience flashbacks of such intensity – not just the sights but the sounds and even the smells. I am fairly sure I am losing my mind – but I will think about that later. Right now, I need to focus on the task of how to get home. There really was a crash yesterday evening, the second one in just over two months, and my car is stranded – undriveable – half in and half out of a ditch near the hotel, where I am staying overnight to break the solo drive back from Scotland. I ring the AA and give them my details. Yes, I say, a lone woman with two dogs. I wait for them to arrive.

A short time later my husband finally responds to the panicky text I sent him the night before. I tell him I am making the 250-mile journey home on an AA truck. He says he has only just picked up my message. He is on the south coast, cold-water training and sharing a room with Nick, a fellow open-water swimmer. He turned his phone off so as not to disturb his companion. I think that makes sense – especially as he is waiting to help me, full of concern, when I finally arrive home with my dogs at 10 p.m. that night. I am clearly in shock, not thinking straight, I tell myself.

Deep down I know there is something terribly wrong with my brain, my life, or my marriage. I don't know which, maybe it's all three, but in any case, I refuse to look too closely. So, in the morning, I do what I always do, what I have done whenever my home life becomes too complicated to endure. I go to work. For more than two decades, I have edited some of the most famous magazines in Britain: planning the content, commissioning writers, directing photographers, approving the layouts and checking proofs. I write many of the headlines and standfirsts – the paragraph in bold type directly under the headline explaining what is to come. Sometimes I contribute an article as well if deadlines allow. But there are two jobs I never delegate. I always write the coverlines myself, the most important 50 or so words for any magazine. And every one of the hundreds of editions I produced opened with a 'letter from the editor', a personal message from me to millions of readers, usually recounting an incident from my own life, to set the tone for the issue. It was invariably upbeat, so I never relayed this story, the one I am about to tell you, because it took me years to process. That night in the hotel in the Lake District I had no idea what was happening. I didn't know that my successful, perfectly bound life was about to unravel so fast it would make your head spin.

Two months earlier, 30 October 2016 – Essex

It is Sunday evening, dark, the night before Hallowe'en. I am driving the route I have taken many times from visiting my mother but now want to get home in time to have dinner and prepare for a busy week ahead, working at the job I adore. My career has spanned many well-known magazines – *Cosmopolitan*, *Esquire*, *Honey*, *She*, *Prima* – but *Good Housekeeping* is my pride and joy. Bringing this grand old lady into the twenty-first century is how I made my name and my reputation, granting me access to A-listers, front-row seats at fashion shows, interviews with politicians and royals. On my watch it has become the biggest-selling lifestyle magazine in Britain.

The road is smooth and dry, not too much traffic. Forty minutes earlier, I put the bigger of my two dogs, Belle, in the back of the car. My mother kissed me goodbye, telling me not to worry about Scarlet, still a puppy, who can't be looked after by our regular dog-walker while I am at work. We had whiled away the afternoon, drinking tea and chatting in the easy way we have always done, until I realised that I needed to leave to get home in time for supper with my husband, who stayed at home to watch the football on TV.

The first half-hour of my journey takes me along narrow country lanes. I grew up in this part of Essex, a finger of agricultural land sandwiched between the rivers Crouch and Blackwater. Although the towns of Southend and Colchester are only a few miles away in either direction as the crow flies, there are no bridges over the rivers that form this peninsula. Laborious road journeys and infrequent public transport have left this part of the county largely untouched by the East End overspill that dominates much of the county. Here, the arable fields stretch for thousands of acres, as flat as the Netherlands, which is just 100 miles to the east across the North Sea; only wind turbines puncture the overarching sky. In Anglo-Saxon times it was known as the Dengie Hundred; the name persists but now those of us who hail from there refer to it simply as the Dengie.

The car radio tuned to Magic FM is playing Cockney Rebel – that was our music growing up. With my schoolfriend Christina, I went to see them in concert when I was just a Judy Teen myself, wearing a black charity shop dress; I thought Steve Harley was singing directly to me. Now in middle age, married to my second husband for 12 years, in a job I adore, my daughter embarking on the career of her choice, my life stretches out before me in an orderly way – straight and smooth as the dual carriage I merge onto, the Southend Arterial which bleeds from Essex into London. I sing along to the radio as I drive, not registering that the song is about betrayal.

Belle lies quiet in her crate in the boot of the car.

I overtake a lorry and see another lorry up ahead, which I will go past in plenty of time before the slip road for the M25. I have had a clean licence for decades now, but even so, I drive as if I have an instructor next to me narrating the driving conditions. Not for me the speeding tickets or bus lane infringements of more confident drivers; I am travelling – as is usual on this familiar road – at a steady 69 mph.

Then without warning, the very rules that govern the universe are upended. The lorry in front has crossed into my lane. He has not simply pulled out in front of me: the cab – and this is bizarre – is at right angles to the road. I watch from a place outside myself as the container slides around behind the cab in a wide balletic arc.

Time really does slow almost to a standstill. Reality is suspended. My first reaction is not fear but incredulity as my slo-mo brain brings up the scene from *Fantasia* with the hippos dancing. In the rear-view mirror I see the cars behind sliding slowly towards me, towards each other. Nothing is where it should be.

An image from my driving test more than 30 years previously pops into my head. The examiner, like a walrus in a brown raincoat, smacking his clipboard against the windscreen to indicate an emergency stop.

I stamp on the brake, holding tight to the steering wheel. Don't steer while you're braking, says the driving instructor/narrator in my head.

Foot off brake. Steer onto central reservation. Brake again.

I take my foot off the brake and the car mounts the grass verge dividing the carriageways. Brake again. The giant side of the lorry fills the windscreen. I will either smash headlong into it or flip over onto the opposite carriageway into the path of oncoming traffic. Brake. Release. Steer again.

The impact, when it comes, is almost a relief.

Am I alive? I don't actually know.

I brace for the moment as the car behind crashes into me. But it doesn't come.

Turn the ignition off. The car might still explode. I open the driver's door and scramble out. I can smell the crushed grass beneath my feet. Does that mean I'm alive?

The carriageway looks like a vision of hell. The lorry is straddling across both lanes. All around, cars are scattered like Tonka toys, drivers and passengers spilling out of them disoriented, stumbling about like zombies. Horns blare. There is shouting some way off. The driver of the lorry, a tall thin man with a navy cap on his head, stands shoulders hunched by his vehicle and places his hands over his eyes. His mate, broader, not quite so tall, stands protectively beside him talking in an Eastern European language. Ahead of us the road is empty, all those other drivers rushing to their destinations, oblivious of the carnage they missed by milliseconds. And there on the carriageway about 20 metres in front of the broken lorry lies the body of a man. I can't work out where he has come from. It looks as if he has fallen from the sky.

Where is his car? There isn't one. Is he a motorcyclist? No motorbike either. Or helmet. A pedestrian? But this is a dual carriageway with no pavements, nothing but trees on either side. I think he must be dead but then he moves, groans.

I have absolutely no idea what is happening. I think, perhaps, I'm the one who is dead.

I must call my husband and let him know.

I get out my phone but my fingers are numb and I can't seem to operate it.

The driver from a car behind takes it out of my hand, slides the screen to camera and starts photographing the front of my car crumpled underneath the wheel of the lorry. I will need the pictures for the insurance claim he tells me.

Belle!

I run to the back of the car and she is trembling but unharmed in her travel crate. I think about getting her out but there are cars manoeuvring all around and she seems safer where she is. I don't think there will be an explosion now.

A woman in a hi-vis jacket, with long, un-brushed hair, pushes through.

'Off-duty Met officer. Emergency services are on their way.'

She stops by me.

'BMW driver?'

I start to say something. I have no idea what.

'Stop talking. You're in shock. Go and sit down over there.'

Obediently, I go and sit by the side of the road. Gradually people from the other cars come and join me. We are lined up on the hard shoulder. I suspect we may all be dead. Everyone dies. I have been waiting for this moment for 18 years. This is almost certainly what the after-life will be like – a queue of dazed souls waiting to tell their tale to St Peter at the Pearly Gates.

As if on cue, the angels arrive. Hell's Angels weaving their motorcycles through the scattered vehicles. Stopping to proffer advice. Clearing a path for two police cars and an ambulance.

Hell's Angels are old these days. One with a long, grizzled beard and a grey plait escaping from under his old-style helmet pulls up by me.

'Take it easy love. They won't get to you for a while. They talk to the people who can get away first. He points at the lorry driver. He's in for the night.'

My fingers eventually start working again and I am able to open my phone and speak to my husband.

'I'll call a recovery truck for you,' he says. 'They'll bring you home and take the car on to a garage.'

An hour passes, it's getting cold. My coat is in the car. I worry about Belle but it still feels safer to leave her there. All attention is on the man in the road, who is still moving and groaning. His grey trousers are ripped and I see shabby loose underpants and pallid flesh. Braces are put around his head and neck before – infinitely slowly and ever so gently – he is lifted onto a stretcher. No one thinks to check me or the lorry driver for injuries, we are still capable of walking and talking while the man in the road hovers between life and death.

'Street lights are out here,' the grizzled Angel says. 'Be sure to tell them that. It's why they do it here. Everywhere else is too brightly lit.'

Who does what, where? And why? I still can't process what has happened. It will be at least a week before I understand that the man lying on the road attempted to take his own life by throwing himself in front of the lorry on this unlit stretch of dual carriageway. He failed because of a million to one chance. That we all – me, the lorry driver, his mate and the people in the cars behind me – survived is nothing short of a miracle. I am unable to process the conflicting facts that I have been in a head-on collision with a lorry at 69 mph and I don't have a scratch on me – physically, at any rate.

My phone rings. The recovery truck can't get to you, my husband says. Road closed in both directions. He tells me he has phoned my daughter, Hope, and she is leaving work in Oxfordshire; she will drive around the M25, going close by our house, from where I assume my husband is calling, to come and get me. It doesn't occur to me to wonder why he doesn't come and get me himself.

It's my turn to talk to the police. I sit in the patrol car, which is warm after the roadside, and littered with coffee cups and takeaway wrappers.

Name, address, date of birth, car registration. My details are radioed over to be fed into a computer somewhere else. Then I am breathalysed. I'm clear, not surprisingly – I have been drinking tea with my mother. Then there's a swab to test for drugs. Which ones I don't know. When that's clear, too, also unsurprisingly, the police officer visibly relaxes and tells me his name is Jason.

I make a statement which he writes down in clear round script.

'How are you getting home,' he asks.

'My daughter – or the recovery truck, or …' I have no idea.

'Your car is a crime scene,' he says. 'We'll need it for forensics.' I realise this is because the pedestrian is very likely to die. People who are hit by lorries usually do. The police officer suggests we walk together to my car so he can retrieve my belongings. Despite my lingering shock, I understand on a deep level that in this melee and confusion the police have to work on the basis that anyone involved could be either culprit or victim, or both. It's a distinction that will return to haunt me.

'I need to get my dog, she's in the back of my car.'

'You get her – she might be upset,'

I realise he's worried she might bite.

'But I have to get everything else.' He means so I can't tamper with evidence. It would be a physical impossibility given the relative positions of my car, the lorry and the pedestrian for me to have been the cause of the crash, but I understand the need for caution – assume nothing, that's what the police must do – even though it means the tow truck won't now arrive to take me home.

Belle jumps out of her little cell into my arms. The police officer gives me my coat, my handbag.

My phone rings. It's my daughter. The roads are gridlocked for miles, she is on her way but how does she get to me?

The policeman takes my phone out of my hand and gives her precise directions that I am still too dazed to follow. Then I get in the squad car again, in the back this time amid a pile of hi-vis jackets, because of the dog. I don't think I have ever before this night sat in a police car; I also have no idea how soon it will be before I am back in one. All I know is the now and the past – and that is bad enough. Jason drives up the empty carriageway, off down an on-ramp and to a brightly lit service station. And there he leaves me.

The dog needs a drink. I'm thirsty, too, and I need to pee badly, but I can't take the dog inside the service station where the toilets are because there is food on sale. I am a law-abiding person, so even though I have been in a head-on collision I still worry about food hygiene regulations at a service station.

Then, out of nowhere, my Angel turns up, the grizzled Hell's Angel. He holds the dog while I go to pee then buys me hot chocolate because sugar is good for shock and the woman behind the counter brings out a bowl of water for the dog and something for me to sit on.

Leaning on the handlebars of his Harley-Davidson he talks to me in calm, reassuring tones, telling me about his wife. And his dog, which is a cockerpoo, the same breed as mine. He tells me his name but I can't remember it now. I am embarrassed that I appear to be in need of care because I have always prided myself on powering through, on being strong. He refuses to leave my side until my daughter arrives, white-faced and tearful, to collect me in her little black Mini.

Hope is shattered when we get home, and goes straight to bed. My husband hugs me tight but doesn't stay up late going over the details. I understand, I am still talking like a robot. As the Met officer said – shut up, you're in shock. I will discover a lot about the effects of shock and trauma in the coming months, learning that in times of great stress blood is diverted away from the brain and other parts of the body to fuel the muscles for the classic fight or flight or for the other more obscure reactions – freeze and fawn. So it doesn't occur to me to ask why he didn't come with Hope to rescue me – or just come and get me himself?

I am Alice falling down the rabbit hole.

I take one of the sleeping tablets I have been prescribed for jet lag and by the time I wake up the next morning Mark has gone for a swim, then on to work. Hope is working a late shift today and still at home. 'Get up,' she says. 'You're going for a drive.' She puts me in the driving seat of her Mini and we drive round and round a nearly empty supermarket car park until she is satisfied that I will get my confidence back.

I call in sick for one day, explaining that I have been in a car crash and am unhurt but a bit shaken, and then on the Tuesday head into work at the usual time. The offices are in London's Soho, just off Carnaby Street; the luxury department store

Liberty is my corner shop. I have cleaved to my work through-out the darkest periods of my life. I love the camaraderie of magazines and the teamwork involved in creating something that will be read and enjoyed by one and a half million women every month. I even love the deadlines, that sense of all pulling together to create something both useful and inspiring, sending it off the press, a brief pause then doing it all over again, month in, month out. We are putting the finishing touches to the January issue of *Good Housekeeping*, which in the bizarre calendar of magazines will be on the news-stands before Christmas. Celebrity chef Jamie Oliver is our cover star, in a red sweater with a string of red and green light bulbs around his neck. I had it in mind that was the image I wanted to capture at the photoshoot back in the summer but wasn't sure how he would take to being decked in fairy lights. Naturally, as the editor, I had to be the one to broach it with him. But Jamie is easy-going and fun, we had met several times before and he trusted me not to make him look foolish. While the shot was being set up, we talked about our children and I tell him that my daughter has become a chef, which pleased him.

Most of the staff work in an open-plan space, but I have my own corner office, painted white, with an intimidatingly large desk, also white. Along the length of one wall is floor-to-ceiling shelving, just as you would find in WH Smith, with all the current British women's magazines arranged as they would be in store. On the deep window ledges are ranged the many awards I have won during my long career, twice named Editor of the Year; a life-time achievement award from the British Society of Magazine Editors; plexiglass trophies for excellence in beauty journalism and interiors photography, for creating a record-breaking website and for pioneering racial awareness in the popular media. I sit at my desk and try to write my editor's letter for January, which will inevitably be about New Year resolutions, then abandon it for a meeting with an executive visiting from our head office in New York. She is warm and friendly, we have known each other for years, but my head is ringing with the sound of tearing metal. After she departs, I close my office door and carefully position my back to the panes of glass, so I can cry without my team seeing their cool, confident boss fall apart.

The next day, Wednesday, I wake up with tears pouring down my face. I can't go to work like this – there aren't enough discreet places to weep, so I go to the GP's surgery. Dr B is young with swingy brown hair. She is very popular but only works a few days a week, so I am lucky to land an emergency appointment with her. She listens to my account of the crash and diagnoses acute post-traumatic stress disorder (PTSD), not surprising, she adds, given what happened. She explains that the normal bodily response to severe threat is the famous 'flight-or-fight' reaction. But in the modern world, after a trauma like a road traffic accident there can be no fighting or running away, both of which would help dissipate the stress hormones released by deadly peril. Instead, there is sitting by the side of the road, waiting to give your statement to the police trying to piece together what happened, and wondering why you are still alive. She tells me the current thinking is that a short course of tranquillisers will give the brain the space it needs to process the trauma and hands me a prescription.

Back home I take the Valium and lie drowsily on my bed for more than a week. I am in the past, reliving not only recent events but the deaths of those I loved years before this. And I feel something else, too: shame. I am so used to being in control that it appals me that a road accident – dramatic as it was – has brought me this low when I have survived so much that was worse.

The police close their report. The pedestrian – they tell me his real name but I am going to call him Peter Swift – spends six weeks in hospital recovering from his injuries. He is in no fit state to be prosecuted for causing the accident, nor does he have any assets for the insurance companies to go after. I assumed the BMW would be written off. One side was completely stoved in under the lorry, but the £70,000 car was nearly brand new and the insurers were convinced it could be rebuilt for less than half the replacement cost, so, technically, not a write-off. I argued with them but got nowhere. I was busy, so much to catch up with at work when I returned nine days later, and they were a reputable company – I had no reason to doubt them. The Beamer was repaired and returned to me. It looked as good as new.

CHAPTER 2

New Year, New You

Christmas 2016: Two months after the crash

It's tough keeping the editorial team motivated and their minds on spring looks and Easter baking when outside the office are the lights of Carnaby Street and throngs of Christmas shoppers. Magazines like *Good Housekeeping* work to long lead times, which meant I needed to send the March 2017 issue to press before I could finish work for Christmas. And in the digital era, it's still December on the website. My brain hurts from flipping back and forth between the spring of print and the digital festive season.

Also, I am sleeping less and less, even by my standards as some-one who has never spent much time asleep anyway. And when I do nod off the nightmares begin. My first family, the husband and child I lost two decades ago, visit me in the small hours. They are alive to me, breathing still. I both crave their touch and fear it. I wake agitated in the small hours, ashamed that I don't want to be with them. I am, above all, ashamed that I am alive, which emerges as constant irritation with the living, storms of unreason-able weeping, descending into temper tantrums. The only thing that's keeping me going is the thought that directly after celebrating Christmas at home, Mark, Hope and I will pile into the car and head to Scotland for New Year with our friends Alastair and Fiona. They were trainees on the same journalism training scheme in the West Country as my first husband John and me and we became such firm friends that, when we moved to London to pursue Fleet Street careers, we even bought flats just a few doors apart in the same north London street. Our children are of similar age and when they all started doing exams and needed somewhere to revise over the holidays away from distraction, they began renting a remote hunting lodge in Scotland and inviting others to join them. It's an eight-hour drive from our home in Hertfordshire and every year since, we have made the journey as a family, Mark and I taking turns with the driving; Hope and the dogs in the back, with all the luggage piled in the boot.

Even now, the children all grown and embarking on careers, we all still make the journey to this Scottish retreat, spending our days on long walks with the dogs or reading in companionable silence in front of an open fire. Peat-brown water gushes from the taps to fill old enamel baths; outside is a *Game of Thrones* wilderness – inside we are warm and safe from the storms. I feel cared for here, in a way I rarely feel at home now. The short break will set me up for another 12 months: 'New Year, New You', as the coverline on the current issue of *Good Housekeeping* reads.

My need to escape to the Scottish wilderness feels even more urgent this year. In the eight weeks that have passed since crashing my car on the Southend Arterial, I have been weepy and bad tempered, so I am shocked and hurt when just before Christmas Mark announces he doesn't want to go.

'You can't pull out now,' I snap. 'We can stay home next year if you like – but we're already committed this year.'

I do at least have the courtesy to ask him what he wants to do instead of going to Scotland for New Year. 'If you're suggesting Paris or Venice,' I snarl, 'then you might have a point.'

'Cold water swim training, off the south coast ...'

Mark and his passions, the latest being open-water swimming; before that it was fishing, competing in triathlons and running the London Marathon. I have my work, I don't do hobbies, and if I did there's no way any of them would involve getting in the icy sea. Spending New Year in an Airbnb with a group of people I have never met doesn't appeal.

So, on 28 December 2016, Hope and I make the 500-mile journey without Mark, in the newly repaired BMW. And it is fine. Some people might have problems about getting back to driving after such an alarming freak accident, but I am a past master at putting unpleasant thoughts out of my mind. If I don't want to think about something, then I don't. I do this so naturally and frequently that I am sometimes at a loss to understand why everyone else doesn't have this same ability. Only much, much later, after the loss of nearly everything I hold dear, do I discover this superpower is, in fact, a trauma response known as 'dissociation'. But for now, I am driving confidently and know the route well from making so many trips over the years.

My friends are surprised that Mark has not come with us. In the 12 years since our wedding they have become very fond of him. 'Do you think he's become addicted to exercise,' Alastair asks? We decide this is probably the case. We think we know all about addiction, what with Ali's long-ago breakdown due to alcohol. It doesn't occur to anyone, least of all me, that I might be addicted to work – even as I while away the wintery after-noons of this supposedly relaxing break writing a 3,000-word article for the *Daily Telegraph*.

The Lodge is in what was former Liberal-Democrat leader Charles Kennedy's parliamentary constituency and we always spent time with him before his tragic alcohol-related death in June 2015, at the age of 55. This New Year's Eve we make a pilgrimage to his grave on a hillside overlooking Loch Arkaig. Ali and Fiona know the remote location but can't give clear directions to the rest of us, so we drive there in convoy, Alastair leading the way, taking his bagpipes to lament our lost friend.

We stop the cars in Fort William where I buy yellow roses to put on the grave before setting off again in our convoy. But as we snake down the single-track roads, pulling into passing places for oncoming traffic, slowing down for sheep that make suicidal dashes into our paths, I somehow lose the rest of our party. I don't know where I took a wrong turn but I am driving endlessly round and round in a landscape of brown ferns, centu-ries-old oaks and tumble-down stone walls covered with moss and lichen.

I am alone in the car; Hope took the sleeper train yesterday evening back down south to be home in time for a New Year's Eve shift at the restaurant where she is working. The roses drip onto the empty passenger seat of the BMW. Eventually, I give up, pull off the road by a waterfall flush with melted snow and cry as I have cried every day since the crash. It has become part of my daily routine.

I cry for Charles and for all the friends and family who have died too soon. And I cry for myself because I am lost and alone on New Year's Eve. Eventually I restart the car and drive some more. I don't manage to find the grave, ending up, after driving around for what seems like hours half blinded by snow flurries, back at the lodge. Somewhere I took a wrong turn in my life – and I have no idea how to find myself again.

Two days later, I set out alone apart from the dogs on the long drive home.

The 2 January is a Bank Holiday in Scotland, so the ferry isn't running, which means I have to drive the long way around the loch, past Fort William where I fill up with fuel and buy water and a cheese sandwich that I can eat as I drive. The narrow part of the A82 takes me back through Glencoe, with its perilous drops by the side of the road. When I reach Crianlarich there are severe weather warnings on the radio, so I don't risk the usual route along Loch Lomond but take the road through Calendar instead, remembering that this is the way Mark brought me when I needed to go to hospital in Edinburgh the year I was having chemotherapy. And then I don't think any more, I need to concentrate on the road in these winter conditions. At Stirling, I join the motorway system that takes me down through Ayrshire, then into England and the M6.

The dogs are quiet in their crates in the back. They travel well this way, even Belle who, like me, shows no apparent after-effects of the crash.

It is raining now and the windscreen wipers are going double speed. Am I nervous? I don't think so. The car feels as good as new. I pull into the middle lane of the motorway to overtake lorries, unafraid that they will swerve in front of me. The lorry that hit me wasn't pulling out, it wasn't driver error – but a freak accident caused by an attempted suicide. What are the chances of that happening again? I push from my mind the one in a million occurrences that have already happened in my life, deciding that whatever Mark's reasons for refusing to accompany me, making this trip on my own has been good for me.

At junction 40, I leave the motorway and nose the car along the winding lanes towards Grasmere where I have booked a room to spend the night, because it would not be safe to do the whole 10-hour drive in one day. It is pitch dark with no street lighting as I negotiate the last bends before arriving in the hotel car park.

I flick the indicator prior to turning into a narrow side road, my mind jumping ahead to the country house hotel which looked so welcoming on the website. I am thinking of a hot bath, maybe, no definitely, a glass of wine ... Except I don't. Instead of obediently taking the corner, the giant German car thunders onwards. I wrestle with the steering wheel but nothing happens. Oh no, please God, not again. Here I am in the driving seat and once more unable to avert disaster. I stamp on the brake as I did in the crash only weeks before and come to a halt skewed across the lane.

I think I must be imagining things. I turn off the engine and then restart it. The expensive car is so sound-proofed that I need to wind down the window to hear the purr of the six cylinder engine. I try again to turn into the driveway but the car goes straight forwards half into a ditch.

I can't turn the steering wheel.

A young couple drive up behind me, waiting to get into the car park. I get out and explain my problem. 'I think the steering may have gone,' I say. 'I was in a crash a few weeks ago, it was supposed to be mended but ...'

The man gets in the driving seat and tries to steer. He can't manage it either. No one can get in or out of the car park.

Somehow the couple and I push the heavy car clear of the entrance, leaving it skewed even more in the ditch.

I thank them profusely and send a panicky text to Mark saying that I have broken down. What should I do? Can he give me the number for the AA? My brain is working so slowly, it doesn't occur to me to look it up online. But my husband will come to my rescue, it's what he has always done in the past. It's why I married him. While I wait for his reply, I check into the hotel and explain why my car is partially blocking their car park. I am outwardly calm and when I see the young couple on their way to dinner, I offer to buy them a drink to thank them for their help, but they demur. I can't go into the restaurant with the dogs, so I sit in the bar to eat supper and wait for my husband to respond.

I wonder if Mark will offer to drive up to the Lakes to help me? That would be like him, I decide. The man who saved me from the loneliness and despair after the deaths of my first husband and eldest child would definitely do that. And the Lake District is one of our special places – only a few weeks earlier we had a mini-break there so he could swim in Lake Windermere. Afterwards we shared a massage in our room and sat in the outdoor Jacuzzi drinking champagne with the snow falling on our naked shoulders. Before making our way to the restaurant we asked a waiter to take a photo of us, arms entwined around each other sitting beside a Christmas tree; it is the screensaver on my phone. Of course he will come and get me.

I ring Hope. She is worried but relieved I am safe. My mother calls to find out how the journey is going and is distressed to hear about the steering failure: 'What if it had happened on the motorway, or driving through Glencoe?'

'I know,' I say. 'But what didn't happen, didn't happen.' Fiona rings. Other friends call. A second potentially fatal car crash in two months, what is happening to me?

I need to be practical and work out what to do about the car, but I can't seem to find the number for the AA. I decide to think about it in the morning and try to sleep. And that's when the horrors begin in earnest, as the walls of my hotel room run red with the blood of my lost family, and I bury my face in the pillows to muffle my screams of despair.

Later it will emerge that after the Southend Arterial crash there was, despite the approved repairs, a deep fracture in the body of the BMW. An undetectable fault line meant the steering was liable to fail at any moment – as it did on the drive back from Scotland. It takes me much longer to understand that running through my perfectly bound life there has been another undetectable fault line obscured by work, success and, yes, love, which chose the exact same moment to give way.

Within one year of that Southend Arterial crash, 10 months after the steering failure, I will lose my home, my career, my marriage and my reputation. But I don't know that yet. All I know is that I am alive – and I am not sure I have any right to be.

PART I

Raw Copy

CHAPTER 3

Saddle-Stitched

7 August 1992, 24 years earlier – North London

It's my birthday and John, my husband, brings me a cup of tea in bed because three-year-old Ellie has woken us up early, in the way that toddlers do. I am pregnant again and suffering badly from morning sickness. We have been married 11 years and are still deeply in love and committed to our growing family. John and I met on our first day working as journalists. I never cared much for hard news and went into magazines. John was, right from the start, a ruthless investigator. His colleague, the veteran journalist David Randall, would later dedicate his book *The Universal Journalist* to John, calling him 'the best reporter I ever met'. I'll quote him here to show it wasn't just me who thought John was exceptional.

This slim, sharp-faced young man had every virtue, and most of the vices, needed in a great reporter. The first thing that struck me about John, even before I realised he was a great reporter, was that people liked him. He was open-looking and he could be funny, but the reason people warmed to him was because he was interested in them and showed it with his outgoing nature. This did not mean he toured the world with a fixed grin on his face, oozing phoney friendship, greeting people like a game show host. But the ability to strike up relationships with perfect strangers was of recurring assistance to him. With rough and ready types (like fellow journalists) he could drink, smoke and swear and with bishops he could drink tea and talk theology. Whatever he thought of people, he could be easy with them and make them feel at ease with him.

But nearly two years previously John had been diagnosed with the blood cancer, leukaemia. In between rounds of chemo at the Hammersmith Hospital he has carried on working full-time at *The Observer* newspaper where he is chief reporter. We have been living with this illness for so long that we have come to think it will always be like this. His red-gold hair has grown back from his last bout of chemo and he looks well and healthy enough, although his blood counts remained worryingly low. A few days earlier I was outside my own office at *Woman* magazine on London's South Bank when a car drew up and the most handsome man I had ever seen walked over and kissed me: my husband. John had been to lunch with Alastair in Fleet Street and was returning to his own office. We stood and snogged in the street like a couple of teenagers.

As I drink my tea John says: 'I don't think I'll live to see this new baby.'

Stricken I can think of nothing to say, so there is silence until he adds: 'You'd better get up now if you want a lift to work?'

Relieved, I laugh. 'You can't say you're going to die and then offer to drive me to work. One or other, but not both.'

A few days later, I am woken in the small hours by the sound of groaning and thrashing around. John appears to be in terrible pain but refuses to go to the hospital; he hated the feeling of vulnerability and always held off as long as possible. It's a Sunday night; he was at work on the Saturday as usual, covering the murder of a young woman, Rachel Nickell, on Wimbledon Common where she had been walking with her dog and two-year-old child. Her body was discovered by passers-by who found her baby son repeatedly crying: 'Wake up, Mummy.' He didn't arrive home until the small hours and so we spent Sunday with my parents, who kept three-year-old Ellie to stay with them for a few days to give us a break.

I struggle getting John into the car. He keeps falling down and I am not strong enough to bear his weight. Eventually I get him onto the back seat and drive fast through the night streets, swerving into the ambulance bay of the Hammersmith Hospital, rather than hunting for a parking space – this isn't the first time in the course of his illness we have been on this particular rodeo. When I try to help John out of the car, he falls on me again pinning me underneath him on the rain-lashed tarmac. Medics hearing the commotion run to our aid, calling in that overly relaxed tone professionals use when they know the situation is grave: 'Are you all right, John? What are you doing down there?'

I stay with him while he is examined. The pain is being caused by a massive internal bleed that seems unstoppable. Bags of blood are produced for an emergency transfusion. I sit by his bed until dawn starts to break. John is dozing; the morphine is finally doing its job and the pain seems to have eased, so I walk down to the chapel to say a prayer – my complex on-off relationship with the Catholicism of my upbringing having surfaced, unsurprisingly, in the past months. Then I buy an armful of newspapers in the hospital shop, from which I plan to read out loud to John when he wakes. This being what we do during his frequent hospital stays.

As I walk back to his bedside John looks up at me and smiles. I remember being struck once more by how blue his eyes are, like Ellie's. Then, as if in slow motion, I see what I hadn't taken in before, that there are doctors and nurses running and flinging back curtains and bringing the crash trolley. A nurse grabs me and pulls me backwards. I keep my eyes locked on John's. 'I love you,' I call out. John can no longer speak but he holds my gaze with his piercing blue eyes as I am pulled out of sight.

A pregnant widow is a walking contradiction: literally full of life yet mourning the reason for the life within her. There was little in the way of grief counselling in the nineties and no understanding of PTSD in the civilian population. I am 36 years old and I have absolutely no idea how to deal with this, how to live my life and support my children, one as yet unborn who will never know her father. So, one week after the funeral ... I do the only thing I can think of and go back to work at *Woman*, the weekly magazine where I am assistant editor.

The editor at the time, David Durman, ran an idiosyncratic, creative and demanding team, which gave me no time to think of what I had lost. The legendary rivalry between *Woman* and *Woman's Own* had been going on since they launched in the boom magazine era between the two World Wars. Both magazines were owned by the same company, IPC, with *Woman's Own* traditionally the bigger seller and *Woman* usually just a fraction behind. Under David's direction, *Woman* had edged ahead for the first time. The competition between the two titles remained intense and was encouraged by our bosses as being good for business. At the time, each magazine sold in the region of a million copies a week – today it is just a fraction of that – and the most popular cover stars were from the soaps. *EastEnders, Coronation Street, Neighbours* and *Home & Away* had taken over from Hollywood celebrities like Elizabeth Taylor who now seemed distant and out of touch. The greatest, most eternal cover star of all was still Princess Diana, who was not only an icon but also a reader. Just before her marriage to Prince Charles she had been spotted buying a copy of *Woman's Own* and a tube of sweets from a corner shop.

To the casual reader it might have appeared that these two magazines, separated by one floor in King's Reach (now South Bank) Tower on London's South Bank, might be cynically taking turns in featuring the so-called scoops of soap opera weddings, divorces and new babies. In fact, we operated not only independently but with such fierce rivalry that every week we each secretly registered our cover scoop with the managing director, who would police the scoops to make sure there was no foul play. On the strength of a hot tip from an agent, one of us would run up the back stairs – to take the lift was to risk getting caught with someone from *Woman's Own* – and slap down a hastily typewritten memo staking our claim to Angie, Den, Deidre, Kylie, Jason or whoever.

Even though male editors of women's magazines have never been as rare as you might imagine, David stood out in the corporate world, with blond hair skimming the collars of his colourful roll-neck sweaters, perpetually puffing on those narrow brown cigarettes called More. His tongue could be savage, his sense of humour gross – I recall a doughnut-eating contest during a high-level editorial meeting, which he won by stuffing a whole pastry in his mouth – but his commitment to quality was remorseless. He may not have lived the life of our female readers but he adored them, venerated them even. Everything he did was to make the magazine better for them. I was frequently told to rewrite even the most anodyne feature. Once he complimented me on a great piece of copy, although when I looked at the proof I did not recognise even one word as mine.

'You totally rewrote it,' I protested.

'Of course,' he replied. 'But you gave me the idea as to *how* to rewrite it!'

Which is probably still the best description of the editing process, I have ever heard.

But he was also very kind. On my first day back in the office, David took me out to lunch and asked straightforwardly between chain-smoking More cigarettes and sipping wine to what extent I wanted allowances to be made for me.

'I don't,' I said. 'Work is a blessed escape from the reality of my life.' And that's how it was to be. In truth, I feared for what kind of mother I would have become if I were cooped up at home with two tiny children, no money and no career prospects and just the endless lonely hours to dwell on the loss of a husband and father. So, I carried on directing photo shoots, writing copy that David inevitably rewrote, and taking the back stairs two at a time to assert our rights to soap opera exclusives. After Hope was born, I took 20 weeks maternity leave, which was generous in the nineties, and went back to work, expressing breast milk in the fashion cupboard and storing it in a cool bag until I got home. I wasn't doing it for the money. In fact, I was so badly paid that if my income hadn't been topped up by a small pension from John's employers, I couldn't have afforded childcare, so wouldn't have been able to work at all. But I loved it.

There was no part-time working, no working from home, just 10-hour days and the joy of not having to think about the aching sadness of John not being around until I got home to my new baby and four-year-old daughter, who were even more distracting. Late at night, after the children were in bed, I cleaned the house from top to bottom because I couldn't afford both childcare and a cleaner. And, also, because exhausting myself was the only way to force myself to sleep, when I knew the nightmares would arrive. I dreamed every night of John trapped in the desert – as a war correspondent he had spent a great deal of time in the Middle East. My sleep was shattered by images of him buried under a mound of sand, calling to me to help him. However hard I scrabbled through the dirt I could never reach him. When I finally shook myself awake, I was grateful to begin another day of distractions.

While I was at work, my girls were looked after by their adored Nanny Su but she didn't live with us. Since I didn't want – and couldn't in any case afford – babysitters to go out in the evening, the camaraderie of so many journalist friends gave me a social life during office hours. The King's Reach Tower complex housed so many titles, from the fashion glossy *Marie Claire*, through *TV Times* to *Horse & Hound*, that it was known as the Ministry of Magazines. There was a canteen in the building where – the rivalry with *Woman's Own* notwithstanding – we gossiped over egg and chips. On Fridays we walked along the South Bank for pizza or, if it was raining, congregated in a wine bar so close to the office that you didn't even need an umbrella to walk there.

I had become friends with Terry Tavner when we both worked on *Honey* magazine, on the 17th floor of the Tower. Petite, sparky, full of wicked good humour, she was a rarity in magazines at the time, being a working single parent. Her children Barry and Hanna were primary school age when their father – from whom Terry was divorced – died a year or so before she and I met. Our friendship was instantaneous and John and I were regular visitors to her home, near us in north London. When, not long into my marriage, I foolishly embarked on a short-lived affair with a colleague – something for which I carry the guilt to this day – it was to Terry's house I fled, so John could remain in our flat. And, not long after, when I came to my senses and begged John's forgiveness, Terry managed that next-to-impossible task of somehow getting us all back on an even keel again afterwards. She is the least judgmental person I have ever met. She loved John like a sister and was a rock to me after he died. Even better, she was working just down the corridor at King's Reach Tower from me as editor of *Chat* magazine. We travelled to and from work together most days and Terry's home was the weekend gathering place for everyone we knew, from neighbours and family, to our parish priest Father Anthony, and an eclectic mix of film producers, writers, actors and politicians.

It was Terry who taught me how to function as a single parent, especially that when you have young children the best way to socialise is to have people come to you. Nearly every weekend she roasted a couple of chickens with a mountain of potatoes and dished up Sunday lunch for whoever was at a loose end. She was godmother to both my girls and we spent most weekends in the warm embrace of her home.

I missed John unbearably but I was still young too, and had my own hopes, dreams, fears and ambitions. A cruel disease deprived John of his future at the age of just 35; it wasn't going to deprive me as well. Maybe I worked so hard because I was trying to have two careers, my own and the one that was cut short?

Two years after Hope was born, I was flown to the Paris offices of Gruner + Jahr, part of the Bertelsmann empire, to interview for – and ultimately be offered – the job of editor of *Prima* UK. A few years earlier, this European import had shaken up British publishing with the offer of a free dress-making pattern every month, a stroke of genius by its founder, the German-born editor and designer Axel Ganz, who noticed runway models sitting around knitting in the breaks between fashion shows. Critics claimed that by devoting space to traditional crafts like sewing, knitting and cooking *Prima* was forcing women back into the traditional role of home-makers. But I had been raised by women who made all their own clothes, and decorated their own homes, not only because that was all they could afford but because they enjoyed it. I had grown up wearing jumpers knitted by my grandmothers or standing on a chair in the kitchen while my mother hemmed a party frock she had sewn for me. I admired their craft skills but few mainstream advertisers shared my view.

Despite being a monthly magazine with extensive fashion and beauty content and printed, like a glossy magazine, on coated paper, the pages of *Prima* were stapled together – like the weeklies *Woman* and *Woman's Own*. This is known as being 'saddle-stitched' and – a bit like my own life at the time – denotes something of a rough-and-ready approach. Not at all upmarket and perfect bound. To the makers of face creams and perfumes we may as well have not existed. I decided I needed a dramatic way to get their attention and remind these potential advertisers that even the most high-powered women could be found enjoying saddle-stitched magazines.

I already knew Cherie Blair, wife of the then leader of the opposition Tony Blair, from the north London children's party circuit, and discovered that like the Fashion Week models she relaxed by knitting in what little free time she managed to eke out between working as a Queen's Counsel or very senior barrister, and as the mother of (then) three children.

In a move that infuriated the mainstream media, to whom she had consistently refused to give interviews, Cherie agreed to guest-edit the 10th anniversary edition of *Prima*. She worked diligently in her guest editor role, arriving unannounced at the office in London's Docklands, talking knowledgably with the knitting editor to design a pattern, writing an article on employment law – her legal speciality – and requesting family recipes speedy enough to cook after a day in court. She elegantly demonstrated that women weren't to be put in boxes labelled upscale or mass-market, career woman or home-maker. Within us are legions.

I arranged for her to be photographed by Anthony Crickmay, famous for glamorous fashion shoots and portraits of ballet dancers. We booked a whole day at his studio, which surprised Cherie who thought it could be done and dusted in half an hour. Always in a tearing hurry, she arrived fully made-up thinking she was camera-ready and was horrified when I made her wash it off and we started again, a process that took an hour and a half. There were tears. When he was ready to shoot, Anthony closed the set, sending everyone out of the studio. I sat in the kitchen with fashion editor Angela Kennedy and Cherie's friend Carole Caplin wondering what on earth was happening.

Eventually both Cherie and Crickers, as we called him, emerged wreathed in smiles.

We would have to wait for the film to be developed but the Polaroids were stunning. With creamy pale skin, dark hair and large expressive features, Cherie's looks were too dramatic to do her any favours in hasty paparazzi snaps, especially since her anxiety over the deluge of press attention contorted her wide, usually smiling mouth into the grimace so mercilessly exploited by cartoonists. Crickers, a true portraitist, had taken his time to uncover her warmth and intelligence and, behind all the dashing from place to place, a serenity.

As we gathered up our belongings to leave, he breathed in my ear: 'Sometimes, darling, you just have to bore them into submission!'

Guest editors were rare back then. And this was just prior to the 1997 election which turned out to be landslide win for Labour. Media interest was so intense that our wholesalers hired extra security for fear of tabloid hacks breaking into the warehouse and stealing copies of the magazine. The issue sold out on the news-stand and was featured not only on all the major news bulletins but even as a running joke on the BBC's *Have I Got News For You*. Advertisers sat up and took notice. I had fought back from the tragedy of John's death five years earlier and was being heralded as the smartest, freshest, most radical women's magazine editor in Britain. My children were thriving. I had rebuilt our lives. Against the odds we had survived. And surely lightning can only ever strike once?

15 November 1997

I am running down hospital corridors holding Ellie in my arms – she is eight years old and I am struggling to carry her, but she is unable to walk, clearly unwell and tearful. As I run, her legs bump against mine and my heart thuds in my chest. Please God, not again. Please God not again.

Earlier in the day I had been called away from a business lunch to take a phone call from the nanny. Both girls had been off school with colds, Hope, aged four, had recovered and returned to nursery school. Ellie was still not quite right and the GP suggested taking her to the local Whittington Hospital for investigations.

While Hope was growing into a rambunctious child, the image of her father with unruly red hair, and given to pairing tutus and wellington boots, Ellie remained the quiet, serious one. Pale skinned, blue-eyed with long auburn curls. She loved reading, ballet and ponies and would invent stories to keep her little sister entertained, even turning them into the little books that she illustrated with pictures of princesses. She remembered her father and often asked me if I missed him. I would reply that she and Hope were each half of him and because I had them both, it was like still having him. I believed that, too.

Just as with John, there are blood tests. And just as with John when Ellie herself was only a toddler, we enter an alternative universe. I don't believe this can be happening again. Ellie is transferred from our local hospital to Great Ormond Street where the doctors are nearly as panicky as me. Could there be any cause, they keep asking, any reason why her blood counts are so low? Had she, for instance, been near any industrial chemicals. Absurd as it sounds, even the doctors were clinging to the outlandish view that a primary school child had been dabbling in carcinogens rather than the truth that both father and daughter suffered from the same rare blood cancer.

I dare not leave Ellie's side. Hope is collected from Terry's house by my mother and goes to stay with her in Essex. When the days and weeks that Ellie stays in hospital turn into months she starts attending the school next door where my mother is a teacher. In the eight months she went there, Hope never stopped wearing the uniform of her original north London school.

Eventually a new and awful routine asserts itself. Ellie is nursed on a ward of individual rooms fitted out for children with compromised immunity. I stay with her. My deputy on *Prima*, Louise Court, is more than capable in my absence and will go on to become one of the longest-serving editors of *Cosmopolitan*. Her relaxed competence means she is generous to me, keeping in touch via phone, pager and fax, this being before digital communications, and allowing me to feel like I am still in charge while she does all the hard work.

At weekends my mother brings Hope to the hospital for a visit and the three of us sleep in the little room on Fox Ward, ordering takeaway food and watching cartoons. We get to know the other children on the ward too, all of them suffering from blood cancers. They join in games, racing up and down the corridors – like regular children except they have bald heads from the chemotherapy – towing behind them the obligatory drip stands delivering medications or plasma. When my mother comes to collect her to return to Essex, Hope takes with her the cardigan I have been wearing all week because it smells of me. It breaks my heart not to be able to cut myself in two and be with both my children. What keeps me going is the belief that Ellie will pull through and life will get back to normal. Leukaemia is so much more treatable in children and surely fate couldn't be this cruel as to take my child from me as well as my husband?

It turns out there is no limit to the cruelty that life can inflict.

CHAPTER 4

Triumph Over Tragedy

July 1998

Just two weeks after Ellie's funeral, I went back to work at *Prima*. I didn't know what else to do. If staying at home after John died had seemed intolerable, the thought of being alone in the house all day while Hope, then five years old, was at school was frankly terrifying. Losing myself in work for 10 hours a day seemed the only way to survive – and, most importantly, to be any sort of parent to Hope, who was understandably traumatised by the death of her beloved older sister.

Only the intensity of my creative output could prevent me from sinking to the depths of my grief. Desperate not to allow my mind time to dwell on my darling Ellie, I launched two more magazines, a parenting title called *Prima Baby* and an interiors magazine, *Your Home*. In 1999, one year after Ellie's death, I was named Editor of the Year by the Professional Publishers Association (PPA) and headhunted to become editor of one of the oldest, most famous and beloved magazines in Britain.

*   *   *

The American version of *Good Housekeeping* began in 1885 and took its inspiration from the pioneering families of the Midwest, describing its mission as 'to produce and perpetuate perfection – or as near unto perfection as may be attained in the household'. In 1922, its owner, the legendary publisher Randolph Hearst – immortalised by Orson Welles in *Citizen Kane* – decided to export his flagship magazine to the UK. Although he personally oversaw the early editions of *Good Housekeeping*, he was happy to permit the British edition to develop its own identity. The first editor was a man, James Young McPeake, who set out the magazine's mission in his inaugural editor's letter:

The burning questions of the day will be reflected each month in articles by women in the public eye, known for their sound grasp of their subject – by women who can lead women and who are fearless, frank and outspoken.

McPeake's editorship was cut short two years later when he died unexpectedly. His place was taken by his young assistant, Alice Head, who was modern and fearless and had even more radical views than the magazine's founder. I was later to meet Alice's great niece, who told me her great aunt always wore a hat to the office and a diamond brooch of such dimensions that – she said – a robber would never guess it was real. Alice was the Anna Wintour of her day and she went on to become managing director of the company – so unusual for a woman that she wrote a book about her experiences, titled: *It Should Never Have Happened*, and edited *Good Housekeeping* for 17 years, making her its longest-serving editor … until I beat her record by one year.

Alice Head set up the Good Housekeeping Institute in London, following the model in New York, testing and rating the domestic appliances that were flooding onto the market and enabling middle-class women to manage their own homes for the first time. But she tempered this domestic advice with articles by novelist Virginia Woolf, politician Violet Bonham Carter (grandmother of actress Helena) and Millicent Fawcett, a feminist at the forefront of the fight for votes for women. Nothing was off-limits, topics included: Should Wives Have Wages, Some Questions on Divorce, and as early as 1927, Sex and the Single Woman. The magazine covers were always charming illustrations, often of children or pets, which along with the comforting logo concealed the ground-breaking articles inside. Under Alice's capable stewardship, and that of the indomitable women who followed her, *Good Housekeeping* became the pre-eminent glossy magazine for British women. And by the outbreak of the Second World War, it was deemed so vital to the public's morale that heavily rationed paper supplies were made available so it could still be printed, albeit in a smaller format later popularised by *Glamour* magazine. Fearful of bombing raids, the editorial team de-camped from the London offices to produce their unique mix of recipes, fashion illustration and fine writing from St Donat's, a castle owned by Randolph Hearst on the Atlantic coast of Wales.

As the twentieth century was drawing to a close, however, the winds of feminism had blown the very words 'good housekeeping' so far out of favour that it seemed inconceivable the magazine could ever regain its former levels of popularity. So when the editorship fell vacant in the last year of the twentieth century, the appointment of the next incumbent was the subject of frenzied speculation in media circles. Could the new editor-in-chief restore *Good Housekeeping* to its former glories, or was the title just too old-fashioned to make it into the brave new world? And then when my name was announced, there was more speculation as to why would I leave behind the huge success I had made of *Prima*, which was the bigger seller, to take on a dying magazine? I gave interviews and talked about the love my mother had had for the magazine as I was growing up. I didn't mention that saving a national treasure felt to me like possibly the only challenge big enough to blot out the darkness that threatened to engulf me.

Good Housekeeping in the late nineties seemed to have little to say to me as a single parent, struggling to provide the quality of home life my fractured family needed and deserved. I felt enraged that the lives and interests of ordinary women, the women I knew and met at the school gates every day, were so being ignored by the publishing industry. I believed I could change it.

Unlike *Prima*, which was saddle-stitched, *Good Housekeeping* was a proper glossy, by which I mean not only printed on shiny coated paper but perfect bound, its glossy pages stuck together with glue, and deriving around half its income from advertising. In the ballrooms of smart London hotels, the big cosmetics houses of Estée Lauder, Clarins, Chanel and L'Oréal hosted nightly celebrations of every new face cream or lipstick they launched. It was my task to attend as many of these as physically possible in order to buttonhole the marketing director, or better still CEO. Resplendent, in a newly acquired designer wardrobe, my hair tinted a brilliant red, and six feet tall in my Jimmy Choos, I rattled off statistics and demographics to any executive I managed to corner and, more than that, I painted a picture of who my new *Good Housekeeping* reader would be.

Every successful magazine editor has an imaginary reader, an archetype crafted from hundreds of hours of market research. For *Prima*, I created Kate, a nurse living in the Midlands with her electrician husband and two children. For *Good Housekeeping*, I invented Claire, a part-time GP living with her solicitor husband and their three children in a detached house outside a big provincial city – Bristol, Leeds or Edinburgh maybe? Away from London and the South East, there was room for two or three cars on the drive and a quarter-acre of garden, which Claire struggled to maintain, what with her job, the kids, checking up on her elderly mother, and keeping up with the friends she made back in antenatal class and at the school gates. I never knew anyone who exactly fitted the photofit of Claire; she was a composite of all the readers I met at events and who wrote, emailed and even phoned me if they liked, or didn't like, something in the magazine. Everything I put in *Good Housekeeping* was run by the fictional Claire for approval. Would Claire wear this outfit? Would she cook this recipe or did it take too long, have too many ingredients? Her life was in many respects enviable, she and her husband had a good joint income and she could treat herself to nice things, but it wasn't perfect. She worried about student loans and how to help her kids afford homes of their own when they grew up, or whether her mother-in-law's care home bills would bankrupt the family first. And she would quite like to lose the half stone that seemed to have settled around her waist since she became peri-menopausal. Claire didn't aspire to be a domestic goddess, just to do her best by her family as she struggled to maintain her career and carve out time for herself. Claire's interests were my concern, her concerns were my obsessions. More than that – Claire was my avatar, she had the life I might have had if fate had treated me differently. I created for her a virtual world that I would have liked to inhabit, and it turned out that one and a half million women felt the same way, turning to the magazine every month for advice, inspiration and entertainment.

Above all, and just like me, Claire didn't have enough hours in her day. The Equal Pay Act and the Sex Discrimination Act in the 1970s had paved the way for women, mothers in particular, to work outside the home. Before that it was commonplace for a woman to be required to give up her job on getting married, and maternity rights and benefits were non-existent. By the turn of the twenty-first century, more women worked outside the home than inside, exploring not only the freedom offered by the new legal protections but also aware that the increasing rates of divorce might mean that marriage was not for life. Social norms, however, were harder to change. My situation was extreme as a single parent, but many women – even those with desirable careers and loving husbands – were working the double-shift with a demanding job by day while taking the lion's share of the responsibility in the home.

I commissioned focus groups and ran surveys which revealed that two out of every three working mothers said they *never* had any time just for themselves and that a shocking one in seven Claires had felt so tired as to be suicidal. I will never forget one reader in a focus group asking: 'If I am doing a pile of ironing but everyone else is out of the house and I can watch what I want on TV while I do it ... Does that count as time for me?'

I launched a campaign called Time For You, appearing on TV programmes and writing newspaper articles calling for the right to ask for flexible working and questioning the inequity of those fathers who claimed not to be able to work the washing machine and referred to looking after their own children as 'babysitting'. Shirley Conran, the hugely successful writer and campaigner who first highlighted the double-shift back in the seventies, got in touch to congratulate me, calling me her natural successor to her unofficial title of Superwoman. The societal change necessary is not complete, yet, of course. I know of so many women still struggling to carve out time for themselves after working and raising children. The rate of progress is glacial.

Editing a glossy magazine in the noughties was what has now become known as a 'greedy job' – one that expects more than can reasonably be given by someone who has a real life to live outside, let alone a single mother. But men had been expected to work like that for decades and women were still rare enough at senior levels simply to be grateful for the opportunity to do likewise and not make a fuss. We called it 'having it all'. So many of my female friends' careers had stalled after they were fired, made redundant or simply edged out when they had their families. As the sole earner for myself and Hope I was intensely grateful for my glamorous, if exhausting, life. I was also greedy for the emotional validation as well as the financial rewards that work offered me. Looking back this was a form of addiction – workaholism – and deeply unfair on Hope who was at primary school, struggling with a form of dyslexia caused by trauma and more usually seen in child refugees.

I took her to see a child psychologist – whom she hated – and we started spending weekends in Essex near my mother and brothers and their families; I acquired a little pony, who helped build Hope's confidence. Astride Rose, Hope learned to read, at last, from the letters that demarcate a dressage arena. From Friday evening, when I left the office as soon as the week's sales figures had been circulated, until Monday morning, when I went back to begin the whole round of insane busyness again, Hope was the sole focus of my life.

Good Housekeeping's circulation began to soar. Taking inspiration from my predecessor Alice Head I explored domestic abuse, commissioned articles on pensions, hitherto confined to the financial pages of the newspapers, and put the word 'menopause' on the cover, causing fainting fits among the ad sales teams. At the time – and this was only 20 years ago – the belief among advertisers of luxury and designer goods was that after the age of 35, women happily settled for a perm and a pair of elasticated waist trousers and showed no inclination to experiment with new brands and products so weren't worth aiming advertising at. I was in my early 40s at the time and knew from myself and my friends that this was far from being the case. But you can't say 40-plus woman to an advertiser, let alone use the phrase middle-aged, or they will take flight. So I christened my readers Grown Up Women and to underscore the point defied the convention governing cover stars which decreed they should be young and white by offering Oprah Winfrey, then aged 47, what was to be her first UK cover and produced yet another blockbuster issue on the news-stands.

I travelled to Paris for the Women in Science Awards sponsored by L'Oréal and UNESCO and recognised that *Good Housekeeping*'s readership probably numbered a great many women like me who benefited from a science education, only to give up in the face of the prevailing sexism and find work in other fields. I worked with British campaign Women in Science and hired former *Tomorrow's World* presenter Viv Parry as the first – and I think still the only – science editor of any woman's magazine.

But the investigation that earned me not so much a reprimand as stunned amazement was when I set the team to work road-testing – so to speak – sex toys. This was sparked by a conversation with Viv who told me that sex toys were being sold online to a new audience who would never have gone into a shop to buy one. But there were no safety checks or guarantees concerning the manufacture of these devices, which after all would be placed on or near very intimate parts of a woman's anatomy. Unregulated consumer products were, to my way of thinking, core territory for *Good Housekeeping* to investigate. We already called out washing machines that didn't remove the stains properly and ovens that burned the fairy cakes, and what could be more essential than investigating vibrators that were unsafe or simply didn't do the job they were intended to do? Along with the ratings on different models, Viv's research uncovered the fact that they were originally medical devices administered to women suffering from 'hysteria', which was itself ascribed to 'wandering womb'. Edwardian women were treated for a wide range of symptoms from grief after miscarriage to sexual trauma by doctors wielding vibrators. Appalling – and only 100 years ago.

Naturally, I didn't bother forewarning my bosses, working as always, even when Cherie guest-edited *Prima*, on the basis that it was better to beg forgiveness than to ask permission. It sounds almost unbelievable now but prior to the 1997 election when Labour won by a landslide, women were not generally assumed to be interested in politics and most magazines steered clear of the subject. My German bosses were appalled when they discovered what I had done just before the magazine went to press, until the sales figures soothed their anxiety. The Hearst Corporation is wholly owned by the Hearst family who remain as interested in their magazine titles as when Randolph Hearst oversaw the launch of British GH. They knew, of course, of my reputation for breaking taboos – it was why they hired me – but even so there was a stunned silence from the Hearst Tower on 57th Street to reports of the vibrators escapade. Shortly before the issue went on sale, I received a call from my opposite number, Ellen Levine, editor-in-chief of American *Good Housekeeping* magazine, who came right out with what they were saying in the boardroom: 'This might just be a hoax but we're hearing something we can't quite believe ...'

Good Housekeeping's market position and sensibility in the US had remained very different from the UK – divided by a common language, Ellen and I agreed. Her pioneer-inspired, apple pie baking brand was still a national treasure in the US and my more feminist and edgy Brit version was equally beloved in the UK. Our bosses never interfered all the time we were making them money, which we were. Ellen and I became firm friends. After that we chatted by phone most Fridays, late afternoon for me before she went to lunch at the Manhattan media watering hole Michael's. When she came to the UK, I took her to visit the Hampshire cottage where Jane Austen wrote her novels. She invited me back to stay at the upstate New York ranch where she spent weekends. Ellen was more than a decade older than me and my secret wish was that when she eventually stepped aside I would be considered to replace her.

I longed to land a New York editorship, following in the footsteps of my idol Anna Wintour at American *Vogue*. But my feminism and risk-taking were deemed too European to play out well with the American Midwest. And, really, what I envied most about Ellen's job was not the work; I felt mine was more rewarding but that Manhattan is more welcoming to high-achieving women. Ellen lived during the week in an apartment on Madison Avenue, directly above a branch of J Crew which she was forever checking out for little gifts to send Hope. There was a doorman to take in her dry-cleaning and her office in the Hearst Tower was just a brisk trot away across Central Park. She could get a blow-dry at 8 a.m. and a manicure in 15 minutes. Meanwhile, I strap-hanged from north London on the Tube to the West End of London for up to an hour every morning and spent weekends running errands and ironing my outfits for the coming week, as well as being a mum. The annual Women of the Year lunch, where I regularly went on stage to present one of the awards, was a particular nightmare. Always on a Monday, there was a photo-call for presenters and recipients first thing, which meant every year I had the drama of trying to get my fine, fly-away hair styled early in the morning: the invisible tax of being a woman. Most London salons didn't open before 10 a.m. and operated on a luxurious, head massage and coffee-and-biscuits schedule more suited to Ladies Who Lunch. Once, I booked with a salon I hadn't tried before. The owner promised to open up early but arrived 20 minutes late to find me seething on the doorstep. My mood? His mood? Whatever was to blame, my hair looked awful by the time he'd finished pulling and tugging it into a 1950s lacquered helmet. I ran back to the office, washed all the product out under a hot tap in the ladies and dried it myself under the hand-dryer, which hardly improved matters, before hightailing it to the lunch where, under a blaze of flash bulbs, I presented an award to a female leader of the Arab Spring uprising – looking as if I had just returned from a revolution myself!

For *Good Housekeeping*'s 80th anniversary in 2002, I wanted to revisit the guest editor idea, but since Cherie's success on *Prima*, every magazine was now boasting guest editors – so how to cap my own achievement? Instead of just one guest editor, I rifled through my Filofax and created an editorial board of the most influential women I knew – a roll call of *women who lead women* for the noughties. Cherie, by now living at 10 Downing Street, was first to sign up, of course, interviewing Dame Cicely Saunders, founder of the hospice movement. Rosie Boycott, one of the founders of the feminist magazine *Spare Rib*, took charge of women's issues. Glenys Kinnock, the MEP and wife of Neil, profiled Aung San Suu Kyi who had revealed to our regular columnist Maureen Lipman that she loved to read *Good Housekeeping* whenever she could get her hands on it during her house arrest as leader of Myanmar's opposition. Ballerina Deborah Bull looked after wellbeing, with particular attention to the eating disorders linked to so-called healthy-eating fads. The fashion editor was Professor Wendy Dagworthy of the Royal College of Art. Rose Gray and Ruth Rogers of acclaimed The River Café were joined in the cookery department by Prue Leith, already famous but pre-*Great British Bake Off*. Leading neuroscientist Baroness Susan Greenfield took on the role of health editor. Interiors were the bailiwick of Kelly Hoppen. Businesswoman Nicola Horlick advised on money issues and somewhat unsurprisingly was the first to file her copy. Cabinet minister Tessa Jowell, yet to lead London's bid for the 2012 Olympics, wrote about sexism in the media. Lawyer Helena Kennedy QC wrote about women's legal rights. Jenni Murray of *Woman's Hour* contributed an article in praise of female friendship. Actress Meera Syal took over the beauty department, confessing to her love of pampering beauty treatments. Gardening was the realm of punk musician Toyah Wilcox. Sarah Ferguson, Duchess of York, reflected on the previous year's 9/11 terrorist attack on the Twin Towers, while Paralympian Tanni Grey-Thompson and round-the-world yachtswoman Clare Francis gave their own advice on making dreams come true. Actress and cake designer Jane Asher inspected the Good Housekeeping Institute on behalf of readers. Broadcaster and intrepid solo sightseer Penny Smith was travel editor. Lady Antonia Fraser wrote an exclusive short story, while the fiction editor was former home office minister – still yet to wow the nation as a *Strictly Come Dancing* star – Ann Widdecombe. I actually don't think it would have been possible to assemble such a roster of talent at any time before – or after. Many of those names, already high profile, went on to even greater heights, some are sadly no longer with us and so many are now Dames and Baronesses that for simplicity's sake I have stuck to the names and titles they were known by at the time. All donated the fees I offered to their favourite charities. Only one on my list of high-profile women didn't return my call – the leading feminist Germaine Greer, although I later heard she never received the message from a junior too terrified to relay a request from a magazine with the name *Good Housekeeping*.

The anniversary issue cover star was Twiggy in one of her first forays back into modelling since her heyday in the sixties and whom I was to feature many more times on the cover. Twiggy was old-school, bringing a wheelie bag of hairpieces, nude underwear and white tops to the shoot, as models were expected to do back in the sixties. She permitted the make-up artist to do a basic look, then took over for her eyes, spitting into block mascara to get the sooty-eyed effect she wanted. I will never forget the moment Twiggy first came on set and photographer Brian Aris invited me to look through the view-finder. If it is possible to say that an inanimate object – a camera – can fall in love with a real-live human being, that is what I saw that day. The undeniably very attractive then 52-year-old woman was transformed into a goddess when seen through a lens. She seemed to glow with the promise of what a grown-up woman could be.

Typically, glossy magazines have modest sales figures, making most of their profit from the advertising, but I managed to create in *Good Housekeeping* a perfect-bound juggernaut, selling twice as many copies every month as *Vogue*, packed with high-end advertising but with the circulation figures usually only seen in the mass-market titles. My secret was a judicious mix of aspirational fashion, interiors and beauty pages mixed with real-life stories ... Or what is known in the business as TOT, or Triumph Over Tragedy – inspirational first-person accounts by women who have overcome adversity. Not an easy combination to pull off in a luxury-ad-friendly environment – but something I knew how to do because I was living it, overcoming unthinkable tragedy to become one of the most powerful women in British magazines.

We celebrated publication day of the 80th anniversary issue with a star-studded party at the Victoria & Albert Museum. The entrance foyer to the museum was dominated by nine huge photo frames behind each of which was a live model wearing the fashions of each decade of the magazine's existence, and who were required to hold their poses for the whole evening. I arrived dressed by Vivienne Westwood, in a vintage Rolls-Royce driven by Peter, my boss Terry Mansfield's chauffeur, as if I were a bride, which in a sense I was. I was married to my work, and this was my wedding day.

CHAPTER 5

Perfect Bound

3 July 2004

I am in the back of another limo, this time wearing an ivory silk crepe wedding dress and an antique diamond tiara. Christina, my matron of honour, is on one side of me in peacock blue satin and on the other is Hope, aged 11, excited to be a bridesmaid, in a princess-style white dress, fresh flowers in her hair. Our car has got stuck behind the annual Pride march wending its way through central London and we are over an hour late. I lean forward in agitation, convinced, as always, that the sheer force of my willpower will make the traffic move faster and we can be on our way. I am getting married again, for real this time, not to my work, and I have no hesitation at all.

I have fallen deeply, passionately, head-long in love with a man I hardly know. He comes from a very different world from me – but I believe in love at first sight because it has happened to me once before, after all. Out of all the pain and grief, I have been blessed with another great romance in my life. And he is waiting for me at the altar to St Bride's Church in London's Fleet Street, the same church where John's memorial service was held 12 years earlier. Mark told me later that as he stood sweating at the altar, he was fretting I had changed my mind. But I would never do that. When I commit, I do so wholeheartedly. I am loyal to a fault. And it is only now I realise it can be just that: a fault.

We hadn't known each other long. Only the previous year, 2003, struggling to find a secondary school for Hope, I put my house on the market hoping to move to a better catchment area. I remember opening the door to the estate agent and seeing a very tall man. I am taller than the average woman at five foot eight, but at six foot three or four he towers over me. He has conker brown hair similar in colour to mine and, likewise, brown eyes. Tall, dark and with a kind face. I remember thinking: 'He seems nice, I wonder if he is single? Probably not.'

He drew up the house particulars and I gave him a set of keys for viewings while I was at work. Then I went away on a business trip – to Barbados. This was the professional life I had created by blocking out everything but work and caring for my surviving child: glamorous, exhausting … and, all too often, lonely. Since John died I had no serious relationship. But being a single working parent means no distractions, right?

Sometimes it is possible to take Hope away with me on business trips. If not, as on this occasion, my family are supportive and, in any case, I can afford to pay for round-the-clock childcare. But no sooner have I checked into the Sandy Lane Hotel than I find numerous messages on my phone from our nanny – in despair because she can't persuade Hope to go to school in my absence. It turns out Hope is terrified the house will be sold from under us while she is at school and I am away. So, when I get home, I ring the estate agent – whose name is Mark – and tell him, regretfully, that my house is no longer for sale. I will have to find another way to resolve Hope's educational difficulties.

Two weeks later, he rings back to say he still has my house keys – will I pop into the office for them? Or perhaps meet up to discuss whether I will be selling in the future? We meet, go for a drink – and it turns out he isn't married. He is younger than me – but only by nine years, a toy boy, then, but not a huge age difference. And he has a great sense of humour, making me laugh in a way I haven't for a very long time. Even now, after all that has happened, I sometimes catch myself giggling at the private jokes we had.

Our first date is the premiere of the *Calendar Girls* movie, the inspirational story of the members of the Rylstone Women's Institute who posed nude for a calendar to raise funds for charity after one of their members – Angela Baker – lost her husband to leukaemia. It was a story that resonated with me for obvious reasons. And it appealed to the readers of *Good Housekeeping*, thrilled at the idea of respectable middle-class women smashing stereotypes, in aid of such a worthwhile cause. The film's stars – Julie Walters and Helen Mirren – are regulars on *Good Housekeeping* covers, so naturally I am on the guest list – and I can take a plus one.

Mark and I walk the red carpet, photographed by the paparazzi – not because I am famous myself but because the paparazzi always photograph everyone on these occasions just in case you do something newsworthy further down the line. This is when he meets Alastair and Fiona for the first time, which could be awkward. Alastair has recently stepped down from his role as head of Downing Street communications, where he was for a while known as the second most powerful man in

Britain. Now he is fund-raising for the charity Leukaemia Research, now known as Blood Cancer UK, just one of the ways he honours the deathbed promise he made to John to look after me and our children. We spend so much time with Ali and his partner Fiona that Hope regards him as a substitute father figure and their children – Rory, Calum and Grace – as her siblings. Ali and Fiona, like all my friends, have fretted about me over the years since John's death; my intense loneliness palpable to all, an open wound that could not, would not, heal. I am anxious about how they will take to this new development in my life, but they are delighted that I have found someone I care about and who cares about me. As a north London estate agent, Mark has never walked a red carpet before, he does not count prime ministers among his friends. He did not go to a famous university, nor has he seen his name on the front page of a newspaper for any reason good or bad. But he has an easy way about him, a natural charm – and he brings the kind of knowledge that no one else in our circle has. He knows about property and cars, and can do practical tasks like hanging pictures and putting up shelves, which makes Fiona very envious because Ali's domestic skills begin and end with making a pot of tea. The children are entertained when he teaches them Cockney rhyming slang, calling a suit a 'whistle' and saying 'Gregory' when he means neck. A born Londoner, he is at ease in the countryside too, escaping from a young age to go fishing in the Lee Valley whenever he could, so knowledgeable about tides and weather conditions. When our friend Tessa Jowell, the cabinet minister, has a cycling accident while we are all on one of our Scottish holidays, it is Mark who tends her wounds then loads her bike, with its buckled front wheel, into his car to bring her safely home. He is a good, kind man, all my friends agree on that. I have more than enough famous, powerful people in my life – what I need is someone who will look after me, and even more importantly Hope. In his groom's speech at the wedding reception, he tells our assembled friends and families that he feels as if he had been put on this earth to look after me and Hope.

Perfect bound, the phrase seemed to describe not only my career but also the home, family and life, straight out of a magazine spread that I fought so hard to create. I am on a permanent adrenaline high every day at work and, wonder of wonders, come home to a loving husband. Hope is thriving with the new-found stability in our lives and having a father figure. She calls him Dada-Bear to distinguish him from her biological father whom she never met. She settles into the new school I find for her in central London, near my office, and starts to flourish, her true potential emerging. We put my house on the market again and move to a smart modern house close to Hampstead Heath, which we decorate together. We are delighted to discover that despite all our differences, we have a shared passion for design, my magazine know-how dovetailing with his hands-on experience. He buys me a framed Beryl Cook print of a couple – her signature plump, joyful characters – dancing together, their bodies echoing each other in perfect harmony. I interviewed the artist as a trainee journalist but I could never afford one of her works. We start collecting art deco and mid-twentieth-century furniture and I quickly realise that he has a far better eye than I do. He studies for an interior design qualification but continues working as an estate agent.

My new-found happiness permeates my work life. So great is the success I make of *Good Housekeeping* that I am promoted to editorial director, in charge of the entire National Magazine Company portfolio, which means I now oversee some of the most famous magazines in Britain – *Cosmopolitan, Harper's Bazaar, Esquire* – the very glossiest of the perfectly bound glossies.

CHAPTER 6

Coverlines

The noughties would turn out to be the heyday of magazines. Something like 5,000 titles were published regularly in Britain, of which about 3,500 were sold on news-stands, the rest by subscription. More print copies were sold each year from 2000 to 2008 than ever before and probably ever will be again, an epic flowering of a form of mass communication that had been around for 200 years. We thought it was down to our brilliance at figuring out what readers wanted – or at least I did. We weren't to know it was a confluence of forces: historically low paper prices and printing costs, combined with stratospheric advertising budgets – and little in the way of competition from the still nascent online world. And of those thousands of titles on the news-stands, I oversaw 19 of the most famous, the most successful, the most beloved. More than that, I was charged with launching websites and creating entirely new projects for launch and expansion.

As editorial director, my office was stacked with towering piles of lesser known and international titles that might be suitable for acquisition or provide inspiration for new projects. I still went to all the shows during Fashion Week and evenings revolved around champagne receptions for new launches. I, along with their editors, was flying the flag for all the Hearst titles now. We swept across London in a fleet of Mercedes, a battalion of glamazons, facing off across the ballroom at our equally glossy rivals from Condé Nast headed by their flagship, the mighty *Vogue* edited by Alexandra Shulman. *Vogue* was, and remains, the biggest draw for advertisers, but Condé Nast managing director Nick Coleridge (now Sir Nicholas) had taken note of *Good Housekeeping*'s impressive circulation figures (which were twice even that of *Vogue*, along with the success of our long-time rival *Woman & Home*, then owned by IPC) and poached publishing director Chris Hughes to work on a rival title for Grown Up Women called *Easy Living*. 'What woman wants to be known for her good housekeeping when she could be enjoying easy living,' Nick quipped in his Old Etonian drawl. Going head-to-head with the urbane, charming descendant of Samuel Taylor Coleridge, I became a scrappy streetfighter from Essex, reminiscent of the editor Magda in *Absolutely Fabulous*. Handbags at dawn, squealed the media commentators as they gleefully chronicled every circulation, advertising or PR blow each of us managed to land on the other.

Easy Living, although it had much to commend it, especially the fashion pages which were never my forte, lasted just eight years before being steam-rollered by the 90-year-old *Good Housekeeping*. Condé Nast put up a good fight but in part due to my remorseless attention to detail and endless parsing of market research, GH spoke more directly to the women of Britain, with an accessible, approachable style that could not be bettered.

No matter which magazine I was editing, whether it was located around my own interests like *Good Housekeeping* or *Prima*, or for women much younger than me at *Cosmo*, or even the men's title *Esquire*, the one job I never delegated, no matter how busy I was, no matter if I was sick or travelling, was writing the coverlines. It was a job that always took at least a day and a half out of every month.

In 80 words or fewer I summed up the contents of a 256-page magazine, the work of more than 50 people, in a way that was topical, seasonal and fresh. Magazines are Fast Moving Consumer Goods – FMCG – selling in hundreds of thousands, but it is not the same as selling baked beans, where having found the winning recipe cans roll off the production line day in, day out. A magazine must be both different yet reassuringly the same every month. And within those parameters my goal was always to attract new readers, serve the faithful audience, and send a frisson of surprise through the ones who might be feeling a little jaded. The formula I came up with, which I called the Golden Cover, was based on a mix of experience and long discussions with the circulation and marketing departments, held together with a dash of neuro-science.

I started always in the top left-hand corner, prime magazine real estate, which I designated as the hotspot. This is the part of the cover that will be seen no matter how the magazine is displayed, whether letter-rack style in supermarkets, or peeking out from behind a cluster of other titles arranged in vertical rows on a newsagent's shelves. The strongest, most welcoming line always goes there.

Directly below go the second- and third-ranking crowd pullers, different for each of the magazines I was in charge of – but this is how it went on *Good Housekeeping*. Generally health, homes and anything to do with appearance jostled month by month for hotspot podium positions of gold, silver and bronze. Health was big in February and June, homes in May due to all the Bank Holidays, fashion and beauty in autumn and the run-up to Christmas. Across the middle of the cover ran my 'banger' line, maybe just one or two words setting the tone for the whole issue and, perhaps, linking several articles on the one theme. Confidence was the top-seller theme for GH – if I could have found 12 synonyms for self-esteem – one for each month of the year – I would never have put anything else on there. In the brave new world of women ascending to professional and executive roles, so many suffered not only from the actual setbacks caused by institutional sexism but, however hard-earned their achievements, from a feeling of being undeserving: imposter syndrome. I thought back then I had all the confidence I needed ... Until I discovered it was just covering up the cracks.

Above the logo would run a ticker-tape offering a line that's nice-to-have ... Not essential but tucked up there above where the eye can skate over it if that's not where your attention lies right now. On GH, travel, short stories or relationships maybe? Not like *Cosmo* where the unspoken questions were: 'Is he the one? Will he commit?' and relationships always went in the hotspot. Grown Up Women – married or single – know that romantic relationships are just one aspect of a fulfilling life, not the whole raison d'être. Those that are interested in reading more will seek it out wherever you put it on the cover, so above the logo it goes.

Bottom left-hand was in magazine folklore where new read-ers looked before deciding if the magazine was for them, so that piece of real estate was always given over to food, the way to any reader's heart. Not everyone likes to cook but nearly everyone loves to eat. Top right-hand corner is the second-to-last location the consumer's eye lands on before deciding to purchase, so celebrity goes there. The star's image is already dominating the whole cover, so just a name and a quote from the interview is necessary, often reiterating the confidence theme – because ultimately we all want to know how our female heroes sustain such enviable lives. And, below the celebrity quote, came my signature flourish as an editor, the line that denoted my involvement in the same way that an artist tags their work to show its provenance. It was what I called the Crackerjack Factor, which could be anything from a rallying call for more women in science to the lines that earned me reprimands from on high, such as when I persuaded male celebrities to strip off to raise awareness about cancer and, of course, the vibrators we so famously tried and tested. The Crackerjack is there to tell you that this seemingly familiar magazine with its century-old name still has a few surprises up its sleeve.

But the real secret to successful coverlines is never to over-promise. Even now, when I pass the magazine racks in the supermarket I cringe at those overly optimistic lines:

Drop a dress size in a week.
Change your life in 30 days.
Reset your finances forever.

We all know that's never going to happen. If it looks too good to be true, it probably is. Equally, I disdain the high-fashion formula of *Vogue* and others, which is basically always a variation on:

New season looks

Or as I used to say, witheringly:

Pink's in! ... So what?

Trend news doesn't mean anything unless you place it in context. What does a new shade of pink mean for me? The mantra I came up with and used on every magazine I edited was Small Achievable Promises, usually shortened to SAP. When writers pitched ideas, I insisted they give me the SAP. If they could sum it up in something that sounded like a coverline, then I would likely commission the feature. If not, forget it.

During 2006, both *Cosmopolitan* and *Esquire* were between editors, so I edited both at once. In the morning I commissioned articles about orgasms and reviewed male centrefolds. Then in the afternoon, I ran down one flight of stairs to tackle Savile Row tailoring and footballing heroes on *Esquire*. Despite having worked for a brilliant male editor on a women's magazine, I knew my own shortcomings – women's issues are my specialist subject, not those of men – so I appointed Dan Davies as acting editor while I was his editor-in-chief. Dan, who subsequently wrote the seminal book exposing the secret life of paedophile disc jockey Jimmy Savile, patiently explained to me the relative merits of footballers Ronaldo Nazario and Zinedine Zidane (nope, still not a clue!), which rock stars, actors and supermodels were cover-worthy and which, in the masculine mind-set, were not. I remember us having a heated debate about supermodel Elle Macpherson, whom I had first booked when I worked on *Honey*, but I can't recall which of us won – or why?

It was satisfying work and I was the queen of all I surveyed. A journalism student sent to interview me for their dissertation reported back on my working day to her tutor, who reprimanded her saying no one could possibly have a job as creative, rewarding and enjoyable as I had. But I did …

And then in the early weeks of January 2007, I flew to New York to interview the rock star Jon Bon Jovi for *Cosmopolitan*. And discovered the cruel fates stalking my life weren't done with me yet.

CHAPTER 7

One in Every Eight Women

January 2007 – New York

It's dark, hot and sweaty in the nightclub – and the music from the stage, where Jon Bon Jovi is performing a live set for just 50 guests, is pounding through my body. Earlier that day I interviewed him in a New York recording studio. I found him charming, softly spoken and passionate about work he does building houses for the homeless, not just writing a cheque but carrying hods of bricks and going up ladders. He likes to perform manual labour, he tells me – it's a satisfying contrast to performing and recording.

As a journalist, I was never the forensic investigator, like John, but I am a good listener and can be empathetic, encouraging confidences and scribbling down the answers in 120 words a minute shorthand. My interview subjects usually warm to me – sometimes, we become friends, as had happened today when Jon Bon Jovi invited me to his concert. I know no one else there, I am in an unfamiliar city far away from home, but I go anyway because if life has taught me anything it is to seize the day – living on a prayer, you could say.

After the concert a town car drops me back at the Mercer Hotel in Manhattan's SoHo. Hot and sticky from all the dancing, I shower before going to bed. As my hand grazes my right breast, made slippery with soap, I freeze. Can I feel something? It is late, I have been drinking. My body clock is still not adjusted to the five hours' time difference ... I can't be sure. The next morning I check again, not a lump exactly, more a sort of thickening.

I am concerned, of course, but years of squashing down fears of cancer affecting my family have been buried so deep I can barely access them. I can quote the statistics gleaned from editing the health features that come across my desk. Yes, one in every eight women will be diagnosed with breast cancer during their lifetime. But – I remind myself equally firmly – nine out of 10 lumps are benign. I am on the young side for a diagnosis, not yet old enough to be called for the NHS screening programme. Then, when I next try to find the thickened area – I can hardly describe it as a lump – it seems to have gone. Maybe I imagined it? Even so, when I get home to London, I make an appointment at the local health centre to have it looked at. The statistics are on my side, I tell myself: seven out of every eight women don't experience breast cancer.

The specialist I am referred to is eminent and larger than life, with a booming voice and peremptory manner that reminds me of James Robertson Justice who starred as Sir Lancelot Spratt in the *Doctor in the House* comedies. No lump shows up on the mammogram, which reassures me, but Sir Lancelot expertly probes the area I am worried about and without any warning produces, like a conjuror, a thick needle which he uses to take a biopsy. It feels exactly as if he has just used a hole punch on my right breast. On my way out, a nurse hands me a pamphlet about breast cancer.

Some women find their partners do not feel the same way about their bodies ever again.

I am two and a half years married, rescued from gut-wrenching loneliness and grief, by a kind man who tells me constantly that he adores me. Is even this going to be taken away from me? I take small comfort in the fact that I feel completely fine in every respect, except for the stinging pain from the biopsy.

Two days later, I undergo exploratory surgery and the next morning Sir Lancelot arrives at my bedside on his rounds. 'I am so sorry,' he says, his booming voice softer than usual. 'But you will beat this.'

It is Mark who breaks the news to Hope that I have cancer.

And it is Mark who calls my mother to tell her what is happening because I am so frightened I seem to have lost the power of speech. The trauma of my diagnosis paralyses my vocal chords leaving me able to communicate only in whispered monosyllables. I am struck dumb with fear to the extent that I can't even talk on the phone to the colleagues and friends who call constantly to find out what is happening to me.

To this day, and despite of everything that came after, I am grateful that I met and married Mark. I do not know what would have become of me, or 14-year-old Hope, had we been left to deal with this alone. During the weeks I am rendered virtually mute Mark becomes my voice, speaking for me, consoling Hope and reassuring my mother that I am getting the best treatment possible.

The good news comes back that the cancer hasn't spread. I am officially classed as stage 2, not as hopeful as stage 1 but it could be so much worse. When we go back to discuss the results with Sir Lancelot, he tells me he wants to operate again to ensure that he has removed enough of the surrounding tissue. 'Borders make all the difference in cancer,' he booms, sounding more like James Robertson Justice than ever. '… And I am known for mine.'

The second surgery takes place on Valentine's Day. Mark, squeezed into the suit he wore on our wedding day, bearing my engagement and wedding rings, which I had to remove before being taken down to theatre, plus a bottle of champagne that the nurses didn't have the heart to deny us, is waiting, complete with red roses, when I come round from the anaesthetic. 'I love you,' he says pushing my rings back on the third finger of my left hand. 'I love you. I love you.'

The next day, a nurse helps me out of bed to use the bathroom. 'I've put a towel over the mirror in case you are upset by what you see,' she says. I rip it down, of course, and stare at the bloodied dressings taped across my chest.

I have never had big boobs, but they weren't small either. In the litany of flaws I can list about my body – big feet, fine hair, no waist – my boobs have never given me any trouble. Other women might weep about their flat chest or engage in a lifelong quest for the perfect bra to tame their embonpoint, but I have a wide rib cage on which moderately sized boobs sit comfortably without noticeable droop even in my 40s. They can be squished together for a commendable cleavage on special occasions but are not so problematic as to trigger an endless search for an industrial-strength sports bra; Marks & Spencer does just fine. And they were functional as well as decorative: I breastfed each of my children for over a year. In short, I had always had low-maintenance boobs. Until I didn't.

The surgeon has performed a quadrantectomy – more than a lumpectomy but less than a mastectomy. I won't need reconstruction; Sir Lancelot has informed me that the right breast was slightly larger than the left anyway, as is often the case, so he has simply evened them up. But I have no idea what it will look like when the dressings are removed. I think about the pamphlet and the advice that my husband of just two years may never feel the same way about my body again. And maybe nor will I? Not that it matters. Sex is the last thing on my mind because I am absolutely certain of one thing – cancer means death. I am going to die. Mark will be widowed, as I was, Hope will be an orphan.

After the second surgery I am given three weeks to recover and then, before chemotherapy, yet another operation, this time to insert a port-a-cath, a plastic valve, in my chest so that blood can be drawn and the chemotherapy drugs given without further damaging the veins in my left arm, which is already starting to look like I am a junkie. My third surgery inside a month. I am woozy from all the anaesthetic in my system and my breasts are a battlefield; the second op has left a seven-inch scar that starts in my right armpit. I am in constant pain and sleep propped up on pillows, waking repeatedly in the night every time one slips to one side.

The chemotherapy sessions are delivered on an out-patient basis. The chemo suite is furnished with comfortable reclining chairs in which patients can read or use their laptops to while away the couple of hours it takes for the drugs to be administered. Mark sits with me as a nurse fixes a line to the newly inserted port-a-cath in my chest, which is still sore from the surgery, and I watch as the bright red chemicals – so toxic that they will burn the nurse's skin if they splash onto her – drip into my veins.

I am warned that each transfusion will trigger nausea for a few days then a dramatic drop in immunity, followed by a climb back towards feeling relatively normal, at which point, three weeks later, the next session will be due. Chemo is best described as a game of Whac-a-Mole: as soon as the fast-reproducing cancer cells start to re-emerge they are 'whacked' by more chemicals.

I am offered an ice-cap to wear on my head during each session, to help me keep my hair. But it is heavy and uncomfortable, giving me a headache, so I abandon it. I will be bald but so what, I am going to die anyway.

Mark drives me home after the first session and I go straight to bed. The nausea starts a couple of hours later. I have tablets to take but I vomit them straight back up again. Even after everything in my stomach has been emptied out, I lie on the bathroom floor retching. Hope stands in the doorway watching fearfully as Mark coaxes me to sip water which I then projectile vomit across floor. And then I start struggling to breathe. In addition to my churning guts, I feel as if my rib cage is being compressed by tight metal bands. I think about the chest X-rays to detect metastases in my lungs. What if they missed a spot and the cancer has spread there after all? I throw up again – and can't catch my breath. Terrified, Mark calls the hospital who tell him to bring me in. No time to wait for an ambulance. Mark will drive me; we take Hope, too, as there is no one to stay with her at home and, in any case, she won't leave my side.

Our night-time dash is painfully reminiscent of other precipitous arrivals at hospitals. As Mark steers the car through the
same night-time streets to the hospital and I struggle to catch
my breath, my brain loops back and forth in time. I am
convinced I am dying, of course I must die. This is how it always
ends.

A doctor meets us at the hospital entrance and I am rushed to
a private room where a seen-it-all-before Irish nurse calmly
administers oxygen and a powerful tranquilliser. I am not going
to die, it was just a panic attack triggered by the extreme nausea.
Even then, just a few years back, no one talked about PTSD-
induced flashbacks. I have lived for a long time with these
intense experiences where traumatic events seem so real that I
can smell the rain on the tarmac, hear the sounds of the ambulance. I simply assume everyone unlucky enough to go through
such things experiences these hallucinations. Why not? I see it
as the price I pay for being the one in my family who survived.

Via the still tender port-a-cath I am hooked up to fluids to
rehydrate me and intravenous drugs to stop the retching, which
work their magic almost immediately. Mark takes Hope home,
and in the morning returns to collect me. But my oncologist
decides it is no longer advisable for me to have my chemo as an
out-patient and the subsequent five sessions will all take place
in hospital where I can be hooked up overnight to the fluids and
the anti-emetics as a precaution. He tells me that my reaction to
the chemotherapy was one in a thousand bad luck – but then I
am used to be being on the wrong side of statistics.

The chemo is effective, very much so. Blood tests show my
white blood cell count falls so far and so fast after each cycle
that I need steroid injections in my stomach to help my immu-

nity bounce back. I am too squeamish to inject myself, so Mark learns how to administer the drugs himself, diligently practising beforehand by injecting an orange. I heartily dislike needles and he is a big man, with big hands, but his touch is infinitely gentle. I could not previously have imagined ever allowing anyone who was not a medical professional to inject me in my stomach – but I have total confidence in my calm, practical husband.

After the second chemo session, normality begins to assert itself, my power of speech gradually returns – and then my hair starts to come out. Locks of auburn hair are strewn across the pillow when I wake in the morning; they settle on my shoulders as I go about my necessarily limited day and block the drain when I shower. It is Mark who sits me down with a towel around my shoulders and using his electric razor gently removes the last bits of fluff, leaving my skull bald and shining. He tells me I am beautiful, that not many women could get away with being completely bald, but that I have the bone structure to carry it off, and that he loves me more than ever.

I get a wig, of course, for the days when I don't feel like telling strangers – shopkeepers and people I meet on dog walks – that I am locked in mortal combat with a dreaded disease. But it feels like wearing a small furry animal on my head – hot, itchy and liable to move around. Most days I simply wind a length of fuchsia silk turban-style around my naked skull.

Even more difficult than the hair loss is that since the steroid injections I have put on 15 lb in a matter of weeks. In the movies, people suffering from cancer are pale, slender and long suffering, like Ali MacGraw in *Love Story*. But soon I am not only bald but puffy as well. And it's not only the hair on my head that has fallen out. My eyebrows are gone along with my eyelashes; with my steroidal moon-face, I no longer recognise myself when I look in the mirror. The steroids have another darker side-effect, too. I start to feel not just angry but filled with a towering rage. Why did this have to happen to me after everything I have been through? Haven't I suffered enough already? What will be the impact on Hope who with the benefit of a regular home, and a father figure, is making real progress at school at last? Why can everyone but me have a normal family life without the constant shadow of disaster? When will I catch a break?

I start down that deceptively reasonable path of lamenting my misfortune that all too quickly descends into a furious howl of despair: Why me, God? Why me? What was the reason for the cancer? Was it caused by grief? From what I can tell, the science doesn't work like that. But certainly the lack of sleep, the amount of alcohol I drank, the careless disdain with which I treated my body will not have helped.

And then my head starts whirling with ever crazier theories. Late one night I read an internet story that grapefruit might be implicated, which sends me running to the bathroom to pour a new and expensive bottle of Jo Malone shower gel down the drain, as if the molecules could escape through the lid, penetrate my skin and kill me in the night.

Another evening, I completely lose it while we are getting ready to go out for dinner and start kicking the kitchen bin in frustration. I keep on kicking despite how much it hurts my slippered feet until the Brabantia bin is crumpled and useless. I am crying and spitting, my nose is running: a bald, fat, screaming banshee. Mark watches me with a fathomless expression written across his face. He says nothing, which makes me even more upset.

The next day, shamed and confused, I clamp the wig on my head and drive to Brent Cross Shopping Centre where I buy a replacement bin from John Lewis. We do not refer to the incident ever again, but it becomes clear that the sight of his wife in the grip of such ugly fury disturbs something deep inside Mark. The rages disappear when the steroid injections stop but an innocence has gone from our marriage.

I sleep propped up on pillows due to the pain from the three surgeries, but now, as well, my nights are disturbed as I wake from a nightmare that I am burning in the fires of hell. The bedclothes soaked in my sweat are too damp to sleep on. The first time it happens I am caught by surprise and have to root around sleepily in the linen cupboard for clean sheets. However, it has become such a regular occurrence that I have a system now with a pile of towels that I layer on the bed to save me from having to change the sheets in the middle of the night.

The possibility of having more children slams irrevocably shut when the chemotherapy crashes me straight into menopause. I have no time to mourn the loss of my reproductive life because to add to the nausea from the chemo and the pain from the surgeries, I now contend with a dozen or more hot flushes a day. Due to the strongly hormonal nature of my tumour – which perversely gives me a greater chance of survival – hormone replacement therapy (HRT) is ruled out. I try to focus on the fact that it's good for me to lose oestrogen because that was fuelling the cancer.

The daytime hot flushes start with a sensation like heartburn just under my collar bones, before irradiating hotly out in all directions, turning my armpits on like a tap and boiling my face like a lobster as my scalp prickles with sweat under my wig. But night-time is hell on an altogether different level.

Trying to get back to sleep on the dry towels laid over the damp sheets, I toss and turn, unable to drop off again even though my body battered by surgeries, radiation and chemicals craves rest. I have never been someone who sleeps easily. My mother still jokes about how as a baby I once didn't sleep for a whole weekend and in the end a doctor prescribed sleeping pills – for her – while I lay wakeful in my cot. Not sleeping was an advantage to me as a single parent when I would arrive home at midnight from a work function only to have to get up at 6.30 the next morning to see Hope off to school. But this takes my lifelong insomnia to a whole new level.

Sometimes in the early hours I creep off to the single bed in the study that doubles as a guest room and lie there wakeful until morning, obsessively thinking and rethinking my diagnosis, bargaining with the God who has already proved so capricious with the fate of people I love. Let me stay alive until Hope finishes school I beg, without any real expectation my prayers will be heard. And I am ashamed to add that I want to live for myself, too. I don't want anything special. I don't care about my high-powered career; I will give it all up if I can just live. And that is the most shameful thought of all, how much I want to live; how scared I am to accept the fate that was dealt to those I loved.

Soon, Mark volunteers to take the single bed in the study, so I can languish in the six-foot wide bed, which I had custommade soon after our wedding. It cost as much as a new car and was engineered to our differing weights – even at my steroid-induced heaviest, Mark weighs several stones more than me. The Rolls-Royce bed I called it, an investment in our marriage.

But even though one or other of us is frequently spending nights in the spare room, there is one loss I had anticipated that never materialises. The loss of intimacy, threatened by that doom-mongering pamphlet, never happens. Even as I engage with the physical and mental battles of cancer, Mark makes it clear that he is as attracted to me as ever, and distracted by the sex I start to believe that is all that matters.

Cancer treatment can be summed up crudely as slash, poison, burn. I have been slashed – operated on – poisoned by the chemo and now I am ready for the burns. I am passed to yet another consultant – this one we christen Brains from the *Thunderbirds* puppet show because his horn-rim glasses look too big for his head – and because he is brilliant. Brains is concerned that despite Sir Lancelot's famous borders, the cancer has penetrated the lymph nodes in my right armpit from where it could travel to other parts of my body: lungs, bones, liver or brain. He requests another surgery – my fourth – these lymph nodes are clear, there had been a question mark over some removed earlier. It's good news, but having had so many lymph nodes removed places me at a lifetime risk of lymphoedema. I am still not convinced I will survive – but if I do, I would rather not be encumbered by a swollen arm. I am warned to be careful not to bruise it or get an infection. Even now, all these years later, if I have a manicure I have to make sure the beautician doesn't trim the cuticles on my right hand. Survival is made up of so many pin-pricks like this. You can't complain, not when you've been given a chance of life denied to previous generations, but it gets tedious when even a trip to a salon means long explanations about what you can't have done.

As soon as the chemo ends, my hair starts to grow back but it comes through iron-grey and weirdly thick and curly in a way that reminds me of a schnauzer dog. I ditch the wig and go back to my hairdresser who cuts this new growth into a chic crop. Mark, refusing to let me think that any of these inflictions on my body make me even fractionally less desirable, says he loves my new look and urges me to keep it that way. But the iron grey chemo curls quickly fall out to be replaced by my more familiar straight conker-brown strands.

Naturally, I had googled the survival rate for my type and size of tumour – 78 per cent surviving 10 years. Not bad odds – but you wouldn't want to cross the road with only a 22 per cent chance of reaching the other side. Until the 1970s, breast cancer killed one in two women diagnosed with the disease – so many lives cut short, so many grieving partners and motherless children. That I am writing this 17 years later is due in no small part to the drug treatments that are now commonplace after the surgery/chemo/rads trifecta has done its job. But no drug is without side-effects. Tamoxifen gives me joint pains and – weirdly – causes my toenails to fall off. I am switched to a different drug – anastrozole – until bone scans reveal I have the bone-thinning disease osteoporosis. It seems to be my fate to experience every side-effect going.

Rads, as cancer survivors call radiation therapy, don't hurt although they do produce a sort of sunburn – mostly it's just a question of keeping very still for 10 to 15 minutes while a huge death ray-type machine is passed over you and the radiotherapist, gowned in lead, shelters behind a door. It's boring and time-consuming.

One day I am kept waiting for more than an hour for my turn and when I inquire of the receptionist the reason for the delay, she tells me – sharply, I think, considering that this is a fancy clinic with elaborate flower arrangements and the latest issue of *Country Life* in the waiting room – that there are more seriously ill patients ahead of me in the queue.

And this is the moment I never expected to see, when cancer treatment becomes mundane, when there are others ahead in the queue who are far worse off. This is the moment that John and, even more tragically, my darling Ellie never experienced. It is the first time I realise that I just might live.

Now it appears that my death is no longer imminent, I switch almost seamlessly from worrying about dying to anxiety about money. Our huge mortgage commitment terrifies me.

Mark finds a buyer through his estate agency connections without even telling me our house is on the market. My friends think this a bit odd that such a major financial decision should have been taken without any proper discussion – but I am still weak and exhausted from the treatment, more than happy to hand over responsibility for something as complex as a house move, while I concentrate all my energies on helping Hope continue to catch up with her schoolwork and rebuilding my interrupted career.

Many cancer survivors object to the metaphor of it being a battle, particularly when the battle is lost, as it so often can be. But, knowing what I know, I think it's a reasonable comparison. Like a battle-hardened warrior returning weary from the front line, I am changed by what I have been through. I have been betrayed by the one person I had always relied on: myself. I have endured terrible events in my life but I could rely on my remorseless drive to power on through. My own physicality never impeded my determination to overcome. Until now. Clearly, my body has been harbouring a seed of weakness, almost undetectable but working silently to kill me.

You never really know the exact moment you lose something, because if you could remember when you lost it, you would be able to retrace your steps. But looking back I see that on some – not conscious – level I made a cold and calculating decision. When I learned the tumour wasn't going to kill me, I could have decided to re-order my life to create more balance – fewer late nights, less alcohol, reduced stress. Instead, what I chose to do was turn my gaze away from anything in my life that didn't please me, including my cancer-prone, hormone-depleted, ageing, aching, scarred, mutilated and – to my mind – ultimately disloyal body. To disregard my flawed physical self would be how I would survive. I had no idea that was also ultimately how I would fail.

Hope is still my number-one priority but after her the over-whelming part of my scant energy goes into my career. I sleep no more than six hours a night, always waking three or more times in a lather of sweat; I stop being able to recall ever sleeping right through. After Hope and work, Mark comes a poor third in the scale of my attention. Fourth if you count the futile quest for sleep as another priority.

In 2008, we move to another, cheaper, house about a mile away, which is fine. I like it very much. I stop thinking about the past at all; too much has happened in my life that I can't bring myself to contemplate. The breast cancer, like a bullet to the chest, stopped me in my tracks, yet I have survived, recreated a home and a family life as well as building a successful career all by concentrating resolutely on perfection.

I had another family once before – and lost them. I will not let that happen again. I will control my life, surroundings, the lives of the people I love. I will make our lives perfect, in the way that I curate every word and picture in the magazines I produce which are loved and read by millions of women. And I will refuse to countenance anything that doesn't fit with my perfectly bound life.

CHAPTER 8

Tried and Tested

While undergoing the chemo and radiation therapy I worked from home for eight months, consulting with editors who came to visit me and researching a takeover bid for another group of magazines. But by the time I was fully back at work after being treated for breast cancer, the credit crunch of 2008 had been followed by recession in 2009, meaning there was no appetite for mergers or launching new magazines. So, when my successor at *Good Housekeeping*, Louise Chunn, left the company – later founding the excellent mental health website Welldoing – I gladly resumed the day-to-day editing of what was always my favourite magazine. But the saying goes that you can never enter the same river twice. As many businesses began to bounce back from recession, print magazines began to struggle as they faced a new and possibly existential rival: digital.

Facebook was launched in 2004 but only really started to take off when smartphones arrived in 2009. Having spent the noughties making *Good Housekeeping* a print title for the twenty-first century I was now tasked with translating this venerable title, nearly 90 years old, into a multi-media proposition.

I was fortunate to be partnered with a talented publisher, Jude Secombe – and together we devised a plan to expand *Good Housekeeping* into a website and a live events business.

The Good Housekeeping Institute (GHI) was our USP – unique selling point – but notwithstanding Jane Asher's explanations in the 80th-anniversary issue, it had come to be seen rather like a mad relative in the attic, occupying smaller and smaller space in the corner of the office, with old-fashioned cookers for recipe testing on which half the gas rings didn't work, the team of testers reduced by successive cut-backs. In my head-long rush to attract the advertising pounds away from younger women's titles, I was guilty of overlooking our greatest asset.

With space in the Broadwick Street offices at a premium, Jude found 5,000 square feet of unoccupied premises down the road in Soho and devised a brilliant business plan that she presented to the Hearst Board in New York, who voiced their unanimous approval. We engaged an architect and work began on constructing an entirely new Good Housekeeping Institute for the twenty-first century.

On the ground floor was a fully fitted-out cookery school where readers would be taught to cook the recipes from the pages of the magazines. Next to that, an event space, fully fitted with broadcast quality electronics for recording radio and TV segments. In the basement, row upon row of kitchen appliances were lined up for testing. Dozens of white plates were painted with egg, pasta sauce and spinach, which were then left overnight to harden before a dozen different dishwashers were put through their paces. Oil, ink, tomato sauce and a smorgasbord of common stains were dripped by pipette onto strips of fabric which were then run through the washing machines to see how efficiently the whites were restored. The most difficult stains to get rid of, by the way, are cosmetics, with foundation being particularly bad. It is after all formulated to stay put on your face, exposed to all weathers. There was a fully kitted-out salon for testing the efficacy of beauty products; a sound-proofed studio for hi-fi equipment; and even a room with a patchwork of different floorings for testing vacuum cleaners – over which we scattered mud, dust and bags of pet hair obtained specifically for the purpose from Battersea Dogs & Cats Home.

It is not often realised, but most domestic appliances are manufactured overseas and tested under entirely different conditions from those that would be found in a British home. Few other nationalities use the oven as much as we do and home-made cake is a particularly British obsession. The Germans and the French, for instance, don't bake nearly as much as we do, ovens being used more for casserole-type dishes that are forgiving of temperature variations. So, our testers baked dozen upon dozen of fairy cakes, comparing the golden – or in some cases burnt – topping with pre-agreed colour charts. The electricity and water supplies to the GHI were regulated to match those found in a residential home and our benchmarks were strictly domestic. *Which?* magazine does this superbly, of course, but their results are only available by subscription – and their readers, at least at the time I am talking about, were largely male. Jude and I reasoned that with women working outside the home as a norm and household help limited or unavailable to many families due to cost, the need for independent advice for women regarding household products was as great or even greater now in the twenty-first century than it had been back in 1924. We put the thousands of test results we generated online, immediately attracting one and a half million visitors to the site. The phrase Good Housekeeping Seal of Approval made famous by our American sister title has a specific legal meaning in the UK, which limited how much we were able to use it. Then I discovered that although *Good Housekeeping* had been the first publication to use the term 'Tried & Tested', for testing consumer products, it had never been trade-marked. With the help of the legal team, I set about remedying that. From my corner office above Carnaby Street I fired off sternly worded letters to any other media outlet who attempted to use either phrase without permission. If a newspaper or colour supplement thought they might run a mayonnaise taste test and call the results Tried & Tested, the editor would find a reprimand from me on their desk the next morning.

In an increasingly online world where many of the magazines launched in the glory days of the early noughties were now in a cut-throat battle for readers and advertising spend – not only with each other but with the Wild West of the internet – I decreed *Good Housekeeping* would be known for its integrity. 'I'll believe it when I read it in *Good Housekeeping*,' readers were always telling me when I met them – and that became my mantra. I even had it printed on coffee mugs produced by master potter Emma Bridgewater.

Stately as a galleon, armed with the big guns of the Institute, *Good Housekeeping* glided above the fray on the news-stands to become far and away the biggest-selling glossy magazine in Britain. The influential Enders consumer analysis hailed our diversification into a website and cookery school as the future of magazines. I was awarded Editor of the Year for the second time – an honour achieved by only a handful of editors – and Jude and I ran hand in hand onto the stage of the Grosvenor House Hotel ballroom to the strains of Tina Turner's 'Simply the Best' to collect the award for Consumer Brand of the Year as well, reflecting that magazines were no longer just about print. Debrett's, the society bible, named me as one of the most influential people in Britain. From seeking out marketing directors to beg for ad pages, my rule became that I would never run 'puff pieces' in return for advertising, something unheard of in an increasingly cash-strapped industry where editorial mentions were increasingly brought into negotiations. I took the Tried & Tested slug-line seriously and tried to ensure that I never included anything in the magazine that either I or one of the team wouldn't do or use ourselves. We triple-tested all the recipes – which few magazines or even book publishers are in a position to do – including on the pearl-grey Aga I had installed in the newly built Institute. I squeezed into the sample sizes of the clothes featured on the fashion pages, used the lotions and potions on the beauty pages on my own face, bought the kitchen appliances recommended by the Good Housekeeping Institute for my own kitchen and, visited as many of the overseas destinations mentioned on our travel pages as I could fit in my diary.

The breast cancer faded to little more than a memory, as faint as the seven-inch scar tracking from my right armpit down to the middle of my ribs which was now just a fine white line. I was working harder than ever and travelling constantly. Hope was away at university studying geography and Chinese – remarkable for the child who at age eight was unable even to read – and Mark had a brand new hobby that was taking up all his spare time. We were all so happy and fulfilled, I thought.

Wild swimming used to be something that made a light-hearted story on Christmas Day TV news, when bobble-hatted enthusiasts plunged into the sea at Brighton and everyone said they were mad! But in 2014 the sport, although nothing like as popular as it is now, was starting to gain followers, and Mark, having tried it, proved to be a natural. He was able to swim longer and faster than any of his fellow enthusiasts – and this discovery led to a new and vaunting ambition that was at least equal to mine.

7 September 2014

We are in the kitchen – my friend Terry, Hope's flatmate Ruby and me – eating pizza and drinking Prosecco, all of us fixated on a tiny icon seemingly becalmed in the blue screen of my laptop. This is the *Optimist*, an escort vessel accompanying Mark as he attempts to swim from England to France. In my north London kitchen, I have no idea what is happening, nor why the boat has stopped. I text Hope and my brothers, Jeremy and Hugh, who are on the boat, asking them what is going on – but they don't reply. I continually refresh the screen hoping to see their position has changed but am filled with dread that Mark has suffered a heart attack in the water and everyone is too busy attempting a rescue to reply to me.

* * *

A widow never has the chance to fall out of love with her first husband and I accept that Mark may have felt jealousy for John although he never showed it. In fact, he became an enthusiastic and committed fundraiser for the charity now called Blood Cancer UK, a name that reflects the greater understanding we now have of what used to be simply known as leukaemia. Tremendous strides have been made since I first became aware of the charity when John was ill and treatment for the most common form of childhood leukaemia now has a 98 per cent success rate, although the certain aspects of John and Ellie's variant of the illness mean it remains stubbornly resistant to advances in medical science. Mark could have chosen any charity he liked to support and I was moved that he chose one that meant so much to me.

Soon after we married, he started taking part in triathlons as part of the charity's Banana Army – so called because they wore yellow T-shirts making them easy for supporters to spot. He is not the fastest runner or cyclist but he is a gifted swimmer. When competing in triathlons his swimming speed and strength gave him such a head start that he would get out of the water ahead of the pack, which gave him an advantage over younger men.

And Mark loves anything to do with water. He is also an expert fly fisherman, travelling to Ireland and Scotland for the salmon and the Caribbean and Panama for bone fish. He is a man who needs to have hobbies – I accepted that. As an estate agent, he didn't have the sort of all-encompassing job that I and my friends had. My life as an editor was not just a way to earn a living but a consuming passion and abiding interest that occupied my every waking hour.

Even if I had the time to swim in lakes and ponds, wild swimming was never going to be an interest I shared. Like many people, I started learning to swim back in primary school. Not that my school had a pool, but, unusually, a nearby children's home had one, which was spartan, icy cold, with flapping open doors to communal changing rooms and a footbath like a petri dish. We were taught by a loud-voiced man in a tracksuit, very unusual apparel back then. For the first lesson he lined us up, all non-swimmers, on the side of the pool and told us to jump in. Those who disobeyed, paralysed with fear in my case and probably the others, too, he pushed in. I plunged into water so cold it felt like being flayed by knives and struggled to keep my balance thrashing and gasping in the chest-deep water, only to have my head thrust underwater by the tracksuited man kneeling poolside. This, he claimed, was the best way to combat a fear of water.

I cried so piteously at the thought of going to school on swimming lesson days that my father took matters into his own hands. When we next went on holiday to the seaside, he taught me breast stroke, which allowed me to keep my head out of the water, and to this day that's the only stroke I do, never really having mastered the crawl.

I wouldn't claim to have developed a phobia of water as a result of that brutal first exposure – but once I was grown up and had a say in the matter, this was never going to be an interest I shared.

I did try to show wifely support and went along with Mark once or twice when he swam in the Serpentine in Hyde Park and also to a lake somewhere in the depths of Buckinghamshire. But I wouldn't enter the freezing, murky water, with the possibility of eels or pike lurking in the deep, myself. And for all the pictures posted on social media by open-water swimmers, there is really nothing to see when you are standing on the shore. The only way I could work out which was Mark's head bobbing about in the distance was that he stayed in the water longer than anyone else, as he turned out to have almost superhuman powers of cold-water endurance.

True open-water aficionados disdain wetsuits, choosing to wear just Speedos and a swim hat – whatever the water temperature. 'Skins' they call it, or 'swimming in skins', I think. I probably have the inflection slightly wrong, I never paid that much attention – big mistake. Afterwards they pull on the towelling dryrobes that have also assumed a fetishistic importance in the sport and those horrible plastic sandals called Crocs. Sexy it's not – but there is an almost Masonic closeness that develops between those who brave the freezing temperatures while chillier mortals like me are left to shiver on the shore.

The shortest distance between Britain and mainland Europe is from Dover on the south coast of England to Cap Gris-Nez between Boulogne and Calais in France, where Captain Matthew Webb first swam across in 1875, taking just under 22 hours, covered in porpoise fat for warmth and fortified by nips of brandy. In the annals of open-water swims, there is none more iconic than swimming the Channel; it attracts enthusiasts from all around the world. And the year before our move to Berkhamsted, Mark decided that he would attempt to swim the Channel to raise funds for blood cancer research.

It was a surprise to me to discover that you can't just turn up and start swimming. Months, even years, in advance, you reserve a boat for a window of a couple of weeks and wait for the skipper to call you and tell you the tide and weather conditions are just right. Throughout the summer of that year, seven years after my cancer treatment ended, we wait. Not knowing when the swim would take place, Mark couldn't taper off his exercise regime as he did before running the marathon. From March onwards when he isn't at work, he's training at the gym or the pool and when he isn't doing either he is sleeping or refuelling, eating prodigious amounts of food to compensate for the massive expenditure of calories. My contribution to this mammoth effort is to keep the fridge constantly filled. We had the previous year moved to Muswell Hill, our fifth address in the 10 years we had been married. I told myself I never minded all the house moves; I would just go to work and leave it all to Mark. I hadn't even been inside this particular house before contracts were exchanged; I seemed to spend more hours of the day in my corner office overlooking Carnaby Street than I did at home anyway.

Finally, with only 24 hours' notice, Mark gets the call that conditions in the Channel are good, not perfect, the tides are strong this late in the season, which will make the crossing more difficult with higher waves, but good enough and Mark is a very powerful swimmer. He will set off at dawn from Shakespeare Beach, Dover. We had already agreed I wouldn't be going along to support him; my chemotherapy experiences had made me wary of anything that triggered nausea – and on a tiny support boat there is no room for anyone throwing up over the side.

My two brothers, both experienced sailors from our coastal upbringing, go instead of me as crew, along with Mark's best friend, Ian. Hope insists on being on the boat, too. She wants to be part of this epic and emotional moment that, even more than the wedding, would unite our family. I stay home in charge of the social media, posting hour-by-hour updates of his progress for the many friends and family who all reached into their pockets to sponsor him.

Not just that, I also need to finish off the packing for our annual summer holiday to Corfu. This is typical – I couldn't just abandon the holiday when he booked the window for the Channel swim; I was so addicted to multi-tasking, so used to a packed diary, that I just thought we would cram it all in somehow. Although, in fairness, Mark was not expecting his swim to be so late in the season. Our flights were early the next morning and there was every chance he would not finish the swim in time to set off on holiday and, if so, I would need internet access to organise changing the flights, which I could hardly do if I was mid-Channel throwing up over the side of a boat.

Mark starts off strongly at 6 a.m., swimming in an easy crawl. Hope sends me updates from her phone when she has signal, which is sporadic, and I follow their progress on the Channel Swimming & Piloting Federation (CS&PF) online tracker, relaying the news far and wide on Twitter and Facebook as more donations pour in. In the middle of the day when all looks set fair, I pause in my monitoring to take the dogs to be looked after by my mother who will be, as usual, caring for my pets while we are away on the holiday that I hope will still happen. I check Mark's position while I am at her house and show her how to follow his progress on her computer. When I return home, Terry comes over to keep me company and then

Hope's friend from uni, Ruby, arrives too – she is coming with us to Corfu the next day.

Although the distance between England and France is only just over 21 miles at the shortest point, the currents and tides mean that most swimmers end up swimming in a letter S shape and covering around 40 miles, an unfathomably long distance. Do I expect Mark to make it? I don't know. He's nearly 50 now and only began serious training a few months previously. All summer we've been following as his new friends attempt the crossing, but no one has achieved it. The statistics tell the story: every year about 300 swimmers set off and only around one in five make it. More people have summited Everest than swum the Channel.

One swimmer he was friendly with got within a mile and a half of the French coast before a big wave dislocated an arm out of its shoulder socket. He carried on swimming with his one good arm but going round and round in circles until the support crew pulled him out of the water before he sank from exhaustion. I know victory is by no means assured.

The day is bright. The water is calm and Hope texts news of dolphins swimming alongside the boat, which I relay to our followers. My brothers mix carbohydrate-rich feeds and lower them over the side to Mark. He flips onto his back to swallow them, then swims on. He can't touch the boat or get even momentary relief by holding on while taking the feed. An official observer on the boat watches closely to see that all the rules are adhered to.

Hours pass. I worry that if he finishes, he will have to do so in the dark. I know there is a support swimmer on the boat who is allowed to swim alongside for an hour at a time. And I know this to be a strong swimmer who will follow him to land in order to give assistance if he needs it, as I've been warned he probably will. And to help him swim back to the boat afterwards. I have been following other swimmers' attempts and it has always seemed to me a cruel way to finish such a mammoth feat, but apparently the pilot boats can't get any closer than 500 yards from the French shore.

The crossing is dangerous, there are poisonous jellyfish and, needless to say, Mark is not wearing a wetsuit that would give some protection. But worse than that, the English Channel is the busiest stretch of water in the world, with 600 tankers and 200 ferries passing through each day, unable to stop or turn for a small craft with a swimmer alongside. People have died making the crossing, I have an unspoken fear that I will be widowed a second time.

At about 7.30 in the evening Ruby is checking the tracker while I answer the door to the pizza delivery and she calls to me that the boat has stopped moving. I think about Mark's friend with the dislocated arm swimming round and around in circles within sight of the shore.

Ages pass. I keep texting Hope but she doesn't reply. I have no idea what is happening and I fear the worst.

Finally, I get the text we have all been waiting for.

'He did it.'

Mark is back on the boat, wrapped in blankets and sleeping. The *Optimist* is heading at full speed through the night back to Dover. They even make it in time for us to catch our flight to Corfu the next day.

Later, as Mark recovers in the Greek sunshine, Hope tells me the full story.

About 500 yards from the French shore, the boat came to a stop and the skipper turned it sideways on. The support swimmer jumped into the water to escort Mark to land and, as secretly arranged between them without Mark's knowledge, Hope took off her jeans and sweatshirt and slipped over the side, too. No wetsuit for her either, just a safety light clipped to her bikini bottoms.

It was pitch dark and the waves were far larger than they had looked from the boat. She, like her mother, is a pool swimmer, unused to open water, but she pressed bravely on managing to keep a few metres behind Mark and treading water by moonlight as after more than 14 hours of swimming he dragged himself out of the water onto French soil.

The rules state that the swimmer must exit the water unaided, clear the shoreline by two metres, stand up and raise a hand.

'I did it,' he called into the darkness. 'I did it.'

'I know you did Dada-Bear,' replied the last voice he expected to hear. 'I'm right here behind you.'

We had been married 10 years that summer, my brush with cancer had tested us to the limits, my sorrow for the loss of my previous family cast long shadows, yet, despite everything, we were happy, fulfilled and in love. Hope had benefited from the security of our home-life and grown into a well-balanced and optimistic young woman. I was overwhelmed with love and admiration for this man who would swim oceans for me. The dark days after the loss of my first family I have described as like living on the seabed so deep underwater that no light could penetrate. Only after several years foundering in the depths, did I start to swim to the surface. On the way up I met Mark, a coincidence maybe that he is a swimmer and a fisherman, happiest in or on water. I thought with his help I would be able to breathe the air again like everyone else. I thought he would rescue me.

I wept tears of gratitude for our deliverance. The darkness was behind us. Against all the odds, we had created a new family as strong and as bonded as the first.

CHAPTER 9

Sidebar: House Beautiful

September 2015

In his espionage novel *The Human Factor* Graham Greene created a flawed hero in Maurice Castle, spy turned MI6 bureaucrat who, significantly for the storyline, lived in the suburbs, a 37-minute train journey from London.

> *... he chose to return to his birthplace: to the canal under the weeping willows, to the school and the ruins of a once-famous castle which has withstood siege by Prince Louis of France and of which, so the story went, Chaucer had been a Clerk of Works ...*

It was the author's hometown too; his father was headmaster of Berkhamsted School where Greene was a famously unhappy schoolboy. The town is still recognisably the same, dominated by the ruins of a motte and bailey castle built by William the Conqueror's half-brother, Robert of Mortain. You can – as I have – recreate the walks that Maurice took to the station and to exercise his dog in Ashridge Forest beyond.

These days, the town of Berkhamsted has all you might wish for a comfortable middle-class existence: a flagship Waitrose, artisan coffee bars, antique shops and a boutique stocking Paul Smith, Hugo Boss and Malene Birger. There is a market twice a week and browsing the stalls selling fruit, veg, cheese, cured meats and sourdough loaves, you might think you were in Provence, were it not for the weather. It is the sort of place my magazine avatar Claire, my imaginary first reader, might live.

Running through the town is the Grand Union Canal, the 137-mile waterway linking London with Birmingham, silently, ecologically, connecting the regions with the capital during the Industrial Revolution. There are 166 locks, which are especially frequent on this stretch as it climbs to its highest point in the Chiltern Hills at Tring. Brightly painted narrowboats line the banks – aboard which you can imagine Toad of Toad Hall escaping dressed as a washerwoman, although now they have engines and are no longer pulled by horses on the towpath. The River Bulbourne, a chalk stream of significant biological interest where wild watercress flourishes in the gin-clear waters, tracks the route of the canal.

That we came to live in this compact little market town was not an accident.

I have been friends with Christina since our schooldays, even though she spent years living abroad, first in New York then Asia. We stayed in touch by phone and letter – before emails made it easier – and visited as often as funds allowed. When she had her first child, my godson Lawrence, she and her husband decided to make their UK base in a family-oriented neighbourhood. A geographer by training and inclination, she pulled out the maps, triangulated commuting times from London with access to the M25 and M11 for visiting family and marked a cross some 25 miles north-west of Marble Arch.

Raising Hope as a single parent kept me closely tied to the magazine offices in Soho, due to the absolute necessity of being able to fall into a taxi and be home within 20 minutes.

But after Hope went away to university, Mark and I began to discuss moving out of London, and Hertfordshire seemed the obvious choice. We had already spent weekends at Christina's house in the Ashridge Forest, walking with the dogs through the bluebells in the spring, and had experimented with living out 'in the sticks' while we renovated one of our houses, so knew the area well. We loved the little art deco jewel of a cinema with its determinedly cosmopolitan repertoire of foreign films, as well as the 'proper' country pubs.

We were tired of London, certainly. Tired of the noise, the dirt and the fact that perfectly ordinary houses in north London were selling for millions. One night, after being stuck on the Tube for over an hour on my way home from work, I started coughing and wheezing unable to breathe. Lung cancer is a typical way for breast cancer to metastasise and the GP panics at the sight of my lumpy shoulder broken in a long ago fall from a horse. X-rays reveal my breathlessness to be simply asthma, but I took it as a sign that my body was telling me we had to leave London. We looked at what we could trade our own terraced house, with walls so thin we could hear our neighbours sneeze – and worse – and found we could buy somewhere with grace and ease and style in Hertfordshire.

To be sure, I was more attached to the area than Mark, although it was he who found the house, most recently used as a printworks but originally built to service the narrowboat trade. You would not know it from the front of the house but open the back door where the garden would be and the ground drops away into the bottle-green water of the canal, the nearest land being the tow path on the other bank, some 20 feet away. There, dog-walkers and cyclists pause to look back at our home crafted from stables that housed the horses that pulled the barges. This was the house I had dreamed of for Claire.

The Canal House had already been attractively renovated to the extent that I thought it was perfect for us to move in. But Mark insisted that, for what he was calling our Forever Home, only the best would do. He went part-time at work to supervise this refurbishment of the original renovation. The priority, he said, was to turn the house upside down, so that the living rooms were on the first floor with views of the canal and the River Bulbourne. From the windows at the Canal House, we would be eye-to-eye with the herons, the cormorants and the boaters as they passed within a few feet of our back door.

This turned out to be no small undertaking. Even getting planning permission for the skylight windows took four months as the Canal House is a listed building. The unused downstairs kitchen was pulled apart and turned into a utility room while we installed a completely new kitchen upstairs, in a configuration that we revised no fewer than 39 times before being truly satisfied. Using my *Good Housekeeping* expertise and with Hope, who once she finished university was planning to train as a chef at Leiths School of Food and Wine, this was to be a kitchen made for cooking in a house designed for entertaining.

Although we were moving away from our friends in north London, our plan was to invite them regularly for lunches, dinners and whole weekends, so we installed three Miele ovens, two fridge-freezers and a wine fridge, as well as a fridge in the utility room just for the dog food, two dishwashers and a boiling water tap. We ripped up the unwalked-on tiles throughout the house and a lorry with some sort of concrete mixer on the back turned up to pour pale grey resin on the floors throughout – elegant, warm and eye-wateringly expensive. It didn't matter to us; we'd made money on the London house and we knew we were going to live here for the rest of our lives. The ground floor was reconfigured to make an enormous study for us to share along with three luxurious bedrooms, each with an ensuite bathroom. Instead of one or other of us tiptoeing to the spare room in the small hours, we had the architect draw up plans for not one but two master bedrooms: his and hers suites.

'Never have separate bedrooms,' my grandmothers used to intone, as they racked up ruby and golden wedding anniversaries. But I never had any patience for their little homilies and nuggets of wisdom. Nothing about my life bore any resemblance to the lives of the women who came before me. No one in my family had ever lived a life like mine. I was the first to go to university, then all the other firsts – good and, yes, tragic – that followed after. There was never anyone to say, this is what worked for me, this is what helps. I was making it up as I went along – and moving from London to Hertfordshire, where I knew only one other household, and having separate bedrooms to manage my chronic insomnia were just the latest in a long line of making it up as I went along.

We are like the family of the Three Bears. Hope, Baby Bear, has her own suite the size of a small apartment. Mark's room features mirrored wardrobes and a black and white bathroom.

It is cool and dark, the custom-made Rolls-Royce bed is installed, firm and unyielding on Mark's side, softer on mine, as per our specifications. My separate suite is decorated in champagne shades, with a softer but no less luxurious bed with a Tempur mattress that, like Mama Bear, I snuggle into on my solo sleepless nights. I have a walk-in wardrobe in which I hang my black Armani work suits alongside open shelving for my Chanel handbags and Prada heels. We install a whirlpool spa bath in my bathroom, which is tiled with sparkling mosaic tiles. Each evening I retreat to this crystal cave where I allow the jets to pummel the knots from my back and neck in the hopes of relaxing enough to snatch a few hours' rest alone in my super-king-size bed. Of course, Mark and I still spend nights sleeping together, mainly at weekends in the Rolls-Royce bed when I don't have to be up early for work, but the knowledge that if I am tormented by sleeplessness, or if Mark wants to get up early to go for a swim, I can retreat not to a spare room with a cheap single bed but to a bedroom worthy of a five-star hotel relieves a lot of the pressure on me.

We buy new furniture to fit with the huge size of the rooms, a dining table that will seat 14 of those future guests, custom-made by Heal's. The light fittings are by designers Philippe Starck and Foscarini. From Liberty we buy a mirror in a baroque frame that, wired up to the mains, flashes the word 'Sexy' across the canal, on and off in neon light. We agree it is both funny and romantic, like our marriage we say.

Inevitably we bust our original budget, and then some, but every time I jib at the cost, Mark reminds me that we will be there for the rest of our lives, even pointing out that the new staircase with its Perspex banister could be reconfigured to accommodate a lift, should either of us become infirm in old age.

'We're never moving again,' he says. There is step-free access to the pub next door – we can drive there on mobility scooters, he adds. 'This is where we'll live out our disgraceful old age.'

It doesn't even take me much longer to get to work than from Muswell Hill where we were living before. In the mornings, I walk along the tow path by the canal to the station, from which the journey time is a little shorter than in Graham Greene's day, just 31 minutes to London Euston. Sometimes I waited that long for a bus to East Finchley Tube station.

There was no suggestion of being able to work from home back then, so I still need to go to my Soho office five days a week and on one or two nights a week out to the beauty events and book launches that have dwindled since the arrival of digital and social media but are still a part of my job – after which I take an Addison Lee car home or stay overnight at the University Women's Club in Mayfair. For Mark the change is more dramatic, something to which I probably should have paid more attention. A proud north Londoner, he grew up within the sound of the Arsenal crowd. When he asked me to marry him, he drove me to the top of Alexander Palace before getting down on one knee. North London spread out below us was his manor. So intent am I on my lovely new home, hanging out with my long-time friends and my fulfilling job, that I overlook the fact that – intent on creating the perfect family life of my fantasies – I am dictating the terms of our relationship and that the move has been more destabilising for Mark than for me. Although it was he who found the house in the first place and insisted on the lavish refurbishment, I don't think he really thought through the implications of moving out of London. He had never before had more than a 15-minute journey to work and the swimming pools and gyms he liked to use daily for training were all now more difficult to reach.

Our *Grand Designs* project takes fully eight months until we can finally move in. The following summer, on 7 August 2016, Mark surprises me with an antique dressing table as a birthday gift. It has a circular mirror and low walnut drawers; it looks perfect in my bedroom suite, the finishing touch. We have been married for 12 years, a year longer than I was married to John, and it will soon be the 10-year anniversary of the cancer diagnosis that overshadowed our lives so soon after our marriage. I believe we have come through the worst. We will be together forever.

29 September 2016: One month before the crash

I am not actually old, I tell myself, this is mid-life – late mid-life if I am being truthful – but I'm as skinny as I was when I was 20 and sporting blonde highlights I could not have afforded back then. Tonight, I am wearing butter-soft suede leggings from Amanda Wakeley with an asymmetric top. This is what is known as a Big Birthday, so I am throwing a party, taking over the premises of the University Women's Club in Mayfair. Champagne all the way. Extravagant, yes, but there are so many reasons to celebrate. The devastating and tragic events of the past that haunted me for so long are now, I pray, firmly behind me. I have so much to be thankful for – not least my hugely successful work life and the support of my loving husband of the past 12 years.

More than 100 people fill the drawing room and library of the club on the night of 29 September: all my extended family, my boss and colleagues from work, Christina and her family, a sprinkling of celebrities from the pages of magazines I have edited, and all the friends and acquaintances who helped me through the dark years. I skitter around on Valentino heels, chatting to everyone, thanking them for coming. In four weeks' time, the man I call Peter Swift will run in front of a lorry – and the agonies of grief I thought I had long ago dealt with will erupt back into the world, destroying my career, my marriage and even – for a time, my sanity. But I don't know that yet.

Fashion photographer John Swannell snaps away all night and sends the photos to me as a birthday gift. I have them still, and there, frozen in time, is Mark wearing one of what he calls his party shirts, raising a glass to me and proposing a toast. The words he uses are so moving that they are repeated back to me by guests in emails and messages the next day:

'This woman changed my life,' Mark tells the 100 assembled family and friends. 'I love and adore her.'

PART II

Unbound

CHAPTER 10

Press Trip

10 January 2017: 10 weeks after the crash

I lean over the basket of the hot air balloon to peer down at the desert below. There is no wildlife to see and precious little in the way of vegetation. The Atacama Desert is famously the most arid place on earth – nothing can live here. It is a moonscape, 41,000 square miles of stony terrain, salt lakes and lava fields.

I arrived back from the Lake District wobbly from the steering failure that sent me and the car nose-first into a ditch, a second crash coming only weeks after the headlong collision with the lorry. I am unable to make sense of Mark's apparent disinterest in these traffic disasters – and I haven't admitted to anyone about the hallucinations of blood running down the walls of my hotel room. I knew there was something badly wrong, but I couldn't work out what was wrong with my marriage or what was wrong with me. So, I did what I always do, what I have become accustomed to doing when confronted with something too painful to look at: I distract myself with work, travel, socialising, preferably all at the same time. I went to my office and I discovered that the travel editor had to pull out of an imminent trip to Chile; it made perfect sense – at least to my fragile brain – to pack a bag and take his place. I was as obsessive about my Tried & Tested philosophy as ever and email and other electronic communications meant that I could stay in touch with the office, editing copy, from thousands of miles away in the southern hemisphere.

I enjoy airports, I love flying, in any section of the plane. I like the anonymity of hotels, the new experiences, and I relish travelling with fellow journalists and writers, the ease with which they strike up instant friendships in a bar anywhere in the world.

This is my working life, or part of it. Along with the colleagues with whom I am travelling, I was woken early that morning while it was still dark and a fleet of 4x4s drove us along dirt roads far out into the desert. We drank hot, strong coffee from flasks while a red dirigible was inflated, then we climbed into the large wicker basket and rose into the sky along with the dawn.

The usually garrulous press corps falls silent, there is no sound except for the occasional roar of the gas jets when we need to gain extra height. Otherwise, we float silently, suspended like a bloody teardrop above the barren moonscape. I think about the vast emptiness of space that is the result of unimaginable explosions at the beginning of time and of the spaces between the particles of an atom which mean that what we think of as a solid world mostly consists of the space between electrons. So very little of what we think is real exists – the rest is just space, internal and external.

The hot air balloon drifts for an hour in the brilliant, cold morning sunshine before we are told to sit on the bottom of the basket ready for landing. We hit the ground with unexpected force and then are dragged a short way – it feels like being thrown downstairs in a laundry basket, I imagine – although not as alarming – and it makes me wonder how honeymoon couples, the more usual clientele for these flights, feel about being brought back down to earth with a bump? A foreshadowing of married life, perhaps?

But then the support car catches up with us, bringing champagne to toast our flight. I think about Mark and how hard it must be to be married to someone who rarely gets home from work before 10 at night and casually ticks off these bucket list adventures on her own. I feel guilty about how he wanted me to go on his swimming trip at New Year but I couldn't even give him that, when I have so much.

I have never before met any of my six companions on this trip but we fall easily into the rhythms and patterns that are the hallmarks of any press trip. There are two pretty young women from fashion magazines – I nickname them the glossy posse – who take every opportunity to sunbathe in skimpy bikinis; an older woman from a tabloid newspaper constantly fielding calls from either her news editor or her teenage sons – who seem equally demanding – and a couple of male hacks, straight from central casting who wouldn't look out of place in a Sunday-night crime drama. Our guide is an extremely capable PR woman, shuffling press releases and flash drives loaded with tourist board approved photos.

Nestled between the Andes and the Pacific Ocean, Chile is the 'long petal of the sea' that borders Peru to the north. It is the closest country to Antarctica in the south. We travel first to the city of Valparaíso, where once pirate ships made land, but at the time of our trip forest fires surrounding the city knocked out the wi-fi and even, for a while, the water supply in our hotel. No one complains. Although, our mission is to write about the opening up of Chile's luxury travel industry, we retain a journalistic longing for disaster. The tabloid woman and the male hacks file news stories, which do not make the UK papers and we are all a little disappointed that the forest fires don't even cause us to depart from our itinerary.

For eight days, we travel the length of this extraordinary country, staying no more than one or two nights in each destination, equably sharing our phone chargers and sunscreen, inevitably lost in the constant packing and repacking, and standing each other rounds of drinks in the bar each night as we bond over our adventures and discover mutual acquaintances met on other trips. It comes easily to me, this being 7,000 miles from home in the company of complete strangers. There are no old hurts, no fresh betrayals, just a friendly group of professionals. I tell myself that this change of scene was much needed. When I get home, I will confront Mark about why he didn't respond when I called him for help, alone and terrified in the Lake District. The story about turning his phone off for Nick wasn't good enough – I will demand to know what is going on. I am so used to telling people what to do, directing teams of people, getting my own way that I am certain I can sort this out.

And I fall in love with Chile. Everywhere we go I am touched by the gentleness and humility of the people, who have endured such suffering in recent memory. During the military dictatorship under General Augusto Pinochet in the seventies and eighties, somewhere around 40,000 citizens were tortured using electric shocks and water-boarding – many of them students. I remember reading the news reports and, being a student myself at the time, joining marches and demonstrations in London against the junta. More than 2,000 were executed, and on this trip, in between trips to museums and art galleries, we visit the football stadium in Santiago where dissidents were herded by the secret police before they were 'disappeared'.

Afterwards we stop off at a flea market where I spot a cocktail trolley and make inquiries about shipping it back to the UK, as I know Mark will love it. I think about the sunrise over the Atacama Desert, a new dawn every day. Isn't that what marriage is about – a constant process of fresh starts? We have been through so much together and my cancer right at the start of the marriage didn't help. I haven't been as supportive as I could have been about his passion for swimming. I resolve to do better. I am good at fixing things. I fixed *Good Housekeeping*; I support the lives of the millions of women who read the magazine. I will fix whatever it is that has happened to my marriage.

Our base in the Atacama has an activity centre where we are offered the options of white-water rafting, mountain biking or a horse ride in the desert. I haven't ridden for years, not since the osteoporosis diagnosis made it inadvisable. But I don't care for white water – or for any water – and have never been keen on cycling. Since it's unlikely that as representatives of the press we will be put in any danger, I sign up to go riding.

The desert is as dry and barren as it appeared from the hot air balloon that morning. Our local criollo horses are sure-footed and pick their way carefully across the scrub. Obviously, neither I or the glossy posse have come equipped with riding gear, so we wear T-shirts, jeans and trainers with borrowed helmets. The late afternoon sun beats down on our shoulders.

One of the glossy posse stands up in her stirrups to take photographs and our guide points out the tiny green shrub whose leaves contain droplets of water, which we could eat if we ever found ourselves lost in the desiccated landscape. I don't look down too much because I have a life-long phobia of snakes – can't even bear to look at pictures of them – but the guide reassures me that nothing can live out here, not even snakes, so I relax and start to enjoy myself. My knees chafe through my jeans and I know I will pay for this over the next few days, but there is something about navigating this elemental scene on horseback that thrills me more than the dawn flight.

We are about an hour out from the stables when the late afternoon sky suddenly darkens. There is a flash of lightning followed far too quickly by a clap of thunder. With majestic irony we are in one of the most arid places in the world and caught in a thunderstorm. The horses stop and paw the ground as our guide circles his mount to address us. He points to a gully several hundred yards away and explains in heavily accented English that we need to gallop as fast as we can into the dip where we will no longer be the highest points around as the lightning travels overhead. Once in the gully, he says, it's vital we keep going at speed following the track as swiftly as possible back to camp before – as happens during these once-a-year storms – the gully turns into a river. From his face and the urgency in his voice we can see it is serious: this is not a drill.

There is no time to be scared. We set off at a gallop, the guide leading the way followed by the glossy posse while I bring up the rear, the criollos moving like the wind, racing the storm. I lean forward like a jockey and clutch at my horse's mane as she gallops, only to have to pitch backwards for balance as she slithers down into the gully. She knows exactly what she's doing, quickly finding her footing again, and I crouch forward, again, in the jockey position as the horses gallop on ever faster, keeping us ahead of the threatened flood.

The rain catches up with us as we reach the safety of the village. Sheltering under the overhang of a building I take the risk of turning around to look behind me. The desert sky is riven by lightning as if an anarchic demi-god is setting off all the fireworks in the box at once and, as predicted, the deluge is turning the gully into a raging river.

In the time it takes to trot the last few hundred yards back to the stables, I am soaked to the skin, my knees chafed. I know I should feel scared – but I never had a moment's doubt that the horses would save us, that they would race against the elements and win. Somehow, I feel more alive than I have felt in a long time.

The next evening, in my hotel room dressing for a last-night dinner that will take place by a roof-top pool, I go into the bathroom and turn on all the taps to drown out the sound of my sobs in order to cry as I have been doing every day for months now. This time I tell myself I am weeping for the 'disappeared'. So much suffering in the world, surely crying every day is a natural consequence?

CHAPTER 11

Fact Check

25 January 2017: 12 weeks after the crash

I arrive home from work just after lunchtime, wheezing and unwell. I picked up a chest infection on the flight back from Chile and although that was a week ago, I haven't been able to shake it off and the cough exacerbates my asthma. I find something in Boots that coats my throat in a sort of sweet gel. It comes in little silver sachets and I gulp handfuls of them to get through the working day before going on to the creative writing evening class I have recently started on top of what by any measure is an already excessive workload. I carry a bottle of water with me too, but every so often I have to run out of the class and sit in the corridor puffing on my inhaler, gasping for breath.

When I stand up from my desk I feel as if I am going to fall over.

The house seems cold and unwelcoming. Hope, I know, was out last night with her cousin Zoe but I can see the remains of a dinner for two – salade niçoise by the looks of it – and an unfamiliar bottle of wine in the recycling bin. I google the label.

More than my husband would normally spend? And it's rosé? In January? I think snobbishly.

Did you have someone over for dinner last night? I inquire when he comes home.

'Yes,' he says. 'Simon.'

I have never heard him talk about rosé-drinking Simon before.

Accuracy is an obsession of mine. Fact-checking is part of the life of an editor. I was trained long ago as a junior reporter always to seek confirmation. Words can be mis-remembered or mis-construed, I tell my team. Never assume anything, text messages don't always arrive, or may not be saved. Keep a contemporaneous record of every important conversation is the rule. So, I decide to send my husband an email asking him to confirm that his dinner guest was a man called Simon. His answer will, I hope, assuage the fears that are starting to build in my mind.

His reply: 'I don't understand why you're making something out of nothing. What are you getting at?'

Well, what am I getting at? I was in my forties when I married Mark, he in his late thirties; we both had pasts that we discussed fully and frankly. We sought marital counselling in the early days when the difference in our backgrounds and expectations showed up, and again when my breast cancer diagnosis rendered me incapable of communicating with anyone including, for a time, my husband. We were united in our belief that fidelity was the bedrock of any marriage. But now I seemed to be accusing him not merely of having an affair but of being sufficiently crass to bring a lover into our home, even into our bed. Really?

It's my own fault that I don't know who Nick and Simon are – I have not made any effort to get to know the friends he has made through swimming. I work too much, dashing off to South America at the slightest sign of conflict. His reply makes me feel ashamed to have accused the good man who so proudly tells anyone who'll listen how much he loves me.

Two weeks later, Hope gets home from an evening out. She finds me lying in the bath where I have been for hours, crying. Tears and snot running over my breasts mingling with the tepid soapy water. She helps me out of the bath, as if I were the child not her, and wraps me in towels. We lie together on my bed.

'Mum,' she says, 'whatever is going on, you've got to start looking after yourself. You can't go on like this.'

The next day I go to see my GP Dr B, and not for the first time it strikes me that she comes as close as anyone I have ever met to my mythical GH reader Claire. I tell her about the steering failure and the terrors that have followed. I am not sleeping I say, usually only two or three hours a night. I have cried every single day since the first car crash, I say. That's over three months ago and I'm not getting any better.

She writes a prescription for the antidepressant citalopram, but as she hands it over she says: 'I know from your notes what you've been through in the past and you're resilient. I don't believe this is about the car crashes. There is something else going on in your life, something you're not facing up to.'

I should take time off work; I know I am not functioning properly. I can only snatch a few hours' rest with the help of sleeping pills and I can't seem to shake off the chest infection. At the very least, I should take a break from the additional demands of my creative writing university course. But the more my life spirals out of control, the harder it becomes to lighten my workload.

I went back to work straight after John's funeral. I worked when Hope was a baby. I went to the office even when Ellie was in hospital … What would it say about me if I stopped now?

Valentine's Day, 2017: 15 weeks after the crash

I go alone for my annual cancer check-up, my head still ringing from the crash, my mind fogged with Mark's inexplicable behaviour towards me.

Dr Bogarde examines me, then I wait in silence while he studies my blood test results and my bone scans. 'So,' he says, without looking up, double-checking the numbers, 'The time has come – I'm firing you.'

I flinch, visibly distressed. I have no idea what he means; since the car crash, I have become hyper-vigilant, seeing threat everywhere.

He is troubled by my response; he has been treating me for a decade, and has not seen me like this, even in the dark days of the early diagnosis and my violent sickness during chemotherapy.

'That was a silly joke,' he says, reaching across the desk to pat my hand. 'I'm giving you good news. What I meant was you don't have to come back and see me anymore.'

Gradually, I start to understand. I am not cured, no one talks of curing cancer, but the chances of a relapse have now receded to a point where they are no greater than if I had never had cancer in the first place. I can stop taking all the medications except for alendronic acid, which is for the osteoporosis, because my treatment for breast cancer is finally over.

He shakes my hand and wishes me well. I stumble out onto Harley Street and text Mark, who stopped coming with me to appointments some time back; I don't remember when. 'Good news x' he replies.

I had a friend, the same age as me – Kate Carr, she was editor of the *Sunday Times Magazine* – who was diagnosed with breast cancer in her late 30s, when she was the mother of two young children. She was given her discharge at five years and I remember her telling me that it was in some ways more traumatic than the initial diagnosis. For the entire length of your treatment you are tested, monitored and reassured that the cancer is being held at bay. Eventually, you become institutionalised, depending on the check-ups like a lifer in prison. And then it ends. You have peered over the side of the abyss and know what monsters live there but now you are on your own. Kate's cancer did come back, in fact, three years after her all-clear. With cancer there are only statistics, never promises. She died the summer I was getting married to Mark. I miss her still – her cool intelligence, her dry wit, her elegant, off-beat style – and it is with Kate that I have a conversation as I start to walk from Harley Street, across Oxford Circus. 'Finishing treatment, it's not always the good news everyone thinks it is,' she says. 'At least they didn't make you ring a bell!'

I don't even notice that these days I am talking more to the dead than to the living.

CHAPTER 12

The Editor's Decision Is …

18 February 2017: 16 weeks after the crash

Saturday morning, and for once, I am awake early enough to go swimming with Mark. I don't usually – too tired from the working week – but I am determined to break an impasse that seems to have developed between us since his refusal to come on holiday to Scotland.

We go Champneys, the health spa at nearby Tring, where I swim 20 lengths of breaststroke, head out of the water like a duck. Even at this stately pace, exercise endorphins flood my system; this is nice, I think. Couples should have hobbies they share.

Mark thrashes up and down in butterfly. The power in his chest and arms is phenomenal. He recently formed a team – I have never met them, obviously, and – this is astonishing – they now hold the world record for a relay crossing of the English Channel in that most inefficient and difficult stroke. 'Punching waves,' he calls it. As I get out of the pool an elderly woman with her hair tied up in a scarf follows me, saying irritably: 'That man isn't usually here, thank goodness.'

So, I wonder, where has he been training if not here?

Mark goes off to work at the estate agency and I go home and get on with mundane Saturday tasks. The insurance on our three cars needs sorting, so I pay it.

The exercise was a good idea. I start to feel calmer. I can't have been easy to live with due to the PTSD from the two crashes and maybe anxiety about my final cancer check-up as well. But a weight has lifted; I love my husband and he says he loves me. I resolve to do better from now on.

In the evening I make chilli for supper and while it's cooking, we walk to the pub next door where Mark buys a glass of Prosecco for me and beer for himself; he thanks me for dealing with the insurance.

Later, after we've eaten, we watch one of my favourite films: Wes Anderson's *The Darjeeling Limited*.

Mark half watches but fiddles most of the time with his phone; busy on social media promoting the swim-coaching business he has recently started up, I assume. I imagine the anti-depressants flooding through my body, restoring my serotonin levels. I relax and lose myself in the film.

A snake appears on screen; I look away automatically because of my phobia and see Mark has gone to the toilet, leaving his phone on the arm of the chair. An email flashes onto the locked screen – he has not bothered to disable the alert. It's from one of his swimming friends, not Nick nor Simon – both of whom he talks about a lot – but a woman … concerning a dinner in Dover in two weeks' time. Time slows. I see the lorry jack-knifing on the road ahead of me. Brake, steer, brake again. Don't panic or you risk flipping over into oncoming traffic. When he reappears, I speak with icy calm: 'You're having an affair.'

A mask slips; his face is ashen; his lips form a jagged line.

'How do you know?'

'There's an email on your phone. If it's innocent, you'll show it to me.'

Instead, he takes his phone and locks himself, with it, in the toilet for 20 minutes.

When he finally comes out, he says nothing.

'We'll talk about this tomorrow,' I manage to utter, before my brain retreats into its long-practised state of denial.

Then – and even now this strikes me as odd – we both watch the film to the end, until Bill Murray is sitting comfortably in his train compartment, the man-eating tiger in another, and the conductor is crooning over the cobra. I don't look away this time but stare steadfastly at the cinematic snake. I don't yet comprehend what is happening to me – it is only much later that I understand I have completely dissociated and gone back to that familiar place beyond pain, beyond reach, beyond everything.

More sleeping tablets from my secret stash get me through the night, and the next day, Sunday, Mark goes out early and is gone for most of the day. I start researching relationship counsellors. We will get through this. Mistakes happen. I transgressed back when I was married to John and we came through it even stronger. I don't know what is going on with Mark but I know he loves me. Only a few months ago he was telling the guests at my party how I had changed his life, how much he adored me. By the time Mark eventually returns it's late afternoon, so I suggest a walk and he agrees. We have been walking up and down the tow paths of the Grand Union canal ever since we conceived the idea of moving from London to the countryside.

In this way, we have laid out our hopes and dreams, fears and possibilities. At this most crucial point in our relationship, I want to be doing what we always do when we make important decisions.

The February air is cold and the sun low in the sky. Hardly any other walkers are about but we talk in low voices and fall silent altogether when someone passes us.

He starts.

'I've taken advice,' he says. 'And we can make a case that we've been living separate lives. We will get a divorce on the grounds of mutual separation.'

Separate lives? It's as if we are reading from different scripts. What was I expecting? The truth, perhaps? An apology, maybe? 'We have a proper loving relationship,' I protest. 'We only moved into this house 17 months ago – we aren't living separate lives. I know you didn't come to Scotland but – um? – we've been on plenty of other holidays together?'

'Blips. They don't count.'

The word hits me like a slap in the face. Strolling hand in hand around the antique shops of Stamford picking out the finishing touches for our new home. Drinking champagne while sitting in a jacuzzi in the Lake District. Falling out of bed laughing after my party at the London club. None of it felt like a blip to me.

He sticks by the word 'blips', using it later in an email to my solicitors, consistently maintaining that our marriage had been 'toxic for years'. And, of course, I didn't share his passion for open-water swimming, was never at the Serpentine in Hyde Park waiting with a warm towel for him while he swam. Not willing to share hot chocolate and a bacon roll with his coterie of friends afterwards. I have been found guilty of being a Bad Wife. Not only have I been too busy with my career to support his hobby. Worse, I have been too desperate for sleep to share a bed most nights.

I spend that night alone, too, knocked out by more of my now diminishing supply of sleeping tablets, before heading into work. Meanwhile, he refuses to admit that he is having an affair.

Pathetically, I need to hear it from his own lips, to believe it's not simply a flirtation or a one-night stand. From the glimpse I saw of the email they were planning a weekend in Dover, so maybe the affair has not yet started, this trip was to be the first? I start to doubt the evidence of my own eyes. I only saw a snippet, after all. And what sort of philanderer doesn't have a second phone? Maybe I have misunderstood and there's an innocent explanation? I think about when my car ploughed into the ditch in the Lake District, how I was incapable of calling the AA, even though I had a fob with the number on my keyring.

I realise I have been unwell since that headlong crash with the lorry four months ago; spaced out and weepy, dependent on sleeping tablets and now on antidepressants. But love does not alter when it alteration finds, wasn't that a quote from our wedding service?

I ring a lawyer friend, Maggie, and leave a message for her. She calls me back from Cuba where she is on holiday and says to 'hang tight', we will discuss it when she gets back. 'Your house is big enough for the two of you to live in without getting in each other's way?' she asks. I confirm that it is.

* * *

On the Monday, I go to work, because whatever is happening in my life I always go to work. I tell no one of my discovery. Same again on Tuesday. On Wednesday, we are photographing a celebrity for an upcoming issue, which will keep me busy all day as I insist on overseeing every detail. At its most basic, that's the job of an editor – to say yes, or no, to all the myriad decisions that go into creating a successful magazine. This colour or that colour? This headline or another – when either looks equally good? These thousands of micro-decisions eventually add up to a creative vision that sells millions of copies every year. It's not written down, well some of it is, but mostly it's held in my head. The downside being that no one can get on with the jobs they are very well qualified to do until I make my decision about which of many equally valid choices to pursue. The editor's decision is final – and that's what I have to do … decide.

It's something I am comfortable with, confident in my choices – plus I know I can make further decisions to fix things if I get it wrong. I have been editing top-selling magazines, and directing celebrity shoots, for over a quarter of a century now, so it's familiar territory; I know how to guarantee a cover that will sell out on the news-stand. Our star must be high-profile yet appear approachable, friendly, with inspirational values. She must be a woman's-woman – not look like she would steal your husband (I joke). And she will be wearing the sort of outfit an imaginary reader – Claire – might want to wear, on a really good day, when her hair is at that perfect mid-point between trims and she's lost that pesky half a stone.

Capturing the image and pictures to accompany the profile inside will take the whole day, so I set off early for an 8 a.m.

appointment with Dr M, the therapist I saw after Ellie died. The sessions had trailed off in recent years: deeply in love again, successful at work, Hope grown into a lovely young woman … I thought I had survived; I thought I was happy. But my GP made me promise to resume my sessions before she would prescribe antidepressants.

After 55 minutes, I leave Dr M's Hampstead consulting room and walk to Swiss Cottage Tube station where I wait on the platform for the Jubilee line train that will take me first to the office. A seasoned commuter, I go to the end of the platform, near where the trains arrive out of the tunnel, to have the best chance of getting a seat in the rush hour. I check the indicator board: Stratford, Train Approaching.

I think about Peter Swift, stepping into the path of the lorry that night on the Southend Arterial. What was happening in his life to make him want to end it? Did he hesitate? Or was it a headlong dash? And there and then the solution to this crisis presents itself. It's obvious, really. It's not our marriage that's toxic but me. I should never have survived either car crash. What right did I have to breathe air and walk around when I was only making everything worse for all around me? It's not fate that has deprived those I loved the most of their lives but my own toxicity. I am the bad seed, the cancer eating away at the heart of my family and like a tumour I need to be slashed, poisoned and burned, although hopefully the slashing will be enough, under the wheels of the next train. Thoughts tumble through my mind in a cascade of self-loathing.

I teeter on the balls of my feet. I don't have to run; one step is all it will take not to feel this pain anymore. I rock back and forth. None of the other commuters is paying me any attention.

Move one foot, then the other and – what – a momentary star-burst of agony? Then nothing. This will all stop. I need never know the truth of the affair, never go through the painful process of dissolving the marriage and picking up the pieces of my life. I need never, ever be alone again.

I rock back and forth again weighing my options, the temptation to join John and Ellie – wherever they are, even if it is nowhere – is nearly overwhelming. The rumbling from the track is getting louder. I feel a rush of warm air. Decide … I'm the editor.

And the editor's decision is final.

I turn and run, pushing my way through the crowd. As the train rushes into the station, I reach the safety of the escalator hall where I sit on the concrete steps between the up and down escalators, panting with fright. I don't think about what my death would have done to Hope or to my mother. I still feel so disgusted with myself that I am convinced they would be better off without me – and Mark clearly has other plans. But I think about the unknown driver of the train, the passengers standing on the platform – it is the thought of them that made me turn away. How could I do to them what Peter Swift did, unwittingly, to me? I don't know how to achieve it – but this pain has to stop. It is not just mental but physical; I have endured childbirth, cancer treatment, broken bones, but this feels worse, like a knife turning in my stomach, like poison flooding my system, as if my brain is melting.

Commuters push past me, each wrapped in their own thoughts, oblivious of the battle raging within me. I don't trust myself to go back onto the platform, so I leave the station and take a taxi to the photographic studio and the shoot.

CHAPTER 13

Shoot

22 February 2017: 16 and a half weeks after the crash

We are photographing one of *Good Housekeeping*'s most popular celebrity interviewees; I have met her before and like her a lot. She is every bit as warm and friendly as when she appears on TV, which is nearly all the time. You would know exactly who she is, if I told you her name – but that wouldn't be fair; she was then, and remains, completely unaware of what was about to unfold that day.

The studio in east London is a bare-bricked barn of a place, busy with people milling around expectantly – everyone waiting for instructions from me.

By the time I arrive the crew have been setting up for more than an hour. Our star has arrived and changed into a towelling robe, her hair wound into heated rollers. Now she is perched on a high stool, in the process of having her face made up, while a manicurist paints her nails. Photoshop is now so ubiquitous that everyone thinks those flawless cover images are achievable with just a few clicks, like on an Instagram filter. But that can easily look fake. I'm not saying we don't airbrush, we do –

although Jane Fonda had 'no retouching' written into her contract with us and I was happy to oblige. But I think there is more authenticity if you get as close as you can to the desired effect with hair, make-up and good lighting. The make-up artist leans in wielding a fine brush to correct an all-but-invisible blemish on our star's otherwise perfect complexion. Within her sight-line the magazine fashion team rifle through rails of clothes, holding up outfits for her to choose between. There won't be any embarrassing disagreements. This is how I avoid conflict, by pre-planning everything, doing all the work behind the scenes.

I start by deciding a colour theme that will be established on the cover and continued subliminally throughout the subsequent 300 or so pages. The issue we are shooting will go on sale in high summer, so I have decreed tropical fruit shades of pineapple, mango and papaya. Lemon is permissible but not lime because one of my 'rules' – and I have so many rules – is that the only celebrity who can get away with wearing green on a cover is Julianne Moore. An assistant is kneeling on the floor of the dressing room, laying out dozens of pairs of designer heels as shiny and colourful as sweetie wrappers, embellished with diamante straps, velvet ribbons and even feathers. I always let a star choose her own shoes – it gives her a feeling of control. And if, later, I don't think they work – well, shoes can easily be cropped out of the picture.

The photographer is consulting with his two assistants – young lads in jeans and plaid shirts, who manhandle scaffolding into place, holding a light meter up to each other's faces and acting as stand-ins for the composition I am looking for. They show me the test shots, I give an almost imperceptible shake of my head, so the photographer instructs them move the entire rig over to the other side of the studio in search of a better angle.

Lounging in the kitchen area are the celebrity's assistant, people from her management agency and PRs for the beauty brand she represents. I am not sure what they are all doing here; they type on their laptops and talk in bored tones to each other, drinking coffee and eating the croissants intended for the crew. In total, I count 21 people, all hanging on my every word, my every decision. I feel suddenly nauseous and go and hide in the toilets.

From there – keeping my voice low – I ring the GP surgery and ask if I can get an appointment with Dr B.

'Is it urgent?'

Outside, I hear the call on-set, they are ready to start shooting … whenever I want? My decision.

Whispering into the phone, I say: 'I think I want to kill myself.'

CHAPTER 14

Deadline

The GP's receptionist tells me to come at once. I leave the shoot in the charge of the beauty director – I don't tell her why – and take a taxi, too fearful to go by Tube after what happened earlier in the day. At Euston the trains are all lined up, innocently, by the buffers. Even those arriving in the station aren't going fast enough to be worth jumping in front of. I climb aboard for the half-hour journey to the country town we so recently made our home. When the train pulls into my local station, I hurry away from the platform fearful that an express passing through might prove too tempting.

At the GP surgery, I am ushered straight past parents with sick children; elderly people who don't look as if they should be out this cold February day; people who are obviously unwell. Dr B greets me warmly, letting me talk on and on, heedless of the full waiting room, until she is certain I am calm and no longer thinking of harming myself. She tells me to book in again with my therapist – it's painful, she acknowledges, but combined with the antidepressants, it will get me through this. 'I'm so sorry,' she says, adding, 'I suspected there was something like this in the mix.'

When I get home, my husband is there – I don't know why he isn't at work.

'You're early.'

'I've been to the doctor's – emergency appointment.'

He doesn't ask for details.

My daughter comes out of her bedroom.

She tells me she is about to work a shift at a local gastro pub. She suggests I come with her and bring the dogs. We can chat before she gets too busy.

So that's what we do. I sit at a corner table; the dogs' leads tied around a leg of my chair. I realise I haven't eaten all day and order the house special, which is bubble and squeak served with a poached egg, hollandaise sauce and several slices of thick salty bacon, rich and filling. I drink two glasses of wine and just before 8 p.m. my daughter calls me a mini-cab and together with the dogs I return home.

All journalists live by deadlines: plural. The submission date for the writer is only the beginning of a process that involves sub-editors and graphic designers all working to multiple schedules that culminate in 'shipping' – the day, and time, when layouts for every page of the magazine are sent to the printers. But even that isn't the final, final deadline. The secret all editors carry is that there is a place beyond the point of no return. A magazine such as *Good Housekeeping* is too big to print in one go. So, even as the presses were rolling, I kept in my head the running order in which each 16-page section was loaded onto the machine, and I could be making changes to the final section even as the early pages were printed and trundling along on the conveyor belt to the bindery. A good editor will always take it right to the wire.

So, although Mark has ignored every ultimatum I set for him to tell me what's going on and is still refusing to admit that he is cheating, I still think I have time to make things better. I have no idea that the Southend Arterial car crash broke open the unhealed fissure of my grief. Like the badly repaired BMW, my steering is damaged. I don't know it yet but the deadline for ending the marriage safely and with dignity has already passed.

The TV is on – but Mark is fiddling with his phone and doesn't appear to be watching. I could go and lie down in the bedroom but I feel self-righteous about staying in the living room – it's my home, too, and I feel as if I've done nothing but lie, sleepless, on my bed for months.

The TV blares but I see he is still not watching; he is texting someone. I walk over to where he is sitting and ask him to give me his phone.

'It's private.'

And then I do something I will regret for the rest of my life – I make a grab for it. And, oddly, he lets me at first. Unlike five days ago when he ran off to the toilet. I see enough in that brief moment, when the phone is in my hands, to know he is texting the woman who sent the email. The woman with whom he still will not admit he is having an affair. But then he stands up and attempts to grab the phone back out of my hand again. I hang onto it momentarily – I want this evidence – before thinking better of it and letting go. He lets go at the same time. The phone flies through the air, landing with a crash and breaking in two, on the pale grey poured resin floor we spent a small fortune installing.

We both lunge to retrieve the pieces nearest us, so we are standing a metre apart, each holding a part of the broken phone. My heart is pounding and I am gasping for breath. This is not what I expected. I still think he will admit his guilt. I think he will apologise. But what happens next astonishes me even more.

'You just assaulted me,' my husband says evenly. 'I'm calling 999.'

Long ago I described the years of grieving for John and Ellie as like living on the seabed, so deep below the ocean's surface that no sunlight could reach me. Mark helped me swim to the surface, to breathe air again. But now the undertow has caught me. My friends, my family, my therapist Dr M and my GP Dr B can only stand helpless on the shore watching me be sucked back under. The one person I thought would help me, his mighty arms cleaving through the waves – the trained lifeguard; the Channel swimmer – is holding my head underwater. I must surely drown.

We will never agree on what happened; his retelling of that evening was, and remains, fundamentally very different from mine.

There are, however, some facts that are independently verifiable.

At around 8.20 p.m., a male called the emergency services and said his wife had broken his mobile phone and attacked him with one of the pieces.

Two police cars attended the scene. They found a woman waiting for them by the front door; they noted she was very quiet and acquiescent. The man was sitting in the living room where the alleged incident had taken place. There were no signs of a disturbance other than a broken mobile phone. No knives in the vicinity, only in their usual drawer in the kitchen, some distance away in this large house.

No one appeared injured. Medical assistance was neither requested, nor offered.

The man gave a statement to the officers at the scene.

The woman was arrested on suspicion of criminal damage and common assault.

According to the notes of the arresting officer, she made no comment of any significance.

For the second time in four months, I am put in the back of a police car. This time instead of being a witness, I am under arrest. I have no idea what will happen next, only that I didn't hit my husband nor intentionally break his phone.

It's half an hour's drive to Hatfield police station. I feel as if I am trapped inside a plastic dry-cleaning bag and, every time I try to breathe, the thin membrane is sucked further inside me, suffocating me. The officers ignore me and chat idly with each other. I lean my head against the cool windscreen and for the first time in months begin to understand what is happening.

I am scared. I can't think about my daughter or my mother, their inevitable disappointment in me is too painful to bear. So I think about my father, dead these past 18 years. Although he left school in the East End of London at age 14, he studied for his law exams while working nights as a reporter to support his family. He remained, throughout his career, proudly a junior barrister, never took silk; a Rumpole of the Bailey. And he didn't have much time for expensive solicitors. 'Always go with a local chap – one who knows the coppers,' he said, although I can't imagine he ever thought his clever, high-achieving daughter would need this advice. 'Much better than some fancy brief driving down from London in a Bentley.'

At the police station, I wait to be processed. I have an officer watching me at all times and I'm not allowed to go to the toilet. Finally, I'm called forward to the desk and surrender my handbag. My purse is emptied, the cash counted: £80 in notes plus change. My credit cards are removed from my wallet and listed: Visa Debit; Platinum Visa; Barclaycard Commercial; American Express. I take off my Tag Heuer watch; my Tiffany bracelet; my diamond earrings and antique gold necklace; they are all sealed in a plastic bag that I sign for. I removed my wedding and engagement rings and put them in the safe at home the night I discovered the incriminating email.

I also sign over my iPhone and my iPad. My diary and notebook are flicked through, then returned to my handbag.

My Ventolin inhaler and the packs of my osteoporosis drugs and antidepressants are inspected and googled to check that are for the conditions I claim.

'You can make one phone call,' the desk sergeant says. I decide to call Alastair. With his own history of breakdown and arrest, I know he won't be judgmental and trust that he will know what to do and, most importantly, will look after Hope. But, in the way of things, the battery on my phone is flat and I can't remember their landline number, although I used to know it off by heart in the days when we all memorised phone numbers. The only number I can recall off the top of my head is my daughter's mobile. It goes straight to voicemail as she is still working her shift at the pub.

'Don't worry,' I say to the recording. 'I'm absolutely fine but I'm at Hatfield police station. Ring them when you get this message and they will explain everything.'

'You have a right to a duty solicitor. It's free.' The desk

sergeant says this in such a firm way that I understand from his tone that I need a solicitor.

In the next bay, I see a young girl, probably no more than 17, skinny, short skirt and bare legs on this cold February night. She turns down her right to legal representation, presumably to get back out on the streets faster.

'Or you can call your own, if you have one?' The expensive watch, all the credit cards. I look like someone who has a lawyer.

I think about my lawyer friend, away in Cuba, presumably her firm has a 24-hour answering service and can scramble a Bentley out to Hertfordshire? But my dear old dad whispers in my ear.

'A duty solicitor will be just fine,' I say.

Then I am 'processed'.

I am body-searched by a female officer wearing blue surgical gloves. I have swabs taken for DNA; facial recognition photos are taken – the classic mug shots – and then my fingerprints are recorded. I dissociate, of course – it's my superpower, after all – which allows me to study my surroundings. I am in a queue behind a big man dressed even more expensively than me. He has the air of this being just a hiccup in his business life. Drug dealer, perhaps? The duty solicitor will be here soon; he will help me explain everything. I understand why this had to happen. It's the same as after the first crash when my car was impounded and I was questioned in the police car, even though I had been travelling behind the lorry that collided with Peter Swift. There is a process. It will soon be over. My daughter will come and collect me. Full of remorse my husband will move out, go to a hotel, or his girlfriend's home, or somewhere?

'Number 27,' the desk sergeant says. And I am led to the cells.

I am told to take off my boots and leave them outside. The policewoman gives me a blanket and asks if I want a cup of tea. I wonder momentarily if they could provide a herbal blend but then remember where I am and just say: 'Yes please.' Adding 'officer' to be polite. I ask for water as well. She locks the door behind her. In the space of 12 hours, I have gone from dictating to a household name what she can and cannot wear, to being deprived of my liberty and personal possessions, even down to my shoes.

The cell is very clean, I hadn't expected that. Maybe eight feet by eight feet square, completely tiled up to the high ceiling, with a bench built into the wall along one side. On the bench is a foam mattress in a plastic cover with a separate moulded shape to serve as a pillow. Bright red like the blanket – a funny colour to choose, I think. Maybe it's to hide the blood? Opposite the bench is a stainless-steel toilet moulded all of one piece, no lid, no seat, and set into the wall behind it a tiny stainless-steel basin like you find on trains, big enough only to wash one hand at a time. I try it out. If you put your hand in one way a tiny trickle of warm water runs out. If you change the angle, there's a feeble blast of warm air. Balanced on the toilet seat is a small box of tissues. And fixed into the opposite corner at ceiling height a closed-circuit TV camera.

There are no windows, obviously, just some glass bricks between the wall and the ceiling way above my head. The processing seemed to go on for ages and it must be around 11 p.m. by now, I guess, and the light that comes through them must be artificial, from another room or corridor.

Minutes pass then the spy-hole in the door opens and I see an eye fixed to it. A flap in the door clangs open and two paper cups appear: one tea and one water. I drink the tea gratefully, even though it has sugar in it, and place the cup of water carefully on the floor next to the bench-bed. I decide to save it, not sure if any more will be forthcoming.

Not that I think I will be here very long. I am just waiting for a solicitor to sort out this appalling mistake. I'm an award-winning magazine editor, for heaven's sake, an ambassador for a well-known charity; I am on the prime minister's Christmas card list. In the cell next to mine a woman throws herself repeatedly at the door banging, kicking and moaning. A male voice shouts at her to keep it down.

Time passes, as it must. But with no phone or watch I have no idea how much. I have never been in this situation before – outside of a flotation tank at a health spa. It is utterly disorientating. A bubble of panic rises in my throat and I want to howl and throw myself at the door like my neighbour. Instead, I sit down on the bench with my back against the tiled wall, wrap the blanket tightly around me and wait for whatever terrors – familiar and new – the night will bring.

Of course, I don't sleep. For months, I haven't been able to sleep at home in my own bed. At intervals throughout the night, I hear boots coming down the corridor and the spyhole opens, the eye fixing itself in the aperture. A bubble of anticipation rises in my chest – my solicitor has arrived? Am I going to be freed? But then the boots go away and I am left locked in and alone. The visions of my first family's suffering are my only company. I remember the time I went to the Hammersmith Hospital to visit John, walking down a corridor when a trolley was pushed past me, and on it a figure, emaciated, covered in tubes, being rushed to theatre, only to realise that was my husband.

Ellie was with me that day, only a toddler then. And before I can stop them, the visions I fight so hard to prevent surfacing flood my brain, exploding out into the jail cell. Ellie in her red dressing gown with matching slippers, running down the corridor of Fox Ward at Great Ormond Street, laughing like any nine-year-old child, calling to me that I have forgotten my mobile and stopping cheekily to put her hand over her mouth because mobiles aren't allowed in hospital. Her nails are painted pink, her favourite colour, because that is how we spend the long hospital days. We have been watching TV together curled up on her bed but now I am going home to make the house ready for her discharge the next day. Just a brief holiday, the treatment continues, but we are both giddy with anticipation. As her father was when she was a toddler, she too now is bald from the relentless chemo. She wears a little cloth cap to cover where her glorious red hair used to be, but is still laughing and running towards mc, towing a medical drip stand, like a puppy.

Time loses all meaning as I whipsaw between flashbacks to Fox Ward and the present of the police cell all through the night. The light visible through the glass bricks remains on and at some point, during a brief visit to the present, I realise I badly want to pee, although the unblinking eye of the CCTV means I dare not. I picture images going viral on social media – magazine editor captured on tape peeing in cell. In the end the pain in my bladder is so great that I have no choice. As discreetly as I can manage, pulling my cashmere jumper down to cover me, I squat over the stainless-steel bowl and wonder who is watching me.

Afterwards, I wash my hands in the tiny basin, there is no soap, and the hot air leaves my hands wet so I dry them on the legs of my Donna Karan leggings. The ridiculousness of the situation – banged up in a cell wearing designer clothes from my day at the shoot makes me laugh hysterically. But again, I remember the CCTV and silence myself, lying back down to wait for the normal course of events to reassert itself.

Sometime during the small hours, I guess, I think some more about suicide; it is still only 20 or so hours since I stood on the platform at Swiss Cottage contemplating ending everything – maybe I should have jumped after all? This sudden crash out of everyday life into a timeless, hostile isolation feels everlasting and unendurable. That's why there is the CCTV and the spyhole. I consider winding a sleeve of my cashmere jumper around my neck, but of course there's nothing to tie it to – just smooth, shiny surfaces. And I wonder how long it would take for the person monitoring the CCTV to see me try. Then as fast as the thoughts arrived that morning on the platform at Swiss Cottage Station, they disappear.

I wonder, almost dispassionately, why the flashbacks seem to be easing off in intensity at last. I had thought they would go on all night until I was released into a world where I could distract myself with work again. I brace myself against the tiled wall, ready to be thrown to the floor again by my demons. But instead, I am flooded with the cool balm of clarity. I still don't have a clue when my marriage started to go wrong. Why did we spend eight months renovating a Forever Home that wasn't to be forever. I have no idea – but it is dawning that my remorseless determination to curate the perfect magazine-worthy life blinded me to reality. And now, after stumbling around as if wearing blinkers for, well, who knows how long, it is only when I am finally alone, locked in a jail cell, deprived of any distraction, that the truth is finally allowed to break through. The gentle giant who cared for me so tenderly during my cancer treatment, my husband of 12 years, wants out of the marriage. And, no, he doesn't want to talk about it.

Well, at least I know.

I hear more boots in the corridor, keys clank and turn in other cells and people are led away. I wonder why they can leave and I can't. What has happened to my solicitor? Surely, they work all night – they always seem to on TV shows?

I think of my daughter, who will be demented with worry, and I wonder if I will get out in time to go home and shower and go to work without anyone knowing of my disgrace. Because that's what I really want to do. I can't bring back John and Ellie, I can't make Mark love me. But I can go to work – my place of safety where everything can be managed and organised. I wonder what my bosses will say about my arrest? When I was a junior reporter in Glasgow, it was my job to ring round the police stations in the morning to see who had been brought in overnight. I don't think newspapers have the resources to do that anymore and magazine editors aren't properly famous. A memory flashes into my mind of the shots of me and Mark on our first date, the premiere of *Calendar Girls* – paparazzi take pictures of everyone in case they are useful in the future. I am grateful that I was arrested in my anonymous married name not my professional name.

I start to feel panicky again and get up to vomit into the stainless-steel toilet bowl, rinsing my lips with my carefully saved water. I remind myself that I live in Britain, not Chile during the junta, that I have nothing to be afraid of. And I am innocent.

At what I guess to be around 7 a.m., the eye appears in the spyhole, then the flap opens and another paper cup appears: more tea. I am asked if I want a cereal bar for breakfast. I do but also something else: 'Excuse me, sir, officer? Could I possibly have something to read?'

Words are my passion – my job and my hobby. I don't much care about food but I have to have something to read.

He returns with a day-old copy of the *Sun*. I drink my tea, which again has sugar in it, and eat my cereal bar, which is also sickly sweet but the glucose and caffeine revive me. I read every page of the paper, even the sport, and do the crossword in my head without a pencil.

It hasn't even been the worst night of my life. I spent eight months – 240 nights, give or take – sleeping next to Ellie on a sofa-bed sharing her isolation room in Great Ormond Street Hospital ... So, not even in the top 100.

The solicitor looks to be in his thirties, he wears a slim fitting overcoat and slightly too tight trousers. He is cheerful and upbeat even at this early hour of the morning as he explains that under English law, common assault is not necessarily a blow, but any unwanted touch – even if it is as 'light as a feather'. It seems to me impossible ever for anyone to prove that they didn't touch someone else. And that makes me think about the Chilean 'disappeared' again.

Next, he outlines all possible outcomes to me.

They are:

- I could be charged with either criminal damage or common assault, or both. This would then mean trial in a magistrates' court.
- I could be released pending charges on either count.
- I could accept a Caution on either charge – in which case, there would be no need to go to court but it would go on my record. For that to happen I would have to plead guilty.
- I could be released No Further Action – this means there is no case to answer and no record is kept of the allegations. Basically, it didn't happen.

I am innocent, I say. I've done nothing wrong.

Then I am questioned by an officer from the Domestic Abuse Unit. This takes place in an interview room and is recorded, my solicitor sitting next to me, the officer across the table, just like in *Line of Duty*. The officer reads from my husband's statement and then gives me the opportunity to confirm or deny each paragraph. I have watched those TV programmes where the accused simply repeats 'No comment', but I have nothing to hide. I ask permission to stand up and demonstrate how we both struggled for the phone and it fell to the floor. I point out it was not in my interests to break it. I was desperate for evidence of the affair, now lost.

And I categorically deny the alleged assault. My husband is nine years younger than me, eight inches taller and fit enough to swim the English Channel. I am a cancer survivor with asthma and osteoporosis; even a minor, accidental fall could break a bone.

'So, why do you think your husband has made this serious accusation against you?' The police officer's face is impassive.

My shoulders sag, from exhaustion of the night before – and the past four months since the crash. 'I am finally realising,' I say for the record, 'that I have had no idea what my husband has been thinking or doing for some considerable time now. Or why.'

After 45 minutes of questioning along these lines, I am taken back to my cell.

I still have no way of knowing how much time is passing but it must be lunchtime as I am offered tinned beans, with or without sausage, in case I am Jewish or Muslim, or vegan. I choose 'with' – and it arrives on a paper plate with a plastic fork. Professionally, I can't help but be fascinated by the catering arrangements. I wonder whose job it is to think up such practical solutions. I know the duty solicitor has been talking to my daughter, attempting to reassure her. She has been up all night, frantic with worry. Her first call when she arrived home at gone midnight and found me missing was to Alastair, of course, who for once in his busy life had turned off his phone before going to bed. So, she called around a troop of her friends, Ruby, who came on holiday with us, and my niece Zoe among them, and these young women, not knowing what else to do, kept an all-night vigil supporting Hope until Alastair could be roused and Maggie, my solicitor-friend, contacted in Cuba. I know nothing of this – but I do wonder if she also thought to call my office and invent a plausible excuse for my absence? I hear boots in the corridor. They stop outside my cell. The spyhole opens. I am sitting on the bench. Keys jangle, the door unlocks.

'You're free to go. No Further Action. On either charge.'

I have been incarcerated for more than 16 hours. The officer walks me back to the desk to collect my possessions – my watch; my handbag; my phone with the dead battery.

He asks where I am going.

Home?

'Isn't there anywhere else you can go?'

The solicitor meets me in the corridor, we walk and talk. 'Don't go home,' he says.

'It's my dream house,' I say. 'You should see it.' I describe the location by the canal, the tiles in the ensuite bathrooms, I may have mentioned the resin floors.

'It's not safe for you,' he says. 'He might make more accusations. You could be arrested again.'

'But I'm innocent,' I say. 'I didn't do anything!'

'It will be a new shift, different police officers,' says my solicitor. 'You'll have to prove yourself all over again. You can't go home.'

CHAPTER 15

Bad Housekeeping

23 February 2017: 16 and a half weeks after the crash

My daughter drives me home, tears pouring down her face.

She stands guard at the front door while I pack my entire life in one hour. I am preternaturally well organised, remembering everything: my passport; my medications; clothes for work; workout kit; books for the course I am studying; my laptop; all the chargers; the special pillow without which I can't even snatch an hour or two's sleep. I have no idea why I am the one who is moving out when he is the one who is cheating. But I know I am too scared to stay.

I even pack for the dogs, their diet food; their raincoats; their favourite toys.

I hear my husband come to the door and ask why he can't come in? Hope says something to him in a low voice. He goes away again.

I load up my new car, a Honda that I only took delivery of five days previously, plain and modest, nothing like the BMW that was too expensive to be an insurance write-off.

There is a gale blowing: Storm Doris it says on the radio. The electronic gates to our driveway have blown in on themselves and don't open when I point the remote control at them. When this has happened in the past, Mark would get out his tool kit, remove them from their hinges until the storm died down, then rehang them.

I don't know what will happen if I wait for him to return, then ask him to do that. The only thought in my head is flight.

I briefly consider crashing my way to freedom, driving the brand-new Honda, with its brand-new smell, straight at the gates, bursting through them with a great splintering of wood. But then I realise I don't fancy being in a third crash in four months.

I get out of the car and together Hope and I force one of the gates open so Hope can hold it in place against the battering wind. Then I climb back in the driving seat and inch the car forward, parking sensors bleeping, through the narrow gap we have created.

My 24-year-old daughter, long red hair whipping around her white face, grimly holds onto the gate, willing me through. She isn't coming with me. She can't get to work from the Dengie, she says. She's like me, she thinks work will save her. She says she can handle the situation. She's my baby and yet she wants me to leave her. I think of how I had to leave her with my parents when she was only five years old so I could sleep at the hospital with her sister Ellie.

Nineteen years later, I drive away from my sole surviving child, from the dream I had painstakingly constructed after the loss of my first family, from the home where I thought I would live out my days and from the man who rescued me from soul-crushing loneliness and despair.

I head for the motorway.

11 March 2017: 19 weeks after the crash — New York

It is snowing in Central Park. I walk around the reservoir, half-blinded by the flurries of snowflakes, unable to see or hear anyone else. Alone in a white world, I wonder if this is wise, but I don't really care. So mug me ... What more can happen?

I am not mugged.

Despite being technically homeless and mentally far from well, no sooner have I arrived at my mother's house after fleeing the Canal House than I repack a small bag and fly to New York on a scheduled business trip. There are meetings with colleagues and dinners with my friend and colleague Ellen Levine. We discuss the rise of popularist politicians across the States and Europe and agree it feels like the end of days, but in truth I feel as if I am watching it from the outside looking in. I no longer care who runs any country.

I am invited to lunch with Mariane Pearl, widow of Daniel Pearl, the journalist who was beheaded by terrorists in Pakistan in 2002. She was pregnant at the time, 15 years ago. We talk about the challenges of raising posthumous children and I tell her how proud I am of Hope and how I have tried to keep her idea of her father alive. I feel profoundly grateful that Hope will never be able to find pictures of her father's death on the internet.

The Plaza Athénée on the Upper East Side is my favourite Manhattan hotel. Most feel anonymous, as if you could lie dead in one of the rooms and no one would notice until it was time to pay the bill. But here the staff are friendly, affecting to remember me from previous visits, indulging my British preference for a kettle and teabags in my room.

I spend the weekend looking at the Klimts in the Neue Galerie with my colleague and wandering around the Met. I dine on room service and read, no longer crying, in the bath. The concierge manages to get me a single ticket for Glenn Close who is starring as Norma Desmond in *Sunset Boulevard* on Broadway: 'I am big. It's the pictures that got small,' goes the line. Sitting alone in the dress circle, I wonder momentarily if magazines are getting smaller thanks to the rise of social media. What will that mean for the grande dame editors, like me, with our glamorous transatlantic lives courtesy of the huge audiences we command? I shudder as if someone has stepped on my grave and dismiss the thought. I can't lose my job on top of everything else.

On my last evening I go to a yoga class on the Upper East Side. Afterwards, I walk back to the hotel, reviewing in my mind how much I have achieved in the two weeks since the arrest. I have survived this trip. While I have been away, my husband has had a surgical procedure which means he can't be compelled to move out of the Canal House anytime soon. I assume his mistress is the 'friend' who is currently caring for him there and about whom he posts on Facebook. I realise now she must have been both 'Nick', who didn't want to be disturbed by a ringing phone after my Lake District car crash, and presumably also the rosé-drinking 'Simon', leaving the empty bottle in the recycling bin for me to discover when I got home from work.

I have never met her. I wouldn't know her if I passed her in the street. But she has been to my house, eaten at my table and is sleeping in the bespoke bed engineered to my weight, with the man to whom I am married.

Hope left the Canal House shortly after me, moving in with Christina. She is shuttling between freelance catering assignments but has received the offer of her dream job, teaching at the prestigious Raymond Blanc Cookery School based at Le Manoir aux Quat'Saisons in Oxfordshire. I make plans to find somewhere for us to live together when I return. I can afford it. I have a great job. I have my family. I have my dogs. It's not what I thought would be happening in my life even as recently as one month ago – but I am surviving. I decide I will make Mark and his lady-friend jealous with the glory of my remade life.

The ground hits me hard and forcefully. I am momentarily stunned. I look up at the wheels of a Mack truck.

Lost in reverie, I have tripped crossing the road and now the lights have turned green. Since this is New York, I wonder if the truck might simply drive over me. It doesn't – but the driver sounds his horn at me as I get to my feet and shuffle to the pavement. Passers-by don't even look at me. No one asks if I am all right.

This is not the first time I have fallen. I seem to have been tripping over a lot recently, although the vulnerability of osteoporosis should make me extra careful. It's as if my body and my mind are out of kilter, so one is never quite sure where the other is going. I think about that morning, still only two weeks ago, on the platform of the Jubilee line. It's a wonder I didn't just fall under the wheels of the train.

My left wrist is very painful. I have travel insurance but I don't feel nearly well enough to negotiate the American healthcare system and, in any case, I am leaving the next day. I catch a little sleep with my throbbing hand propped on many pillows. And in the morning head out early to JFK airport.

The plane is full. I can't use my left hand to lift my bag and I worry about someone knocking into me. I make a sling from a scarf to keep it out of harm's way, resting diagonally across my chest. A bruise is spreading like soot nearly up to my elbow. I tell myself I'll get it X-rayed when I get home. But in the event, I don't bother, even though it is painful for weeks, so much so that I can't hold anything heavier than a pencil in my left hand. I have always been neglectful of my own body, my own pain, ashamed of the good health that was bestowed on me and not on my family. Not for the first time I wonder why I didn't die from the breast cancer let alone in the crash with the lorry back when I believed I was loved, when I thought life had come good again after all the sorrow.

I awake in my mother's spare room at 5 a.m. and open the curtains to see her creeping across the garden in her dressing gown, mobile phone in hand. I pull on a fleece and Ugg boots and follow her out … Is this the start of dementia? She hears me and gestures to leave the dogs inside.

I shut them away and follow her over to where she is standing by a bushy shrub.

She points silently.

There is a nest, so perfectly made it could be from the John Lewis Easter collection, and sitting on it, her feathers puffed up around her in a matronly way, a small brown bird.

'She has an egg,' my mother says, and takes a picture with her mobile phone.

We stand and look at the nesting bird for some time. Is it a thrush? My mother gives me a look.

'Blackbird. You know the female is brown, right?'

When I was a child we walked everywhere: to the shops, to the bus stop, to post a letter. My brothers, who are younger than me and close in age, in the double buggy, usually pushing and shoving each other. Me trailing along the dusty pavements behind.

To distract us my mother would point out the flowers growing on the verges: bluebells, celandine, violets, cowslips. And the birds in the suburban gardens: robins, chaffinches, bullfinches, thrushes and starlings. We had a cat who caught baby birds and brought them to us as offerings. I tried to nurse these fledglings back to life but they always died, even if they didn't appear outwardly injured. Shock does that, apparently.

In all, I spend a month living back in the Dengie with my mother. After her long career as a primary school teacher, my mother tackles the ageing process like a homework assignment. French conversation lessons to stave off Alzheimer's. Tai Chi to guard against falls. Daily interaction with neighbours and friends in the community to prevent the loneliness that she tells me science has proven is more fatal than smoking – obviously, she doesn't smoke either. She is abstemious, slender and hard-working, only having recently given up tutoring local children. She recycles, saves paper and string, uses her bicycle rather than her car for trips under two miles. Every Sunday we walk the dogs for three hours across the flat arable fields of my childhood. We call it the Divorce Walk, as I have already filed the paperwork. Even in the hell that my life has become I know how lucky I am to have the chance to get to know my mother even better.

From Essex, I take the train to work every day where I am busy with the summer issues. I spend a lot of time on the phone to Downing Street trying to arrange an interview with the prime minister, Theresa May. I have interviewed the previous three prime ministers and met Mrs May many times; once she crashed into me rushing late into a meeting, her mind on matters of state and I caught her before she fell to the floor, astonished at how little she weighed. I don't share her politics although I admire her as a principled woman and for her strong stance on modern slavery. But demonstrating the tin ear that resulted in her losing her majority later in that year, she has agreed to do only one women's magazine interview – with Anna Wintour's American *Vogue*, not even the British edition – while rebuffing the opportunity to speak through *Good Housekeeping* to a huge audience. Oh well, not everyone understands how magazines work …

The pictures from the shoot I abandoned when suicidal ideation threatened to overwhelm me turned out just fine thanks to the beauty director and will appear in the next issue. I draft some coverlines:

- Fabulous at every age. What you need to know about your body, health and lifestyle now
- How property gurus add value to their homes
- Look younger instantly hairstyles
- Midweek suppers to save time and money
- Confidence: How to carry on without anyone guessing you want to kill yourself

… Well, not the last one, obviously.

I meet my friends for early suppers near Liverpool Street station before getting the last train back out to Essex.

One weekend I ask after the blackbird and her egg.

Both gone, my mother says. The chick has flown, the nest is no longer needed.

There is no distinction in law between the cheater and the cheated and, so, no automatic right for the spouse for whom the collapse of a marriage has come as a sudden and profound shock to remain in the marital home. Morally most people would say the innocent party should not have to move out. Even leaving decency out of it, on a purely practical level, the one who did not see this coming has had no chance to make alternative arrangements. But in my traumatised flight to my mother's house, I ceded that position. Nor does an adult child – and Hope was 24 – have any rights at all in a divorce. As for our beloved dogs, well in law they are just possessions, like a table or a chair. Who lives where will be resolved during the divorce proceedings, or in a separate case in the Family Court to award an Occupation Order, granting the right to live in the family home. As it happened, we did have a second home that Mark could have moved into if he had wished to spare me further trauma, a tiny rental property, near where we used to live in north London. Impossible for Hope to commute to her new job in Oxfordshire from there and unthinkable for me to be separated from her as I struggled with the collapse of my world, let alone be parted from the dogs who could not live there. The flat was only half a mile from Mark's office; however, he declined to serve a Section 21 No-Fault eviction notice asking the tenants to leave. While I was in New York, he entered hospital for an elective procedure and after that chose to remain in the Canal House, citing health and other issues. To be honest, I wasn't even sure that I wanted to go back to our house of broken dreams. The knowledge that while I had been in Chile making inquiries about a cocktail cabinet as a gift for him, another woman had been in my home sharing a glass of wine – and more – with my husband meant it was all tainted for me now. I couldn't contemplate my home without thinking of the pair of them making love in it. And, in any case, Mark had changed the locks!

My friend Maggie, one of the most famous divorce lawyers in London who acted for Princess Diana in her divorce from the then Prince of Wales, shrugged and advised me it would cost more in court fees to file an Occupation Order than to pay rent for a few months, so better to push on with the divorce. Little did either of us known that the Section 21 would come back to haunt me. That the editor of *Good Housekeeping* was to prove so bad at holding onto her home was ironic – very Bad Housekeeping as it turned out.

The house, elegant and modern, stands on its own surrounded by grassy fields, one of a collection of converted barns on 100 acres that were formerly racing stables, and it is available to rent. Horses graze in the surrounding fields; baby rabbits scamper in the grass. The long driveway is lined with daffodils and protected by electric gates. It will take most of my savings to live here but what choice do I have? I tried some estate agents who jumped at the idea of my substantial budget – but then wrinkled their noses at the suggestion of my two dogs. My mother will take them in for me, I know. But I don't want that. I have lost my home and my marriage; at least let me keep my dogs. Finally, in desperation I call a property developer who occasionally rents out properties before they are sold. She does have one she says – but it's enormous and expensive: Hope and I go to see it anyway.

A few years back I got involved in some pro bono work for the homeless charity, Shelter. I travelled around the country interviewing families living in temporary accommodation. This wasn't the homelessness of sleeping on the streets; these people had a roof over their heads, some of them had wide-screen TVs and they all had mobile phones. What they didn't have was the confidence of where they would be living next week, let alone the week after.

At first glance some of the houses and flats offered to these technically homeless seemed quite nice, some, outside of the cities, having a garden. But there was never a dining table for serving home-cooked food or for the kids to do their home-work. And usually the gas had been turned off due to non-payment of bills so there would be a fire-hazard collection of cheap electric heaters with tangled flexes and damp washing hung in front of them. And what good is a garden if you are too far off the beaten track to get your kids to school or yourself to work and can't afford to run a car?

But these practical issues aside, what struck me forcibly was that without a secure roof over your head it's practically impos-sible to get to grips with any other aspect of your life. The parents I interviewed couldn't hold down jobs because they had to take time off to up sticks and move house at short notice, often ending up somewhere without transportation – especially difficult if you work in a minimum-wage job that demands unsocial hours. The kids had to change schools and sometimes couldn't go at all. Or even wouldn't go because, like Hope all those years ago, they feared their home would be gone when they got back.

Now Hope and I – although by no means in financial distress and being supported on a practical level by concerned family and friends – are emotionally homeless. I can't focus on my work and some days Hope is unable to travel to her freelance jobs, so losing a day's pay. She stands no chance of being able to cope when she starts her demanding new position with Raymond Blanc unless we feel secure at home.

The Divorce House, as I name it, is let unfurnished. I arrange for a removal firm to take exactly half the furniture, half the kitchen utensils and linen from our three-person Canal House, which isn't enough for our new household of two, so I order more from John Lewis. Hope needs a bed, so we order that too, and she sleeps on the floor until it is delivered. My brothers and nephew come over and assemble all the flat-packs into furniture. They spread out all the components beforehand on the floor to check they have everything, working silently, efficiently, handing each other the parts they need without being told.

I have no storage, so I order cheap sets of shelves from Amazon – which also arrive flat-packed. Unable to wait for the weekend for my brothers to show up I assemble them myself using scissors and kitchen knives as tools. They look wonky but I feel a sense of achievement nonetheless.

I left behind the big sound system at Canal House, so I go online and buy something white and elegant from Bose that doesn't have a slot for CDs but runs entirely off my phone, which suits me, because Mark kept all but six of the CDs. Fair enough because I took all but six of the books. I download Beyoncé's album *Lemonade* and play it continuously.

'She's the most beautiful woman in the world – and she got cheated on,' says Hope. 'It happens.' And it becomes a joke between us to list all the goddesses – beautiful, powerful brilliant women – who have had unfaithful husbands.

Organising the inside of my house is time-consuming but it's satisfying to get everything back under control. This is a minor hiccup – my life can be put back together to resemble something from a glossy magazine. The pages may have been scattered by divorce but I can put them back in order, my life can still be perfect bound.

The Divorce House is five miles upstream from the Canal House. It has white walls and marble tiled floors and I have brought from the Canal House my favourite sofa and armchair, upholstered in the exact shade of a Cadbury's Dairy Milk wrapper. I launder white linens; plump up silvery grey cushions and set out the mis-matched blue china I have collected over the years. My collection of black and white photography and the Beryl Cook print are propped up on the mantelpieces; they look stylish that way and I don't want the bother of putting nails in the walls of a rented house.

So precipitate was my flight, so dizzyingly short the time that elapsed between the joint project of furnishing our Canal House and setting up separate establishments, that we still have items of furniture on order. A purple velvet chaise longue and a white dressing table stool circle the M25 like the Flying Dutchman, before being finally redirected to the Divorce House.

With so much space and not enough furniture, Hope and I set aside one room to use as a yoga studio. We discover an English sparkling wine that we like and buy by the case so we will always have some on hand. I light candles scented of fig and distribute potted orchids that are fake but look alive; real ones quickly die, which is how you know they are real.

The garden, however, is another matter. An alien world full of difficult tasks and constant retribution. I have assiduously avoided gardening all my adult life. At *Good Housekeeping*, even though I obsessively edited every page – chasing commas, reuniting split infinitives – I still would pass gardening articles to my deputy. My parents were both ardent horticulturalists, roping in their children as unskilled labour. Lawns that needed mowing twice a week; weeding every weekend; armfuls of scratchy prunings to be piled onto the compost heap where a grass snake was reputed to live. As an adult, patios are about as much outdoors as I can be bothered with. At the Canal House, we had a breakfast terrace that got the morning sun and a gin and tonic terrace … You get the picture. However, the Divorce House has a proper full-on, full-scale garden.

There are shrubs with labels still attached, a sign that my landlady chose them deliberately and they are not just any old weeds. I will have to look after them, water them; maybe even prune them. There will be a way they are supposed to look and they will need to look like that when I leave this place – whenever that may be.

I also need to mow the grass. But I don't have a mower and the lawn taunts me with my lack of capability.

Even worse, there's an oil tank that needs to be filled, the depth measured with a stick, and some strange man phoned and an arrangement needs to be made for a lorry to arrive and fill it up so we can be warm indoors. Will we even be here in winter? Who knows? There is a manhole cover in the middle of the lawn. Why? Where does it lead? I assume I need to know about it, in case there's a flood?

Beyond the garden are fields and trees. I have always found it easier to look to the distance than focus on what's up close. The open countryside requires no input from me. There are oak trees that have been growing since a hundred years before I was born and will still be there a hundred years after I am dead.

What's the point of gardens anyway? It's just trying to impose man's will on nature, which would get along perfectly fine without us. Wherever I end up after all this is done, I'm not bothering with a garden again. Gardens are like husbands. Just endless chores, then you go sick for a short time and poisonous weeds flourish in your carefully tended bed. Really not worth the trouble. Pave it over my London grandmother used to say. Grass only encourages cats.

I order more furniture online and set up a guest room. My mother comes to stay, arriving on a Saturday afternoon. She can't rest because of the state I have let the garden get into. We attempt to start the ancient lawnmower one of my brothers has lent me but fail. It is necessary to pull the cord sharply in an upwards motion to fire the motor. Neither of us is strong enough to manage it. My mother is driven nearly mad by this and goes to get a trowel from the back of her car – who keeps a trowel in their car? – with which she starts digging up weeds in a kind of repressed fury.

She can't put my life right but she can make my rented garden look nice.

As the light fails, I pour wine to make her stop and Hope arrives home from work and cooks dinner for us. We drink more wine. My mother and I get quite tiddly. I smash a glass trying to load the dishwasher and my mother can't walk a straight line. My daughter goes to bed in disgust at the pair of us.

In the morning, my mother gets up at 4.30 a.m. and takes all the dogs for a walk. When I get up at 6.30 a.m. she is drinking tea, working on her laptop and has no sign of a hangover. Hope, who works weekends, comes downstairs at 7 a.m. and is immediately accosted by my mother who wants her to start the mower for us.

'The neighbours …' protests Hope, but weakly. The grass needs to be cut and she's the only one who can start the mower for us, so she does. My 82-year-old mother pushes the mower up and down scything the long, wet grass; slicing the heads of the thistles; dumping her anger into the garden waste bin until it, and I (and probably the neighbours) can take no more.

Then she changes her shoes and we walk the dogs along The Ridgeway footpath for two hours. There is no end to the energy that anger produces. Back at the house while I update her iPad for her and check her social media privacy settings, she carries on with the weeding until I persuade her to stop for lunch.

I don't bother with lampshades or curtains. We aren't overlooked. And I rarely think to put the lights on anyway. As the earth moves towards the summer solstice, it stays light until gone 9 p.m. When my daughter is out with her new boyfriend, Jamie – they appear to be getting serious about each other – I roam the darkening house, listening to music until, having been awake since dawn, I am usually in bed by 10 p.m.

The dogs accompany me upstairs. My bedroom is huge and filled with light from dormer windows. I have put in there the art deco dressing table and six feet wide Tempur bed – not the Rolls-Royce one engineered to our differing weights, now contaminated by infidelity but the Mama-Bear bed that wraps me in its soft mattress.

The dogs sleep with me. Belle positioned like a spouse with her head on the pillow next to me. Scarlet chooses the crook behind my knees. When I roll over in the night there's a soft flump as the pup falls onto the carpet, followed by a scrabbling as she climbs back up, finds the crook on the other side and snuggles down. Why she doesn't choose a more secure position than this I don't know, but all through the night it's flump, scrabble, snuggle until I barely wake up even as she does it.

The weather that spring breaks all the records: the driest March; the warmest April and May. A general election is called. A terrorist drives into pedestrians at Westminster. Another blows himself up at a concert, killing children and teenagers, the youngest only eight. The terror alert in Britain is at its highest level: critical. And still the sun blazes unseasonably as if trying to flood out the darkness in our collective souls.

Sometimes at night, the weather breaks – because it has to – and rain lashes down. I lie in bed watching through the dormer windows as lightning splits open the night sky. The dogs tremble under the bedclothes but I like these storms; they suit my mood.

Then in the cool, misty morning I walk with them around the fields. The long, wet grass reaches over my wellies brushing my knees, reminding me of country walks as a child. I listen to wood pigeons and look out for pheasants and deer. I will pave over my heart and look beyond into the view. The foreground is a dangerous place.

Tomorrow will be three months since I discovered Mark's affair, since I was arrested. It's Sunday afternoon and I am home alone. Hope is busy in her new job. I have walked the dogs for two hours; talked to my mother on the phone for 45 minutes; written in my journal. I unpack a bedside cabinet that has been delivered. One of the legs is chipped but I know I won't bother to return it. Arranging for deliveries when Hope and I are both out at work all day is hard enough without sending stuff back, too. It is packed in polystyrene that disintegrates into bobbles all over the guest room. I vacuum them up. Stack the cardboard packaging to be recycled and make myself an omelette for lunch.

The entirety of my solitude engulfs me.

I am married but exiled from my home; from the life I thought was mine right up until three months ago. Now someone else has that life. Are Mark and his girlfriend cooking a Sunday roast in the kitchen I designed? Do they sit down at the dining table to eat under the chandelier he and I picked out together. Do they take their glasses of wine out onto the canal terrace and watch the narrow boats pass, as we used to do? How is it possible for my life to have been so comprehensively stolen from under me?

8 June 2017: Seven months after the crash

I arrive at the canal-side pub straight from the office dressed in a black Paul Smith trouser suit, so sharp I could cut myself. He is more casually dressed in track pants and a T-shirt bought during our 10th wedding anniversary trip to New Zealand two years earlier; I wonder if that is deliberate? We have not met or even spoken since the night he picked up the phone and dialled 999, but I have seen him at a distance.

With me and Hope in the Divorce House, Mark has been determinedly carrying on with life in our home town for all the world as if our break-up had been mutual and amicable. He goes everywhere with his new love: shopping in Waitrose, drinking in the pubs we used to frequent. He introduces her to the neighbours and stops for a chat with our dog-walker on the tow path. They even go together to the little cinema where we had so recently celebrated our wedding anniversary. I know this because I was there on the same night with a bunch of girlfriends. I arrived late from work after the film had started, so I didn't actually spot the man who is still my husband with his new partner at the nearby table. It was only after the film ended that I wondered why Christina, Liz and Julia formed a praetorian guard, frog-marching me out of the auditorium while the credits were still rolling. I had been attuned in my life to operatic levels of tragedy; I didn't realise the end of my second marriage would turn into a Brian Rix farce.

Now the divorce is proceeding, we have a court date set for next month but I can't bring myself to press Go without meeting him one last time and hearing his side of the story.

He finally admitted the affair, in an email, copied to my lawyers, having abandoned the claim that we were living separate lives. The stark acknowledgement came as a relief to me after all the gaslighting, and meant the divorce would proceed more quickly on the grounds of his adultery. This is enough for the court. The law does not require him to tell me or my lawyers when the affair started, or whether there were others before this one. Was he already cheating on me when he stood up in front of 100 family and friends to tell them that I changed his life, that he loved and adored me? I will never know. Financial documents reveal payments for rooms in a local Premier Inn around the time I was retreating further into the fog of PTSD. What would I have seen if I had dragged myself back to the present? How would I have managed the situation if I had been mentally well?

We speak in guarded, painfully general terms for half an hour. He tells me how the cat is doing – she doesn't appear to be missing me – and asks after the dogs, who I can confirm aren't missing him. He says he wants to see Hope. I remind him that she's an adult and that's her choice to make not mine, nor his. I want to ask him when it was our marriage failed? But I don't dare? I can't trust myself not to cry. I cried a lot during our marriage and when I did he would accuse me of shouting – I think crying and shouting feel like one and the same thing to him.

It is early evening and we are the only people in the pub. We have chosen a table by a window looking out on the canal, and the barman has disappeared out back. What if Mark doesn't merely accuse me of shouting, what if he later claims that I attacked him? He could say I hit him right there in the pub, while the barman was changing the barrels? I can't risk it. The taint of the accusation, even unproven, lingers on; no smoke without fire. It closed me down then and is closing me down now. The moment passes.

I realise that the divorce will go ahead, with just the bald admission of his infidelity. He is never going to apologise for smashing up the dream we had of our life together. And I am never going to be able to ask him when he stopped loving me nor why he came to hate me so much that he would rather see me arrested than talk to me. Let alone why he believed it reasonable for me and Hope to leave the family home when he was the one breaking his marriage vows.

Which means, perversely, that now I can only tell my side of the story. I assume my grief for John and Ellie, transmuted into workaholism and insomnia, made me very difficult to live with. The PTSD constantly bubbling under the surface erupting amid times of stress. Put like that it sounds like a lot, too much maybe, for any marriage to bear.

We finish our drinks and get up to leave. 'I will write about this one day,' I tell him.

'I know you will,' he says heavily. I was writing my first memoir when we married and he was proud to be the subject of the final chapter – my knight in shining armour come to rescue me from the years of loneliness. He featured often in my newspaper columns, the blog I wrote about breast cancer, and was a recurring character in my editor's letters at the front of the magazines I edited. It was only ever my interpretation of events, I realise now. There is a version of the narrative – his version – in which everything he did was necessary, reasonable even. I didn't know then – nor will I ever know now – what it was.

As we say goodbye, I lean in to kiss him, a reflex action based on the 13 years we spent in a physical relationship. He seems surprised, taken aback, quickly turning his face away from me so my lips graze the stubble on his cheek. And then it is over. Our marriage is dead but there is no body for me to bury.

We have not met since.

CHAPTER 16

Spiked!

5 July 2017: Eight months after the crash

The dining table is decorated with glitter reindeer and sparkly baubles. Christmas carols are playing on someone's phone and from the kitchen comes the smell of roasting turkey. On the wall is projected a flickering image of a roaring log fire. Outside in Soho it's 30 degrees – the hottest day of the year so far. Which, really, I could have predicted because the day in July on which *Good Housekeeping* holds its Christmas planning session always seems to be bathed in glorious sunshine.

The December issue of *Good Housekeeping* sells twice the number of copies of any other issue and carries millions of pounds worth of advertising. Getting it right today will be the most important task of the year. My avatar, the *Good Housekeeping* archetype Claire, loves Christmas – the turkey, the fairy lights, the gift-giving – but worries that it is exhausting, over-commercialised and expensive.

I gather my trusted team around me and start with my usual preamble, setting out the importance of the work we are about to do and how December *Good Housekeeping* must uphold all the festive traditions while feeling to Claire as fresh as snow falling on Christmas Eve.

We look at location shots of the manor house we have hired for later in the month. The editorial team will decamp to the country to photograph all the fashion, food, beauty and decorating features, giving the entire magazine a coherent visual identity. It will take two full weeks at the end of July, after the schools have broken up for the child models but before the photographers start going on their summer holidays. During the course of the shoot we will decorate around 17 Christmas trees, cook at least three turkeys, use five different photographers and assorted hairdressers, make-up artists and set builders. We will play host to three adult models, seven child models – and their chaperones – five dog models, with their trainers, plus a horse, which I have booked to be part of the fashion photography. 'At heart, most women still harbour their pony-mad childhood dreams,' I say.

Today is coincidentally the anniversary of my first day at *Good Housekeeping*. I joined on 5 July, 18 years earlier, and the Christmas conference was one of my first tasks. Hope was just six years old at the time. While my own Christmas that year would be drowned in grief, the mythical Claire's Christmas with her family was to be a magical fantasy of everything we all hope the festive season to be. In editing the magazine, I was always creating a life I wished I could have lived.

But this year I have been, for nearly two weeks, in formal consultation over my role. The company that owns *Good Housekeeping*, like many other publishing houses, is restructuring, in the face of changing consumer habits and the rise of digital media. The fear that I will lose my job intrudes on my thoughts constantly but I push it away. There is no suggestion that I had been anything other than diligent, despite my unexplained 24-hour absence a few months ago, and *Good Housekeeping* continues to out-sell every other glossy. But times are changing. Over at *Vogue*, Alex Shulman, one of the only major-league editors to have been in post longer than me, has announced she is leaving. So, too is Condé Nast MD Nicholas Coleridge.

Suddenly it hits me this might be my last ever Christmas conference. I look around at my team sitting at the table, their expectant faces waiting for me to decide what the theme of our big opening celebrity feature will be:

'The last supper.'

Huh? The team look baffled.

'No, that was a joke.' I recover quickly. 'I mean the ultimate fantasy Christmas dinner.'

I go on to outline my plan – we will photograph a dozen celebrities around a groaning Christmas table, as if they were all spending the day together. Such set pieces have become a trademark of my time at *Good Housekeeping*, fabulous extravaganzas that require months of wrangling competing press agents and publicists who all want top-billing for their stars.

After that the rest of the planning flows. We schedule 12 pages of Tried & Tested foodstuffs that every year gets picked up by the national press. Whichever supermarket wins for its mince pies they are inevitably cleared out of the shops. I commission a beauty feature about the fragrances worn by the women we most admire and plan glamorous fashion makeovers for six deserving heroines of the tragedies and atrocities that have struck Britain during the year: the Manchester bombing, London terror attacks and Grenfell Tower. I ask for a short story from a famous author and insist the issue should be multi-faith, something that stumps the team who ask, not unreasonably, for more time to think about how to achieve that. I ask the food team to devise recipes for a Christmas dinner that can be on the table in fewer than 90 minutes. All this takes four solid hours without a break until I truly feel that this, my 19th Christmas issue for *Good Housekeeping*, will be my best yet.

The next day promises more glorious hot weather. In the morning, after Hope has driven off to work at the cookery school, I set out on what is now my regular journey from the Divorce House, taking the train to London and walking from Euston station to Soho. I still do not trust myself to take the Tube. The divorce will go through shortly, I hope. Hope is loving her dream job and we are safe and happy in our rented home. Life is beginning to pick up, except for this cloud hanging over me of my role being formally 'at risk'. Turning the corner into Broadwick Street, I feel the strap on my overloaded handbag snap, scattering the contents onto the warm pavement. I kneel on Broadwick Street, gathering my scattered belongings: purse, make-up bag and diary along with the notebooks and ballpoint pens, part of every reporter's essential kit and which I still carry with me despite it being nearly 40 years since I first embarked on my journalistic career.

Back in the 1980s

My path to becoming an editor started as a trainee reporter with what was then Mirror Group Newspapers. Fresh out of university, I learned shorthand, typing, media law and the British constitution while working on local newspapers owned by the group in the West Country. On my very first day, I met a tall gangly red-headed young man ... who was late for our introductory session because he was out chasing a proper news story.

Within weeks John and I were living together in a succession of tiny rented flats in Plymouth. He distinguished himself even in those early days, collaborating with the *Sunday* and *Daily Mirrors* on exposés of conditions in Dartmoor prison and other hard news. Meanwhile, I took on the showbusiness beat, interviewing celebrities visiting the West Country to work on films or appear in summer seasons at the Hoe Theatre.

After two years John was welcomed with open arms by the investigations department headed by Dan Ferrari – father of the LBC presenter Nick Ferrari – on the *Daily Mirror* in London. I meanwhile was posted to Glasgow to work on the *Daily Record*, not merely a Scottish version of the *Daily Mirror* but a national newspaper in its own right, at that time read by one in every two adults in Scotland, which made it a cultural institution. I missed John dreadfully and spent hours on the phone to him every night, scheming to land a job in London, preferably on a magazine.

To say the *Daily Record* did not know what to do with me was putting it mildly. This Essex-accented Catholic female – at the time Glasgow was divided along sectarian lines and my colleagues worked it out from the school I went to – who showed no aptitude whatsoever for hard news.

I started work at 10 in the morning, late-ish – but I was expected to have read every Scottish and British newspaper by then and to have produced a list of feature ideas. Then while the senior team were in the editor's office pitching stories that would make the day's news agenda (rarely any of mine), I was given the jobs that went to the lowest of the low: writing up the weather and tide timetables and ringing round all the police stations in Glasgow, asking what had happened overnight. Anything serious was passed to the crime team, a hardcore bunch of grizzled men at least as frightening as the gang warlords they hung out with and turned over when the time was right – while the quotidian pub fights, drink-driving and burglaries appeared in a side-bar under the generic byline Pat Roller (say it out loud). I didn't even get my own name in the paper.

But one particular day, when I hadn't been there very long, I heard from my flimsy showbiz contacts that the actress Rula Lenska – still riding high in public awareness due to the success of TV's *Rock Follies* – was rumoured to be filming somewhere near Loch Lomond. Amazingly, this suggestion made it through conference and I was assigned to find and interview her.

Off I went with a photographer and we drove around the Scottish countryside all day, asking in pubs if anyone had seen a film crew, until finally we found them in a fold in the hills. Rula – the daughter of a Polish countess – was as gracious as she was beautiful, and during a break in filming invited me into her trailer, answered all my questions and posed for pictures. We arrived back in the newsroom at about 7 p.m. where the features editor quickly ascertained that, yet again, I had not landed any sort of scoop, just a colour piece which could be written up in the morning for use on a slow news day.

As I was leaving the building, I became aware of consternation on the back bench, where the overnight team of sub-editors and night lawyers headed by the night editor had begun the work of shepherding the day's stories through to press.

There was shouting: 'Fuck! Fuck! Fuck!' Reporters who had been drifting towards the door and the pub turned back in that time-honoured way of all hacks, moving towards trouble rather than away from it. I dithered, assuming that whatever was happening I was not senior enough to be affected, and having already worked a long day looking forward to supper on a tray in front of the TV in the West-side flat I shared with other young journos.

'Stay where you are,' the features editor warned me, as he picked up his notebook and headed into the editor's office. Blinds were pulled down. The lift doors opened and the chief executive, in black tie, called away from a dinner with Scottish politicians, emerged. The lift doors kept opening as more suited men – lawyers and executives – arrived.

We loitered. We waited. Journalists love chaos, the adrenaline was palpable.

Out came the features editor.

'OK, Nicholson. Got your notebook? Write up that Rula-bird interview NOW! It's the spread with a front-page trail.'

Out of the corner of my eye, I saw my snapper running – and he was a stout man – to the darkroom to process the photos.

Back then, there were no laptops. Reporters were expected to bring their own manual typewriter to work. So, I sat down at the portable my father had passed on to me, threaded in five sheets of paper, interleaved with four sheets of carbon, and began typing straight from my shorthand notes onto the page.

When I had completed two paragraphs, the chief sub-editor snatched the pages out of my typewriter, snorted and impaled them on the spike – literally a metal spike on each desk where rejected copy was collected ... Spiked. 'Keep going,' he said gruffly. 'It'll get better.'

By now a crowd had gathered around my desk. The features editor and chief sub stood reading over my shoulder, silently counting the lines as I typed them. No word-processing packages in those days but subs had a sixth sense for how many lines of type it took to fill the centre pages of the next day's paper.

Somewhere on the other side of the newsroom, which was the size of a football pitch and open plan, although you could barely see from one side to the other due to the fug of cigarette smoke, the news reporters were hitting the phones, hunting down a story from their contacts to provide a front page 'splash'.

Phones were ringing. People were shouting. I still didn't know what was happening – but like the dog that didn't bark, there was one sound missing. In those days at the *Daily Record*, in common with most other newspapers, the printing presses were on-site. Giant noisy manufacturing plants in the bowels of the building, presided over by the highly unionised printers or 'inkies'. Derogatory yes, but we journalists were hacks or scribblers, PRs were flacks and photographers were snappers so ...

At this time in the evening, the presses should have been cranking up ready for the first run, the Highlands and Islands edition. But not tonight. The presses had literally stopped.

In the days before the 24-hour news cycle of TV and digital media, newspapers produced several editions, updated throughout the night, finishing with a 5 a.m. or City edition. This meant that breaking stories – train crashes, political upsets, terrorism – could be updated throughout the evening. And if you had a scoop, you might let the early editions go with a more vanilla story and only release your scoop around midnight when it was too late for rival media to come up with a spoiler.

But this was different – the presses that were warming up for the first edition had been shut down. Unheard of … the presses always rolled, through wars, terrorism, political strife. I later learned what had happened. The splash and centre-spread were devoted to an exclusive about a rock star, very popular in Scotland a few years previously, who had been discovered living on the streets and confessed in tabloid parlance to a 'drink and drugs hell'. The story was written up, laid out with pictures and, at an unusually late stage, a proof shown to the night editor – a clever young man of saturnine good looks.

'It's nae him,' said the night editor.

There was no Wikipedia back then. No Google images to double-check. The only facial recognition software was human – and fallible.

'He's changed a lot. Thrown himself in the Clyde a couple of times. Drink and drugs will do that to a man …' The scribbler was convinced of his scoop.

'It's nae him … It's nae fookin' him,' shouted the night editor. And then the words you hope only to ever hear a few times in your life as a journalist: 'Stop press. Stop the fucking presses. This will kill us if we print it.'

He was not wrong. Libel laws being what they were – and are – the real rock star could have sued for millions, bankrupting the newspaper, even though it was an honest mistake, the journo having been misled by a lookalike chancer who gained a few drinks and some cash out of it. Even today, more than 40 years on, I dare not name the maligned celeb.

But I was told none of this. I just had to keep typing, translating my notes straight from shorthand to key strokes, and every time I finished a page, the chief sub snatched it out of the typewriter and made his marks on it. When I had written enough, he shouted: 'Boy'.

Journos, even editors, were rarely allowed to cross to the print side of the building, so a copy boy – old enough to be my grandfather – shuffled forward, jeans low over his lean haunches, fag in the corner of his mouth, to take my typed pages through to the compositors' room – known as the 'stone'.

In the days of 'hot metal' every single letter that appeared on every page of the newspaper was fashioned individually out of molten lead, while photos were etched onto metal plates in acid baths. Words and pictures were then assembled in wooden frames known as 'forms' by highly skilled compositors – a job that has completely disappeared now – among whose skills was the ability to read upside-down and back-to-front so that every word appeared in the right order. A difficult, messy job. Sometimes, in transferring the completed forms to the presses, one would be dropped scattering lead bullets of letters on the floor, holding up production while it was reassembled, during which there would be a clattering of metal rulers – em-rules – on the compositors' work benches accompanied by shouts of: 'The print's pied.' It was bad enough when a unionised compositor dropped a form – unthinkable if a journo did – the cry then would not be 'the print's pied' but 'everybody out', so usually only one member of the National Union of Journalists (NUJ) – known as the stone sub – was allowed to cross the threshold to do the final pass.

'You'll be seeing your story off-stone then.' The night editor came over and indicated to me. I was conscious of his good looks and his cleverness – although he was far too old for me, must have been in his mid-thirties and I already knew I was going to marry John. Hands clasped firmly behind our backs so there could be no accusation that a member of the NUJ had touched anything rightfully the territory of one of the print unions, I followed him, aware this was a great honour.

The compositing room smelled of molten metal and a tall muscular young Glaswegian silently swept an ink-covered roller across the forms containing my story then transferred it to sheets of newsprint, slapping the still-wet proof pages down in front of us. There was my name in bold type, no longer Pat Roller but my own name. I quickly read the story and the night editor did likewise and nodded, saying: 'Print it.'

The heavy wooden forms loaded with metal letters and pictures were loaded on trolleys and taken through to be inserted into the presses – please let this not be a night when one was dropped – and together, hands still clasped like the late Duke of Edinburgh behind our backs, the night editor and I were ushered onto the print floor – the beating heart of this nightly manufacturing process, where journos were even more rarely welcomed than the stone. Here sweating men, in stained vests and grimy trousers, threaded miles-long rolls of paper through presses the size of double-decker buses. The heat was oppressive and the noise deafening. A dirty, dangerous job; sometimes, if there was a paper jam, a man – they were only ever men, the job passed down from father to son – reached into the maw of the machinery to fix it, because stopping the presses meant unacceptable delay, a shortened print run or missing the ferries to the Islands. Although I soon moved to the calmer waters of magazines, I never forgot that our creative jobs in Soho offices were just the start of a heavy manufacturing and distribution process. For more than a quarter of a century, *Good Housekeeping* was printed by the family firm, Jarrolds of Norwich, and it was always a thrill to go and see the Christmas issue roll off the production line, so big and fat with adverts that it took 10 days to print and perfect-bind. My love affair with printer's ink began that night in Glasgow. As the first copies of the night's reworked newspaper rolled off the press, an inky ran forward, grabbed a completed edition, flicked through to ensure all the pages were the right way round, then – was that a glimmer of a smile? – handed it to the night editor.

He checked the splash, then turned to the centre spread, which fewer than 60 minutes earlier had been squiggles in my shorthand notebook. It looked fine – like a spread on any other day of the week: TV's Rula Brings Glamour to the Trossachs – or some such headline.

'They'll be wanting to see this in the pub, Nicholson,' he said, which was all the praise I got – and more than I expected.

Outside in the cold night air the lorries were lined up in the van-way with their engines running. Bales of newspapers were being loaded on pallets. There would only be one edition tonight. It was doubtful whether islanders would have anything to read at their breakfast tables – but the mainland was saved and, if memory serves, we even made the night train to London where in pre-internet days ex-pat Scots bought their news from home at the mainline railway stations.

It was nearly closing time when I arrived at the pub, but after such a day there would naturally be a lock-in. My colleagues – the crime team, the hard news guys and the subs – were waiting, already celebrating and drinks for me – gin and tonic, no wine in Scottish pubs back then – lined up on the bar. No longer the pointless English lassie, I had earned the respect of gritty – hairy-arsed, they used to say – Glasgow newspapermen. I had earned my stripes.

I never forgot that night – that feeling of being a cog in the wheel that got the paper to bed. Like playing in an orchestra, or being part of a winning football side, I imagine, not that I have done either. It's something I have since aspired to in every job I have had, even, or especially, as the editor – and that is to be a team player. My husband John was to be acclaimed as the greatest investigative journalist of his generation. That was never me. But I was quick, capable and, above all, I loved being part of a group working towards a common goal. You don't have to be the best, you just have to do your bit and step up when needed. And, if you get it wrong – as that scribbler who was misled by the chancer did – then the team will come to your rescue.

More than 30 years have passed since then and I have pursued a career that has brought me real pride and joy every day, often all that could get me out of bed in the morning when tragedy engulfed my private life.

But now as I scrabble for my belongings on the pavement for the tools of my trade I know in my heart that my time on *Good*

Housekeeping has come to an end. That the company-wide restructure has no place for me. That it is my turn to be spiked and I am to be made redundant. The presses have stopped rolling. The print of my life is pied. Just a few months ago I believed my husband loved me, until today I believed I was an editor. Mistaken identities abound. We won't only miss the early editions.

I don't blame my employers, who are kind and generous throughout the whole formal process. I have been part of many restructures in the past, always rising higher, taking on more responsibility; it was inevitable that one day I would be the one to receive the bad news that I had in the past been responsible for delivering to others. But still it devastates me. I have lost my team who could always be relied upon to save me. More than that, Claire, my avatar, the fantasy me with the perfect life, has died – another death on top of so many.

CHAPTER 17

The Real Meaning of Good Housekeeping

August 2017: 10 months after the crash

The summer drags on unbearably hot. I ask people if they think it is as hot as 1976, except most of them weren't even alive then, so they don't know what I am talking about. The dogs flop panting on the cool marble floor of the Divorce House.

It's too hot to walk far in the middle of the day, so I wait until the evening to take out the dogs, which also serves as a device to delay opening the Sauvignon Blanc.

I try making a rule: No drinking until the dogs are walked and fed and my own supper is on the go, otherwise none of us might eat at all.

That Sunday, after the shocking news that I am about to lose my job, in addition to the end of my marriage, I take the dogs out along the gallops, a circular track of about a mile where racehorses used to exercise on a soft sandy surface free of potholes and other perils. To the left of the two-metre wide track are thick knots of woods and brambles; to the right, the paddocks where once brood mares and their foals grazed peacefully, surrounded by four feet high fencing keeping them safe from the testosterone-fuelled stallions quartered at the stud farm nearby. The wooden posts and slats have an uncared-for appearance but are still reasonably sturdy.

The sun is low in the sky. The dogs run on ahead chasing rabbits. The mercury has fallen from earlier in the day but it is still hot, and muggy; a storm is coming. I make a mental note to close the dormer windows or the bedroom carpets will be soaked. I have not rented on my own since I was a trainee journalist and I am appalled at how much effort there is in looking after other people's property. And then, inevitably, I go back to ruminating on the impending divorce.

My hairline is damp with sweat and particles of dust and grit from the sandy track have worked their way inside my trainers. I look up, scanning for the dogs but I hear them before I see them, barking their heads off. And galloping towards me, with my dogs in hot pursuit – a fully grown stag, the size of a small horse but with antlers.

I am caught on the track between the thicket on my left and the high stallion-proof fence on my right. The stag is so close I can see his velvety red coat and liquid brown eyes. Those antlers could easily tear apart what's left of me that hasn't already been savaged by fate. We must surely collide.

I don't suppose he wants to hurt me. But he's terrified.

I'm terrified.

I spent that afternoon working on a heart-breaking list of demands from Mark's solicitors:

- Itemise everything you have spent on clothes in the past two years.
- Provide an inventory of everything you took from the house when you left.
- How much will your mother leave you when she dies?

He's scared. I'm scared.

The stag is almost upon me and I have the feeling I have so often now that I don't even mind that much if I die. I don't actively want to kill myself anymore, but trampled by a stampeding 12-stone creature – well, who could blame me for that? A tragic accident. Another tragic accident?

Nonetheless, a last vestige of survival instinct causes me to flatten my body against the paddock fence, hoping to make myself into a smaller target. It's too high for me even to attempt to climb; if I did, I would be even more likely to fall and be trampled. The hooves of the stag are flailing. The gallops are narrow and curved. Even though I am espaliered like a peach tree, I can't be sure he won't strike me.

And then, without appearing even to slow, he executes a sharp jink to the left and hops over the high stallion fence in an elegant bascule. And he's off, galloping across the field out of harm's way. The dogs trot up to me, wagging their tails and looking sheepish.

We are all absolutely fine.

The Divorce House is set back so far from the road that there is no mobile phone signal and the only working landline socket is in the boot cupboard in the hall. When the phone rings I sit on the floor in the hallway, back against the wall, legs straight out in front of me, and field calls from lawyers, therapists and ambulance-chasing insurance companies, promising a quick buck from my two car crashes.

My note-taking is so copious that I buy a cheap white desk, which like everything else needs assembly. When it looks relatively stable, I place upon it an A4 ruled notebook with a poison green cover that I use as a day book. I number all the pages, creating an index at the front and a log for future events, as if for an imaginary magazine. I draw up week by week To Do lists with deadlines attached. With no job to go to, my life shrinks down to nothing but therapy and admin. In the morning, after Hope has left for work, I go to my little white desk where I take phone calls and answer emails and letters. I make dated and timed notes of every conversation and transaction which I cross-reference back to my index. The poison-green notebook faithfully records every fact and every detail.

I get myself a second mobile phone with a new number and set up a new email account. I tell only 12 family and close friends the new number and email address. That's all you need really, 12 people, like the apostles. Hope is my main support, despite losing her home, too, and worse her relationship with the only father she has ever known. She is stoical and practical, taking it one day at a time, although I later learn she confides in Alastair about her fears for me. She changes the passwords on all my social media accounts, keeping them secret from me so I can't post anything rash. And at 5 p.m. every evening I turn off the old phone that the lawyers, insurers, former colleagues, my soon-to-be-ex-husband and the world in general use to reach me and hide it in a desk drawer until the next morning so I am not tempted to look at it.

August is a drowsy month, the lawyers start to disappear on holiday, I begin to sleep a little more. Five hours at first, sometimes six.

And then, just when I begin to feel as I if I am surfacing again, I am served a Section 21 No-Fault Eviction notice. My landlady told me when I first signed the rental agreement that the Divorce House was for sale, but the market was sluggish and she didn't expect it to sell ... Except now it has. Hope and I and the dogs will have to leave in 12 weeks' time. We are homeless again. I was the longest-ever serving editor of *Good Housekeeping* but I can't keep a house – I have lost two homes in six months.

Tectonic plates start to move somewhere deep within me. Whereas before I had been frozen, stuffing my feelings down under the dead weight of busy days, wine-fuelled evenings and sleepless nights, now the demons are unleashed and what emerges has the smell of sulphur.

It is as if I hear a rumbling, quiet at first then growing louder and louder, building to an almighty roar that encompasses my whole being – a howl of rage that seems as if it could engulf the universe, an infinite number of universes. What more must I do? I have tried to be such a good girl no matter what fate has done to me. When a fatal disease deprived me of my family, I prayed for their souls to the God who had betrayed me and them, then struggled to my feet and went back to work to keep a roof over the heads of my fractured family. I paid for childcare, pay my taxes, donate to charity, never in debt. I keep my BMI below 23, have my teeth scaled and polished every three months, my legs waxed every three weeks. I recycle. I campaigned for better maternity benefits and part-time working that had never been an option for me. I fought for more opportunities for women than I had in my own career. I turned a legacy magazine that was slated not to make it into the twenty-first century into the biggest-selling glossy in Britain. I told the Claires of Britain how to organise their wardrobe, which bread-maker to buy – as well as which vibrator – how to decorate every room of the house for Christmas and put a meal on the table for a family of four in under half an hour, never having had my own family of four all alive together in this world. I kept smiling through breast cancer, writing an upbeat blog about hair loss and surgery scars. I married a man I fell in love with and who I thought loved me. I disdained merely living together because I believed in commitment before the eyes of the God who had already proved so capricious. I encouraged my daughter to love my second husband as the only father she had ever known. I always played by the rules and coloured inside the lines. And still ... still it came to this: homeless, jobless, betrayed, humiliated – and at an age when I had thought I would be winding down, finding peace at last after all the struggle and grief ... Not to be starting all over again. What had being a good girl brought me, except anguish and pain? The glue of my perfectly bound life did not hold, the spine is broken and the pages lie loose and scattered, they cannot be reassembled now.

And so, finally, I allow myself to do what, perhaps, everyone expected me to do decades previously after first John died, then Ellie. I let go of every ounce of restraint, caution and decent behaviour. I don't bother getting dressed in the morning but walk my dogs around the fields wearing my nightdress and a cardigan, my feet stuffed into a pair of wellies, bottle of wine in hand.

I start drinking straight after breakfast and carry on all day, right through until I pass out at night. I ring Mark and slur down the phone, fighting for my marriage in the way I perhaps should have done when there was something worth rescuing. I tell him Hope and I are homeless and that I want to move back into the Canal House. And then, when he refuses yet again, I instruct my solicitors to obtain an Occupation Order. There is a backlog in the Family Courts and I must wait weeks for my case to be heard – and, even then, there is no guarantee I will get my home back.

Autumn arrives as a cold, hard shock. My lovely Divorce House is no longer a place of shelter and appears to turn on me, becoming overrun with spiders and daddy longlegs while the garden grows thick with toadstools: tiny black ones; regular brown ones and even, in the roots of trees, bright red with spots, as if destined for a witch's cauldron. Every morning there are more – the lawn is thick with them. The weather forecast on the radio says it's been the hottest, wettest summer on record, which probably accounts for these natural phenomena, but I feel as if poison is seeping out of the ground and evil creatures are running amok.

I'm not scared of spiders but Hope is, so I try to keep them under control. The dogs play their part, pouncing on them, then spitting out the legs in disgust. My mother tells me that country folklore has it that a bowl of conkers will keep spiders away. It's a good year for conkers too, and it works like the charm it probably is. But nothing can keep at bay the depression that rolls in like the morning mists.

I rarely leave the Divorce House as if – like Hope refusing to go to school all those years ago – I fear the door will be barred on my return.

Although we are living on borrowed time in the Divorce House, my niece Zoe comes to stay, bringing her guitar, cat and yoga mat. She is not technically my niece but the granddaughter of my beloved godmother Jo. Now in her late twenties, she resembles the actress Lily James. A theatre director and yoga teacher, she has broken up with her boyfriend and needs somewhere to stay, but I suspect she has been despatched by my family – whether those living or deceased, I am not sure – to look after me and Hope, which she does, cooking nutritious vegan meals and taking us through yoga routines in the studio.

21 September 2017: 11 months after the crash

I win the court case securing an Occupation Order in my favour, which not only requires Mark to vacate the Canal House within six weeks of the date of the hearing but also rules that he will be arrested if he so much as sets foot on the property after that date; this feels like some small vindication. With no salary coming in, I am relieved not to have to keep paying rent. But more importantly, after eight months of living in exile, Hope and I will be going home.

We – Hope, Zoe, the dogs and I – move back on 30 October 2017, exactly one year to the day from when Peter Swift threw himself under the wheels of a lorry, unwittingly ending my life as I knew it rather than his own. Just 12 months have passed since I stepped out of the broken wreckage of my car onto the central reservation not sure if I was alive or dead.

By remaining alive for the subsequent 365 days, I have lost not only my marriage but also my job and twice been made homeless. My fall has been precipitous and brutal. I am not even sure I want to go back in the Canal House; it's so tainted for me by what has happened in my absence. But I have nowhere else to go. With the demolition of the life that I thought I had created for myself, for us, I have absolutely no idea what should replace it. Should I retreat back to London? But why, when for the first time in four decades I have no office in which to spend the largest part of my day? Should I go back to my family in the Dengie? Perhaps? But I am too unwell to contemplate buying or renting another home – so the Canal House it has to be.

Narrowboats nose their way along between the locks. As I make tea in my kitchen I can see out of the window into the cockpits of *Girl Betty* or *No Place Like Home* as the skippers drink tea from mugs brought by their mates.

At night, I smell the smoke from their barbecues, hear the quiet murmur of voices drifting on the evening air. In the morning they are gone, heading north towards Birmingham or south towards London.

Mark has taken what remained of the furniture I left behind when I moved out. All that is left is the giant bespoke 14-seater dining table, presumably too big for wherever he is going; a reminder of all the dinner parties we had planned to give together. Otherwise, the house is empty, echoing, a dream we had spent so long working on prior to moving in, making it perfect, exactly how we wanted our lives to be. And for what? Our time together in our so-called Forever Home was just 17 months. In the utility room the shelves of the laundry cupboard still bear the Dymo labels I made, Martha Stewart-style, denoting the linen and towels for each of the rooms. Mark did not peel them away after I fled and I wonder whether every time he saw them he remembered the hopes and dreams we had for our life together – or was he simply irritated afresh at my obsession with neatness and order?

He also left behind the cat, which puzzles me. Mark was the cat-lover; I prefer dogs and, in any case, am mildly allergic to cats.

I am not sure if Lulu minds this double abandonment. She is part-feral and I don't think she really cares much for humans, but she consents to sit alongside me on the sofa in the evenings as I watch TV. She is now quite old but still capable of catching mice, bringing them into the house, dabbing at them with her claws to show me how they run, until they hide trembling under the furniture. Remembering how I used to rescue baby birds when I was a child, I shut Lulu in the utility room then scoop up a quivering mouse in one of the takeaway coffee cups that I wash out and save for this specific purpose, before carefully depositing the victim in a safe spot, far down the lane where she will not venture. No matter how many times I do this, no matter how unscathed the mouse appears, nor how determinedly it ran from Lulu, I still find it dead in its coffee-cup coffin when I go back later to check.

Other than the table, and the cat, little remains of my and Mark's intended life together, but there is still the mirror we bought together in its baroque frame with the light that flashes on and off across the canal, one word seeming to mock me: Sexy … Sexy … Sexy!

I know I need to get a job – and not just for the salary but because I have never not had a job. I have no idea how to structure my days without the backbone of work. Magazines have been my life but are now changing out of all recognition.

Budgets and staffing levels are being cut to the bone; even the very job description 'editor' is being phased out in favour of the more managerial sounding 'content director'. I am known for big-budget, big-selling titles, for risk-taking and turn-arounds, for headline-grabbing campaigns, dominating the market and fighting off competitors with publicity-garnering special issues. I couldn't see any employer feeling brave enough to take me on in this scaled-back landscape for fear I might embark on another extravagant project requiring a roll-call of famous names, gala evenings and interviews on *News at Ten*. The premonition I had watching *Sunset Boulevard* had proved right: magazines really had got smaller. Brutally, for someone who had made their name by predicting consumer trends, I was no longer in fashion. I need to do something else – but what?

In a moment of supreme hubris, notwithstanding that I am by any definition in the middle of a major nervous breakdown, I decide to become a life coach. Yes, I really do think that despite being jobless, divorcing, dependent on antidepressants, and drinking far too much, my new calling should be telling other women how to live their lives. The real attraction though is that the training course is based in California: planes, travel, strangers – my favourite escapes – I will be running away but on the pretext of finding my next career.

I leave Hope and Zoe unpacking our possessions in the Canal House and head for the airport.

1 November 2017: One year after the crash

I am in Heathrow Terminal 5 when I realise I have mislaid my identity, almost as if it were a carry-on bag that I put down absent-mindedly, only to turn and, with a lurch of the heart, discover it missing.

The attendant at the check-in desk for the BA flight to San Francisco repeats herself: 'You don't appear to be who you say you are.'

The world tilts slightly on its axis; I shake my head trying to clear the fog that has been filling my brain for months. I hoped that despite losing nearly everything, I would still be me? But maybe not? The fragile bond that anchors me to the planet has become so frayed and weakened by recent events that now I fear it may snap altogether and, untethered, I will float away into the vast empty darkness of space.

'Your paperwork is not in order,' she clarifies, adding: 'You won't be getting on a plane today.'

Metaphorically, and perhaps actually, I smack my forehead in despair. I have recently acquired a new passport, reverting to my maiden name ... But amidst the chaos and panic of the past year, I have forgotten to update the ESTA, the document allowing me to travel without a visa to the United States, which is still registered to my old – now irrevocably lost – identity.

'I have to fly. I'm booked on a course that starts tomorrow. In California.' A cliché. I know, I am heading out West for a new beginning. This was supposed to be my fresh start, a last throw of the dice that I am using my redundancy pay-off to afford. A mad attempt at reinvention on top of all the foolish things I have done lately, and then I start to cry, right there in Terminal 5.

The check-in attendant – her name tag says she is called Barbara – softens her tone, maybe because I am a top-tier frequent flyer or more likely because I am no longer young and my tears are not pretty: 'The US authorities say you have to allow three days for an ESTA to be issued – but if you're lucky you might be able to do it online and still make the flight.'

She tells me to go into the first class lounge – she will advise her colleagues that she has authorised it. I am no stranger to business travel but since I am paying my own fare today, I will not be turning left when, or even if, I get on the plane. In the lounge, I am to find a quiet corner, sit down and go through the process calmly. 'Don't allow yourself to get rushed,' she says. 'If you make a mistake, the system will spit you out and you'll have to wait, maybe days, before you are let back in.'

First class this side of passport control is not luxurious, it is simply an empty space, screened off from the rest of the travelling public. There is no seating because VIP travellers don't linger here but are ushered through at speed, the sooner to get to the free champagne in the Concorde lounge that is their due. So, I sit on the floor and as I do so, I remember the trip to New York earlier this year when, despite all the indications that the life I had worked so hard to construct was dissolving like a gossamer cathedral, I still had faith in my abilities to cope – misguided as it turns out. Now I don't even know who I am anymore, no longer sure of my own name, nor when – or if – this cascade of misfortune will come to an end.

On top of everything else, I am out of work for the first time in my life – and I'm not the only one. All that summer the major league magazine editors have been falling like crowned heads of Europe after the First World War. Among us, only Anna Wintour continues her reign into the new uncharted digital era, rising to even greater heights as Creative Director of Condé Nast. The inspiration, it was alleged, for the satirical novel and smash-hit film *The Devil Wears Prada*, is still the most successful, admired and in some quarters feared magazine editor of all time; she be-strides the modern media landscape like a designer-clad Colossus.

The glare of the fluorescent lighting is preventing the US Border Authority website from picking up details of my passport photo page. I shuffle around on my knees, bending this way and that, searching for the best angle for the light, trailing the spillage of my wheelie case behind me. All the wine I've been drinking lately means few of my smart clothes fit me anymore. I feel the elastic waistband of my trousers slide down, probably revealing bum cleavage.

And it is while in this position on the floor – more or less looking like a homeless person, which was so nearly my fate – a pair of high-heeled boots clicks past me. And I look up into the dark glasses and signature blow-dried bob of Anna Wintour herself.

We used to nod to each other at London Fashion Week and chatted over a lunch where she was the guest of honour and I had just picked up a major award. She was wearing Chanel and a fabulous necklace; I wore my favourite Donna Karan. Anna is known to be shy but I found her warm and friendly – nothing like her Nuclear Wintour reputation. I noticed she ate rather more than the usual number of potatoes, stretching past me to spear second helpings. I could not claim we were friends. And even if we were, I doubt she would have expected the weepy person in fat-pants sitting on the floor of an airport terminal that afternoon to be anyone she actually knew. I hide my face anyway in shame as she strides on by, noticing as she passes that not only is she not trailing luggage like me and every other passenger, but she doesn't appear to be carrying a bag, nor even a phone, just her passport and boarding card held lightly in one hand, her transatlantic path smoothed by unseen helpers. Her identity so beyond doubt that unlike every other woman in this airport, she doesn't need to carry a handbag – not even one by Prada ...

'I used to be someone like that,' I mutter to myself, then again with more force: 'I used to be someone.' On my previous trip to the US, only months before but with another name and life, there was a limo meeting me at the airport whisking me to the Plaza Athénée Hotel, every step of my trip itinerary planned out by my super-efficient PA.

Now, left to my own devices, I am stranded, like Oscar Wilde at Clapham Junction, in the chains of my own humiliation. And it looks like I won't even be getting on the plane, my new life aborted before take-off ... How has it come to this? How have I fallen so far – and so fast?

My relationship with my own given name is complex. I have never used the name that appears on my birth certificate, being double-barrelled not because of any aristocratic connections, rather the reverse. My great-grandfather was rumoured to have been a jockey, known as Cuffo. He had a muddled private life and two families, necessitating the adoption of two surnames. I have only ever used one of those names, Nicholson, for work, and omitted – due to feminist pride – to take the opportunity to change my name to my John's surname, Merritt, on my first marriage. With hindsight that would have made my life a lot simpler than finding myself a single parent to two children who did not bear the same name as their mother. After I married Mark, I put feminist considerations aside in favour of practicality and changed my name, my bank accounts and my passport to his name (Johansen). Why do I always seem to be one surname behind my current status?

Somewhere in the midst of all the house moves, job loss and divorce proceedings, I changed my name again by deed poll, giving myself a middle name I never had before, in memory of my beloved godmother. And in that stressful, disorientating and confusing time managed to change my passport, my bank accounts, my driving licence … everything but the damn ESTA which was organised for me by my PA back when I had a job, status, and people who made things happen for me.

I cannot, however, explain all this to the US Border Authority website. And I cannot afford to waste the money already spent on the Californian course, nor the hotels which are booked.

I have no choice but to remain sitting on the floor, working away at my phone with anxious fingers, until the gods who rule the internet suddenly take pity on me and the website accepts my new passport and grants me an ESTA. Back to Barbara at the check-in desk, who is delighted, ringing ahead to warn the gate I am on my way. And then with only minutes left to catch my flight, dragging my hastily restuffed wheelie case behind me, I run through the airport, as if on my way to meet a lover.

* * *

I found out about this course from my favourite magazine, O, *The Oprah magazine*. And my fellow participants are nearly all women, mostly American, some from as far afield as New Zealand, no one else from the UK. They seem to be mainly mid-lifers, some on the run from reality like me, but most just wanting to transition out of jobs as corporate lawyers or bankers into something more meaningful. During the lunch break on the first day, I am approached by a tall, slender woman a little younger than me – flanked by two others of similar age.

'You're Lindsay, right?' A Canadian accent. 'You're in our group.'

'There are groups?'

Mired in my grief and anxiety, as well as the move back to the Canal House, I had not only failed to update my ESTA but barely glanced at the pre-registration documents. In fact, I had very little idea of what we were going to be studying. I just had a vague idea that I could build a career giving the women who until recently had been my readers personal tips on prioritising and time management; I just needed a qualification that said I could do it.

The Canadian is Lisa, a former marketing executive. Her wing-women are Elizabeth, an HR professional from Texas, and Betsy, a child psychologist from Colorado. Our tutor is Martha Beck, a 50-something from Utah. She is tiny and pretty with cropped blonde hair and I am reassured by the fact that she has three Harvard degrees – her work informed by psychological research not New Age woo-woo – especially as my own family are of the opinion that I have run away to join a cult!

She starts by telling us that 'gut reaction' is more than just a saying and that paying attention to what is going on in the body can be more helpful than listening to the stories our minds continually weave. I have a jet-lag headache and I am not enjoying the seminar at all. Here's a physical reaction, I want to say, my gut says you're talking rubbish.

But I have paid good money to be here, so I remain in my seat.

To demonstrate the difference between a stressed body and a relaxed body Martha proposes students compare their physical strength while first thinking about someone who loves them and then again while thinking about something that is a demonstrable lie. She invites volunteers on stage asking them to hold out an arm while repeating an obvious lie over again. 'I like vomit' is her suggestion. When they do so Martha can easily push their arm down to their side. But when she tells them that instead of repeating the lie about liking vomit, they are to concentrate hard on an image of someone who loves them unconditionally, she can't push their arm down no matter how hard she tries. Or appears to try; I am not buying any of it. Maybe my family were right and this is a cult?

By the time the session ends, I am in a thoroughly bad mood. I tell my new friends that I am too jet-lagged to join them for dinner – and go to bed ridiculously early.

The next morning, I wake in my hotel room at 2 a.m. local time, which my body is absolutely convinced is 10 a.m. See, I say out loud into the darkness, the body does lie – the reality is I am on Pacific Standard not Greenwich Mean Time. The room is all beige – curtains, bedspread, carpets – with a mustard-coloured chair to ring the changes. There is a TV on the wall which I don't turn on for fear of disturbing sleepers in adjoining rooms. I start to feel anxious. It was being alone and stressed that triggered the traumatic flashbacks in the Lake District and in the police cell. I don't think I can survive a rerun. Distraction, I need to distract myself …

Thinking about someone who loves you unconditionally will make you stronger, Martha said. So, I concentrate on Hope, living her life with such grace despite never knowing her father and losing her sister at age five. She supports me unfailingly even though I was absent at the hospital with Ellie or busy at the office for so much of her childhood. My mind floods with images of her beautiful face and waist-length strawberry-blonde hair, such a capable confident woman she has become when no one, least of all me, would have blamed her for going off the rails. When she picked me up from the police station that morning after the arrest, 'Oh mother,' she said, her voice gruff with emotion. 'This was always supposed to be the other way around.'

Then I think about Zoe, my niece. She is at the Canal House now, supporting Hope, telling her to get back on the yoga mat, while she unpacks the boxes, creating for us a home in which we will want to live again.

I try conjuring up images from a year ago when I was, I believed, happily married. When did it go wrong? Why didn't I notice? I have no idea. Or rather my conscious mind has no idea, but perhaps my body knew all along: the insomnia, asthma, falling over all the time, the extreme reactions to medication and other frequent illnesses, the frantic burying myself in work trying to convince myself all was well … I like vomit.

Dwelling on the failure of my marriage, I feel myself sliding back to that place where the walls run red with blood and my bed bucks and rears … Quickly, I think about my 82-year-old mother, driving 75 miles to tend my rented garden. And – unbidden – more images of friends and family crowd into that dimly-lit hotel room. And not just the living. My grandparents are there, too – indomitable survivors of two World Wars, although long dead now.

My Essex grandmother, grew vegetables, skinned rabbits and slaughtered chickens for the pot, raising her four children alone while her Royal Air Force engineer husband was stranded and starving on the besieged island of Malta, before being torpedoed not once but twice in the Mediterranean on the way home.

My paternal grandfather spent the war in the London dockyards, fitting out warships, finishing off the job as they sailed down the Thames, highly vulnerable targets for enemy action. His wife, a matriarch straight out of *EastEnders*, bleached her net curtains, prayed daily with her rosary and haggled ruthlessly on the black market to stretch the rations that were barely enough to feed her family. We lived with her for a while when I was very young, in the Stratford house they remained in for decades after being bombed out of their former home in the Blitz until it was demolished as a slum. Every week she would kneel in the street in apron and curlers, and vigorously scrub clean her front doorstep, so as to keep the horrors of the outside world from being trodden into the home. Fortitude was the defining trait of both sides of my family.

My grandmothers would have disdained domestic goddess fantasy of housekeeping just as they would have found the concept of a life coach risible – if not downright unbelievable. They would have derided poured resin floors and whirlpool baths as foundations for a marriage. Their homes were not showpieces, let alone investments, but places of refuge from a harsh world. They were in my life long enough to know I had gone to university, the first in my family to do so. My country grandmother called it 'the university' not realising there was more than one. Neither knew I would go on to become the editor of a famous publication. Not that they read *Good Housekeeping*, preferring *Woman's Weekly* or *The People's Friend*, printed on porous paper and saddle-stitched – they were not interested in being glossy or perfect bound.

What 'good housekeeping' meant to them was living according to their values and making life better for the children and grandchildren who would come after them. That innate knowledge, rather than anything material, was their legacy to me.

Of course, I had no time for what were known back then as housewifely skills – I was a feminist, a career woman ... Only as a single parent did I realise the overwhelming importance of creating for my children – and myself – a safe place to go out from in the morning to do our work and to return to when the day is done.

While the mythical Claire was my imaginary first reader of every issue of the magazine, my true inspiration came from my grandmothers and all the women like them, who did whatever was necessary to keep their families going in the hope of better days ahead. They were the ones who taught me the real meaning of good housekeeping. And they are with me still, urging me from beyond the veil to take things one step at a time: eat properly, look after myself, my surroundings and those I love. Above all, just keep going.

It is starting to get light now, although still too early for breakfast, so I get up and go for a walk along the beach. As the sky turns from pewter to violet, pelicans fly low, like fighter planes, along the shoreline while dolphins play out in the bay. My grandmothers never saw such sights, their lives limited by poverty and circumstance. I have travelled further than they could imagine and along the way I have struggled to reconcile my successes with the eternal questions of grief and betrayal. It is the nature of suffering to think we are alone – when all that is really happening is that we are becoming more human.

The women who made me did not have my fancy education, nor my opportunities, or freedom of choice, yet they possessed the more ancient knowledge, which is how to find your way home. Without recognising their influence, I was paying homage to them every day, with the small achievable promises that made up the magazines I created.

A wave rushes in to cover my feet then draws back to the ocean, sucking the sand from under my toes. I am momentarily unbalanced, then right myself. As I do so, I realise that all I need to do to survive is to start to live according to what I have always known to be true.

The time for editing my life is over, the time for living it has begun.

CHAPTER 18

The Golden Cover

November 2017: 13 months after the crash

The brave intentions formed on the beach at Pismo Bay disintegrate into a fog of cold and jet-lag when I return. It doesn't help that I continue seeking solace in wine. Hope is working long hours and spending increasing amounts of time with her boyfriend who lives nearer the cookery school than we do, so she often stays over. Long, lonely evenings marooned on my own in Canal House are made tolerable by the company of my good friend Mr Sauvignon Blanc.

The witching hour is 6 p.m., when I turn to this most reliable lover, the one who will never die, never cheat on me, who is always by my side softening the passage from the hard-scrabble day by which I have lived for so many years to the blurry evening. Depression descends like a fog, or perhaps like a blanket thrown over a parrot's cage, putting a stop to the ceaseless activity that has ruled my life for so long. The adrenaline that powered me through the house moves, the divorce negotiations, the redundancy, evaporates. The blind energy that drove me back to work after John's death, even after Ellie's, not daring to

217

stop and think because thinking was unbearable, not daring to sleep because then the nightmares came. Now in a fog of alcohol and medication, I sleep late every morning, turning off the alarm that rings at 7.30 and dozing until 10 a.m., or later. Sometimes I lie there even longer nursing my hangover; there is nothing to get up for anyway.

My weight, that ever reliable barometer of my mood, has been increasing steadily, the heavier my mood, the heavier I become physically. When I am finally able rouse myself, I select the least objectionable from an ever-growing pile of stretched-out leggings and musty sweatshirts on the bedroom floor. The simple tasks of keeping myself fed and the house and my body reasonably clean seem to require immense amounts of energy that I, the person who regularly worked 16-hour days, can no longer muster.

I develop a cat-like horror of getting wet. Taking a shower feels like being pelted with hail stones and washing my hair brings on a headache. So, I don't bother. For someone who operated on a strict regime of brow shaping, eyelash dying, bikini waxing and root retouching, now even brushing my teeth feels like an assault. The stainless steel twin-sinks in the high-spec kitchen become crusted with limescale, a grubby ring forms around the whirlpool bath. Dust bunnies roll unimpeded across the poured resin floors. I see no reason to change the bedsheets: why bother stretching a sheet across a six-foot wide mattress that only I will sleep on? Putting on a double duvet cover is a two-person job for a reason.

The dogs insist on being walked every day and often that is all I can accomplish in any given 24-hour period. Some days I can't even face that and ring my friend Mary and pretend that I am snowed under with work so she will exercise the dogs for me. Then I lie on the sofa wreathed in clouds of self-loathing, shovelling chocolate into my mouth as if the sweetness will offset the sour curdling of my mind.

One day, I walk into town to collect my antidepressants. But there has been a mix-up in the pharmacy and the drugs aren't ready. This is disaster, I am pretty sure I won't be able to sleep without my medication. And all I really want, crave, is sleep, not to be conscious. I start to argue, quickly becoming hysterical. The pharmacist hustles me into the private interview room, where every year I have my flu jab. She talks to me gently until I calm down. Then she rings the GP practice and sorts my prescription: 'Yes,' I hear her say. 'An emergency.'

It is only with hindsight that I realise the picture I must have made. I had never really had off-duty clothes. When a cashmere sweater became too bobbly for the office, I downgraded it to my off-duty life – paired with Sweaty Betty leggings, no longer smart enough to be seen at the posh gym where I did Pilates – emblematic perhaps of the lack of care I took over my non-work life? For my trip to the pharmacy, I was dressed head to toe in black, wearing huge sunglasses despite the fact that it was a dull winter's day, face smeared with purple lipstick, a leftover from one of the lipstick launches. A tall screechy woman dressed as if for a funeral – with purple clown lips. The finishing touch, a hippy-style necklace of brown beads. One of the stalls in the market is run by a woman who makes simple jewellery out of semi-precious stones. I got talking to her and she told me that tiger's eye – amber in colour and striped with black – is reputed to give the wearer confidence and strength. That's what I need, I thought. Fearful of seeing Mark who is still driving around town in his car that still bears the personalised number plate of our entwined initials, I hardly leave my home. I am a scientist by education, a journalist by training, but the protection of the magic crystals gets me out of the front door.

Since my abrupt departure from the world of the glossies, I have thought about magazines very little. Mired in my own despair, humiliated by my failure to leave at a time of my own choosing, I scuttle past the supermarket racks, the branch of WH Smith at Euston Station. It is over, none of it means anything to me now.

But, still, I think best in ink and so one day in between endlessly cycling through the Sauvignon Blanc nights and the chocolate-inhaling afternoons, I sit at my kitchen table and amuse myself by roughing out some coverlines for a magazine based on my life now:

Dress like nobody can see you
Eat whatever's in the fridge – no plate required
101 reasons not to exercise – you will only need one

It brings a rare smile to my face, so I carry on:

How to get ahead at work? Master the 16-hour day
#1 tip to ruin any relationship (clue, see above)
Why redecorate – no one visits anyhow …
Crisis of confidence? What made you think you were so special
  anyway?

I pause, my hand hovering over the sheet of paper. It goes against my instincts and training to commit such negative thoughts to paper, although I would sometimes do it, just to get the creative juices flowing. And then, hardly daring to venture back into positivity, I try turning them around. If I made myself a magazine to guide me now, what would it look like? Those Small Achievable Promises float around in my brain. What if I devised a Golden Cover for the way I want my life to be now? It seems worth a try. What else is there to lose?

The hotspot would be devoted to my current priority because, despite the court battle to return here, the Canal House still feels alien and despoiled for me, so:

Turn your house into a home

Directly underneath that would be the obsession I shared with every Claire I have ever met:

Get a great night's sleep, tonight and every night

And below that – but still significant even though fashion is so often described as trivial, because I have to accept my appearance is scaring, if not children or horses, then certainly pharmacists right now:

Find the look for your lifestyle

On the bottom right-hand corner, food of course. We all have to eat:

Cook yourself happy
No-stress suppers
On the table in under 30 mins

A banger in huge type across the middle of the page:

Confidence!
3 surprising ways to increase self-esteem

There must be some – other than medication – even if I don't yet know what they are.

For the nice-to-have above the logo, I might steal the line that Alice Head used as long ago as the twenties:

Sex and the newly single woman? What relationships look like now

I have no idea what the Crackerjack will be. It sits like a blank page in my mind. But then it always was, until I knew it when I saw it ...

PART III

Small Achievable Promises

CHAPTER 19

Turn Your House into a Home

December 2017: 14 months after the crash

The Decree Absolute has been granted and my 12-year marriage is over. It turns out that Mark got both Waitrose and Tesco in the settlement, so I have taken to shopping in the nearby Marks & Spencer in order to avoid seeing him and his girlfriend, and that is where I bump into a woman I know from the local yoga studio. Despite being tiny, Angie is always easy to spot in a crowd, with her flowing purple and orange robes, hooped earrings and extravagantly winged eyeliner. Today, as is often the case, her mass of jet-black hair is captured in a turban and she moves like a queen steering her younger son in his push-chair down the grocery aisles. Angie wants to know where I've been lately, so I pour out my tale of woe. She listens intently, then: 'You need a cleanse,' she says briskly.

I assume she's telling me get to grips with my personal hygiene as she can probably tell I'm still sporadic about wash-ing my hair and brushing my teeth. But it turns out the cleanse she is referring to is shamanic and she means for my house. Angie was born in Chile, coincidentally the country I fell in love with just when my life was falling apart. As a child, her family was forced to flee Pinochet's evil regime, settling by a roundabout route in this small Hertfordshire town. She is now a highly regarded alternative therapist, describing herself as a shaman and modern medicine woman. So, without really thinking it through, I arrange for her to come and give the Canal House a spiritual cleanse to rid it of the bad energy surrounding the end of my marriage. Not that I actually believe in this stuff – but it has to be worth a go.

I was raised Catholic, and despite the support of our former parish priest, Father Anthony, my relationship with religion fades in and out like a badly tuned car radio. But you can't be raised a Catholic and not be intrigued by the idea of a ritual.

Unlike Christianity, which has little to say on home improvements but also hasn't so far provided much comfort in my current dilemmas of divorce and redundancy, dipping my toe into shamanism at least provided a much-needed incentive to clean up the house. In the run-up to our appointed day, I vacuum throughout and scrub the scum from around the bath. I do this mainly because 'feasting', as Angie calls it, is an important part of any shamanic ceremony and she has instructed me to organise a party for the evening after the cleanse. I have invited a dozen girlfriends and it is their critical eyes – not the gods – I fear. Hope does not want anything to do with the ritual. She physically shudders at the thought – and instead offers to cook for the party. Zoe will mix the cocktails.

On the day itself, Christina arrives to accompany me as Angie traverses through every room of my house waving what she calls a 'smudging stick', made of leaves of dried sage lit with a taper that smoulders like a home-made cigar, emitting a heady smoke that reminds me of incense. To be honest, it's all a bit Ab Fab, especially when Christina feels woozy from the fumes and has to lie down on my bed. While she recovers, Angie instructs me in the South American traditions of truly inhabiting a home, rather than just making it look nice.

Altars are key in a home, Angie tells me, which makes me think of the giant statue of our Lady of Lourdes my London grandmother kept in her bedroom, lighting a candle before it every Christmas Eve to keep vigil as the Virgin laboured through the night bringing Christ into the world. But shamans have a different interpretation. 'We do everyday altars,' Angie tells me. 'Start with one in the kitchen to celebrate the changing seasons. Dress it with flowers and leaves you gather on your dog walks in the summer or maybe bird feathers or pretty stones, anything that catches your eye. On no account buy imported flowers in winter, just use bare twigs or make paper flowers.' It is very nearly Christmas, so she produces tissue paper and pipe cleaners from the Mary Poppins-style bag in which she stored the smudging stick and her sacred drum and shows me how to fashion simple decorations. It feels a bit odd, sitting there in my kitchen making paper decorations and inhaling the sage-scented air, but creativity is one of the ways you anchor yourself to your home, apparently. In my study, Angie decrees, I must have another altar – to celebrate the work that has been so important to me and to remind me of what I have yet to do. Under her watchful eye, I retrieve the silver platters, plexiglass trophies and assorted gongs accumulated over my years as an editor, which are all still stuffed in the cardboard box in which they followed me home by courier after my abrupt departure from

Good Housekeeping. I arrange them where I can see them while I am at my desk.

Then, and most importantly, Angie says, I need an ancestors' altar, a staple of South American homes. 'How can we ever be sure of who we are if we do not remember where we came from?' she asks.

Do I have pictures of John and Ellie and mementoes of their lives? Of course, dozens, and so precious to me. But after I married Mark, I put them in storage or placed them into Hope's room out of consideration for Mark. Since moving back to the Canal House, I have been too despondent to do anything with them. Everything is just too painful a reminder, so they are stacked in crates against the walls, which makes the rooms seem smaller, compressed by the artefacts of my past life that I cannot bear to look at.

In Chile, when someone dies an altar is placed not in the most central part of the house but slightly off to one side, so as not to dominate. It is somewhere that the family can pause for a moment whenever they pass, until eventually remembering becomes not a trauma but an accepted part of life. I use a small desk just off the hallway and place there pictures, not only of John and Ellie but also my father as a young man and my grandparents' wedding photos. Dusting and refreshing these altars – or as I, more Britishly, decide to refer to them: tables! – should not be regarded as housework, Angie tells me, but a sacred act of remembrance and commitment to my past, my present and the future. And that is what it turns out to be – a ritual that extends to keeping the rest of my surroundings clean and habitable as well.

The ceremony Angie has customised is scheduled to end with me burying something in the ground to commemorate my family's time in this home. Something that might be dug up in centuries to come by people who will wonder about who lived here. With my distaste for gardening and because the light is failing outside, I decide not to dig and instead to cast something into the canal that flows past the back door. But what? It needs to be meaningful Angie says, but preferably not precious. Inspiration strikes in the form of a box of broken trinkets stashed at the back of a wardrobe in the spare room. In my working life, I dressed every day as if for a cocktail party, which was tough on my jewellery. Statement necklaces became unstrung, brooches shed gemstones and earrings lost their mates. None of it was valuable, I never liked real stones, much preferring the fun of costume jewellery. It would have cost more than I paid in the first place to have them mended and they had no value even on eBay, but magpie like I kept these pretty gew-gaws in old shoeboxes. Now I sort them into a ritual offering, choosing those that I think will best survive a long immersion in water.

There is another important task to complete, too. Because we have not spoken since that June evening at the pub, I have been working on a letter to Mark, a final farewell, reminiscing about the joy we felt the day we married. Of coming round after surgery to find him pushing my wedding and engagement rings back on my fingers and my gratitude for the way he supported me and Hope through those dark days. Of the triumph of his Channel swim which united us as a family far more than mere words could ever have done. I have copied the letter out by hand and now, with Angie's help, I fashion it into a paper boat. It is getting dark now and cold when I go out alone to the canal terrace with my sacrificial offerings. First, I launch the paper boat into the water, leaning perilously over the water's edge to light it with a taper and send it on its way. After the arrest, the exile from my home and Mark's refusal ever to talk about when he stopped loving me or why, I was never given a proper chance to acknowledge the death of my marriage nor to mourn its passing. Now, at dusk falls, I can give our love, which was real and true at least for a time, a Viking burial. I salute the tiny ship of our marriage as she floats out to mid-stream before disintegrating into flakes of ash upon the water.

After that, it is almost a relief to pitch a shabby evening clutch, stuffed with treasures from my former life, upwards into the darkening skies. At the zenith of its trajectory, the fragile clasp gives way and the bag bursts open, raining diamante, glitter and paste down into the bottle green water. My campaign medals from gala dinners, fashion shows and premieres quickly sink into the depths where, presumably, they still remain entombed in the mud as proof that, yes, I did exist, I lived here, with my family – and we were happy for a time.

No sooner have we finished these ceremonies than Christina emerges refreshed after her nap, and Hope and Zoe invade the kitchen; slicing, chopping and mixing drinks. The doorbell rings and friends arrive, greeting each other on the doorstep laughing, chattering and letting in puffs of sharp night air that cut through the smoky fug of remembrance. They shed winter coats to reveal elegant outfits – having dressed up for the occasion – and bring gifts of chocolate, wine and even a festive wreath to hang on the door.

I won many awards for the interiors content in *Good Housekeeping*; I launched the successful magazine *Your Home* and, as editorial director, oversaw that war-horse *House*

Beautiful. To think that all the design advice I dished out, all those room-sets I created for visual effect, all those artfully placed objets d'art and plumped cushions, and I never before understood that it's always the people who turn a house into a home.

CHAPTER 20

Get a Great Night's Sleep Tonight and Every Night

February 2018: 16 months after the crash

My home has started to feel like a welcoming sanctuary once again, but despite that I am still not sleeping. I follow all the rules we covered in endless articles on the subject in *Good Housekeeping*. I keep the bedroom cool and dark, avoid caffeine after midday, turn off devices an hour before bed. But my nights seems to be getting worse, not better. Sometimes I am not even sure if I sleep at all, just doze in an agitated trance. I go back to see the GP who changes my medication from citalopram to mirtazapine, which is more calming, and I go for weekly sessions with my long-term therapist Dr M. Her analysis is my dreams have become so terrifying since the crash that every time I drop off and the nightmares begin my brain wakes me up so I don't have to endure them. 'When you are able to process your trauma by day, it won't need to visit you at night,' she says and instructs me to go back to keeping a journal by my bed to write down anything I can remember in the morning. Except I don't remember. My mind is blocked. I am even retreating into the mute state I experienced after the breast cancer, barely able to speak during our sessions. Until finally, during one of these silences, something from the night of my arrest pops into my head. The Dixon of Dock Green desk sergeant itemising the contents of my handbag asked what the antidepressants were for, I didn't bother telling him about the loss of my first family so long ago, but I did explain about the Southend Arterial car smash into the jack-knifed lorry, and then so soon afterwards the steering failure on my supposedly mended car.

'You want EMDR,' he said, in a thoroughly Dixon of Dock Green way. 'Any of the lads here have something nasty happen, we send them off for a few sessions, they come back right as rain.'

In everything that happened that night and since – fleeing my home, filing for divorce, losing my job – I had forgotten his words. Indeed, why should Dixon of Dock Green know more of what would help me than my own GP or my therapist? But now his words come back to me like a lifeline. For something to say, I ask Dr M about EMDR, which she tells me stands for eye movement desensitisation and reprocessing therapy. She explains it was developed in the early nineties and has good results with the police and military returning from war zones, helping them process the horrors they have experienced. It is not something she is trained in delivering herself, so, with her blessing, I find a practitioner in Harley Street and make an appointment. Another therapist, on top of lawyers, rent, mortgage and no job. I don't care. Anything to keep me anchored to this earth rather than constantly peering into the next, trying to find the people I have loved and lost.

Dr D has the bubbly presence of a children's TV presenter, being young, pretty and no-nonsense. Not at all my idea of someone who spends their days unfreezing patients trapped in post-traumatic stress. She later confides that her first impression of me was of a drowning woman clutching at the last piece of driftwood. We spend the first session taking notes about my history – the loss of my first husband and eldest child, the breast cancer, the two car crashes, the arrest, the loss of my home, the divorce and the redundancy. 'You're in deep trauma,' she says, adding, briskly: 'Hardly surprising.' She concurs with my other therapist and my GP that the shocks of the past year have awakened still unresolved trauma from the deaths of John and Ellie, nearly 20 years previously. I am pitifully grateful that she says this. Marital breakdown is so common, 40 per cent of marriages end in divorce, redundancy is even more frequent. Why can't I handle these everyday stressors when I have powered on through so much that was worse?

Dr D explains that EMDR is thought to work by allowing the brain to reprocess memories. Normally, even very distressing events are processed by the brain over time, probably during the REM phase of sleep, then filed away, so while still retrievable they don't intrude on everyday life. For reasons that aren't clear, some experiences are never properly metabolised; one theory is that repetitive nightmares wake up sufferers before the REM sleep has processed the images. The sights and sounds, even the smell of a traumatic event remains as vivid as the day it happened, causing flashbacks and even the hallucinations I have been experiencing. Dr D diagnoses me as suffering from not only acute PTSD from the car crashes and arrest – but complex long-term PTSD as well. I have never heard of any of this before, living for so long with images of John and Ellie's suffering, which I believed was simply the price you pay for love – one I was more than willing to endure. Until that first crash broke the dam between my night terrors and daytime competence.

Even listing all the trauma of my life at that point was enough for the first hour-long session. We would start the reprocessing later in the week.

In the second session, Dr D asks which memory I want to start on first. The long-time, deep-seated trauma of my family's deaths will be more difficult to treat than something more recent and straightforward. We decide on the crash on the Southend Arterial.

As I sit in a chair in her consulting room, Dr D asks me to imagine I am travelling on a train, looking out of the window, and to describe the view as we pass places I know. After a while she suggests, I look at the road on which my other self in the BMW was driving along that mild autumn evening, dog in the back, Cockney Rebel playing on the radio. While I talk, she passes a pen back and forth in front of my eyes, on which I am to focus while keeping remembering.

From the safety of my seat on the train, I see what I hadn't seen from my car: that troubled, desperate man running out in front of the lorry as if pursued by a swarm of bees that were only inside his head. I see the lorry driver take evasive action catching the pedestrian, Peter Swift, only a glancing blow but causing his vehicle to jack-knife. And I see me innocently in my car, coming from behind, braking, steering, then mounting the central reservation, the terrible clash of metal on metal and the left front wheel of my car disappearing under the wheels of the lorry.

Tears begin pouring down my face, Dr D remains calm, passing the pen back and forth across my sight line. 'Stay on the train,' she says. 'And while you are safe there tell me what you are thinking?'

'I can't stop terrible things happening,' I sob. And the full horror of human frailty engulfs me. 'I can't save anyone. I couldn't save John for long enough for his second child to know her father. I couldn't save Ellie in time to see her 10th birthday. I couldn't save a stranger in so much pain he stepped in front of a lorry … Why should I bother trying to save myself?'

I go back to Dr D for three or four more sessions spaced at two-weekly intervals and, in between, I notice something strange: even though I didn't consult her about my insomnia, I am starting to sleep through the night for the first time in a long, long time, on some nights seven hours or more with no wake-ups. At our last meeting, Dr D once more has me envisage the crash from a place of safety.

'The train is still moving,' says Dr D, continuing to pass her pen in front of my eyes, and she describes it taking me away from the scene of the crash, which is becoming small and grey and more distant as I am borne safely away.

'Where would you like the train to take you now?' she asks. 'Choose somewhere safe.'

The 1960s – Walton-on-the-Naze, Essex

The wind from the North Sea whips across the beach and the four ponies tied to a half-sunken wooden post swing round their rumps to avoid the sand stinging their eyes. There are two bays, brown with black manes and tails, and a skewbald, like a cow pony; they stamp their feet and toss their heads as if impatient to be off. A grey stands quietly, head drooping, maybe conserving her energy for the next rider. The name painted on her browband is Jane.

Walton-on-the-Naze on the Essex coast has a fine, sandy beach and the second-longest pier in Britain. We have been coming here every day for the past week, my two brothers and I sliding about on the back seat of my father's tank-like Ford Zephyr, because petrol is cheaper than a bed and breakfast. And if it rains, which it does frequently even in August, we can go home early.

We bring our black poodle with us and she rushes in and out of the sea, barking at the waves. My mother makes tomato sandwiches for lunch, which end up as more sand than tomato, and we change into our swimming costumes under haphazard arrangements of stripey towels. Better-organised families have towelling tents under which they shimmy in and out of their costumes without risk of embarrassment. They also have purchased – from where we know not – windbreaks, strips of canvas anchored by bamboo poles, that protect their picnics, and their dignity, from the bracing North Sea breezes and in whose lee we take care to pitch ourselves.

I am seven years old; my youngest brother, Hugh, only 18 months, plays happily in a sand boat sculpted by my father. Jeremy, three, has already scared my parents by wandering away in an unguarded moment and completely disappearing from sight. My mother and father run up and down the famously long beach screaming for what seems an agonisingly long time before they find him, safe and well, hidden behind one of the wooden ramparts mostly rotted away by sea and salt air that protect the beach from erosion.

All that wind-blown, lost brother, sand sandwiches week, I am transfixed by the ponies making their way up and down the sands giving rides to other children, the ones with wind-breaks.

I have never ridden a horse but I am already a bookish child weeping over *Black Beauty*, thrilling to *National Velvet*, and immersing myself in the Jill saga by Ruby Ferguson. I identify with the young heroines who take up the reins of untameable beasts in small but capable hands, all the better to triumph over more entitled peers.

I am too young to have deciphered the mythology that horses represent beauty, power and the freedom to escape from our mundane existence. It will be decades before I discover that, in shamanic tradition, it is the horse that takes us on our life quest, delivering us without being told where we need to be. But on some level, I have intuited that to be able to ride a horse, you must have not only physical balance but something more, something within that is deserving of the trust of a wild creature. And at seven years old, on a windy Essex beach wearing a pink summer frock and a yellow cardigan knitted by my grandmother, I am pretty sure I have neither.

For six days I watch Jane walking to and fro carrying plump ice-cream eating boys and little girls with long plaits while I try to summon the courage to attract my fretful young parents' attention long enough to ask for a pony ride.

On the last day of our holiday, I realise, it's now or never. As my father lifts me onto Jane's broad back, a trickle of urine runs down my bare legs in a mixture of fear and anticipation.

I gather the reins in my own small not very capable hands; a gruff-looking, silent man with unkempt hair and a greasy waist-coat stretched over a small pot belly, sets off at a slow pace and, after a moment, Jane follows.

The rough felt pad of the saddle chafes my damp legs as the pony steps out beneath me and I hastily abandon the reins preferring to grip the front of the saddle for fear of falling. Hardly daring to breathe, I allow myself to be led one length of the sands and back, at first discomfited but then settling into the easy four-time rhythm of Jane's gait. That's all that happens, just a walk of a few hundred yards, but in those minutes there is that blinding realisation – the first but not the last time it happens to me – when I truly understand the gift that horses give us. Jane is only a pony, not a horse, but she is bigger than the man at her head and much bigger than me. She has hooves and teeth. She doesn't have to do this. She could have ripped her halter rope from the wooden post, reared up and galloped away. Her calm generosity in consenting to carry me on her back blows my seven-year-old mind.

After one turn, up and down between the groynes where my brother was so recently lost, my father lifts me down, back to the sand, back to earth and my own two by now shaking legs. The holiday is over, it is time to get back in the Ford Zephyr. On the way home my father smokes his pipe, which combining with the smell of wet dog and the sliding round corners on the back seat makes me nauseous. We stop at a country pub, my mother cleans me up with a hanky moistened with spit and then disappears with my father to the bar where they buy a pint of bitter for him and a gin and bitter lemon for her. They return giggling and pass through the car window glasses of lemonade for us children and crisps that come with salt packaged in little blue bags.

We could not afford for me to have a pony but I did take riding lessons, until, when I was 13 years old, my father was diagnosed with cancer. Despite his attempts to continue working from his hospital bed, his illness decimated our family's already fragile finances. Because of the War, my father had no formal education after the age of 14. My mother, managed to hang on at school until age 16. It was only after they married and started a family that they both resumed their studies in what little free time they could salvage between looking after three children and earning a living. My father studied law at night school while working as a news agency reporter, finally qualifying in his early thirties. He had barely established a legal practice before the cancer struck at age 39. Meanwhile, my mother was also making up for her own thwarted ambitions by enrolling at teacher training college. It is only now with hindsight that I understand what an example they set for me, but also at what great cost – emotional and financial. As a student teacher, my mother received a maintenance grant. During my father's treatment, other than the work he did while ill and the occasional late payment cheque from better days, we lived on her grant which would have been barely enough for a young single student, let alone a family of five. My school uniform had been bought on the large side for me at age 11 and saw me all the way through to age 18. My weekend clothes were from charity shops, which probably accounts for the eye-watering sums I was later to spend on designer clothes. We sold our house in the newly popular commuter suburb of Brentwood, Essex and moved into a vicarage, which was being sold off by the

Church of England because it was unmodernised, lacking proper amenities, without even central heating, and therefore not suitable for a vicar. It was located in the Dengie, at the end of the line for trains out of Liverpool Street.

The move meant a commute of more than an hour by train each way to my convent school back in Brentwood, but it saved us in many ways, not just financially. There was more than an acre of overgrown garden, which my parents, inspired by the seventies sit-com *The Good Life*, turned over to food production. We grew potatoes, marrows, lettuces and tomatoes and went out to scour the hedgerows for blackberries to make bramble jelly. We kept chickens for the eggs and even, for a time, a Jersey cow called Little Moo. With so much space, we children were allowed to have as many pets as we wanted; I once brought home a stray dog and was allowed to keep her. My brother Jeremy kept birds of prey, training them to fly to a lure from a glove on his wrist. My younger brother Hugh went more or less feral, camping out in the garden all summer long and only venturing indoors for meals.

There was never any pocket money but Jeremy, Hugh and I signed up for weekend and summer shifts waiting tables at the yacht clubs in nearby Burnham-on-Crouch. During the annual regatta week, we cheerfully cycled the six-mile round trip to serve breakfast at 7 a.m., only returning home again after dinner service ended at midnight for a few hours' sleep before doing it again the next day. As my father's health returned, he resumed full-time work and my mother qualified as a teacher, landing a job in the school next door to the old vicarage. The pressures on the family finances eased and we became quite comfortably off, although the coping strategy of hard work as the best cure for heartache never left me. My brothers developed an interest in sailing, working as crew on the yachts for the owners we served dinner to. Hugh later served as a lifeboat skipper in his spare time. Jeremy tinkered with old cars and even had some success motor racing; he still teaches race driving skills on the big circuits. But I was nervous of anything to do with water and had no interest in cars. I had the one dream, and that was to have a pony. Finally, when I was 16 years old, a fat dapple-grey pony was installed in the garage, which had been hastily converted into a stable.

Trophy was a barely-broken youngster, newly imported from Ireland. A generous, friendly mare but in no way suitable for me as a novice rider, especially with parents who knew even less than I did about horse care. Even so, for hours at a time, I rode undaunted and alone across the Essex marshes, this being long before mobile phones were invented.

I fell off Trophy repeatedly, breaking my fingers, my nose, and even an ankle when she bucked me off going over a jump, which resulted in three months in a full-leg plaster cast. After it was sawn off, leaving my right leg withered and temporarily useless, I got straight back in the saddle. Who else was going to exercise my beloved pony? The risk and physical pain were totally meaningless to me. I was a tall, skinny, academically bright though emotionally immature teenager in a family committed, perhaps obsessively, to achievement. It wasn't easy but our unrestricted access to nature felt like more than enough reward. One time, while cantering alone across the marshes, Trophy put her foot down a rabbit hole and I went over her head, hitting the ground hard with my left shoulder and causing such pain that I was unable to get up and remount, which was my usual modus operandi. Showing remorse, perhaps, for letting me down, Trophy waited beside me for several hours, until finally my father came bumping along the farm track in his Land Rover looking for me and then we bumped back down the track and on to the Chelmsford and Essex Hospital Emergency Department, some 20 miles away, where X-rays revealed a broken clavicle. The fracture mended badly and, fully 30 years later when I married Mark, I still needed a shoulder pad stitched into the left side of my outfit to even up my posture for the wedding photos.

The memory of going to visit my father in hospital after an op, seeing him with books and paperwork piled up around the bed, because this was the only way to keep the money coming in, has never left me. His health was permanently damaged by the overwhelming amount of radiation therapy it took to save him. Over the years he was diagnosed with various cancers three more times, the final one taking him aged just 69. Such a lot of cancer in our family. But the other motif that runs through us is that we never, ever stop. We plough on through no matter what is happening. My father working from his hospital bed. John reporting on Rachel Nickell's murder two days before he died. Had I forgotten, or perhaps I never knew, what it took to make me happy?

In my mind I am no longer in the Harley Street consulting room but sitting in my father's car, in the pub car park. The cold, fizzy lemonade cures my car sickness and I think about riding Jane up and down the beach daily. With more practice, we might have trotted or cantered. But it's not just speed I crave: it's connection – a word I don't even understand yet, except to know that I long for it. Nonetheless, I decide that when I grow up, I will write books not just read them – and I will have a horse of my own. That would be a fine way to live, I think.

And all the while Dr D moves her pen back and forth, reordering the paperwork in the filing cabinets of my mind, assigning the painful memories that trigger the nightmares to their proper place, which is in the past.

CHAPTER 21

Find The Look for Your Lifestyle

11 April 2018: 17 months after the crash

Christina and I sit draped, like the nuns who taught us at school, in plain white scarves to hide our hair in natural daylight by a window to ascertain our unvarnished skin tones, our true colours.

Superficially we look alike, with what was originally dark brown hair, now artfully streaked to hide the grey, and brown eyes. Our long friendship is based on the way our differences align. Christina is measured, her speech considered to the point of what can be disconcertingly long pauses while she thinks through the impact of what she might say, wary of giving offence or causing harm. I talk a mile a minute, frequently making statements which on later reflection turn out to be not what I meant to say at all.

Christina has olive skin that tans easily as opposed to my very pale complexion. I am the taller of the two of us and she has curves while I go straight up and down. Over the years, we have travelled the world together. Christina always overpacks; she once astonished me by taking two dressing gowns and five belts on a mini-break, when I hadn't even packed enough under-wear. I travel strictly hand-luggage only – shamelessly borrowing everything I have forgotten from her bulging suitcases. Christina has been happily married for over 30 years. Before having her two sons, she was a stockbroker, now she offers her clever financial brain and limitless energy to working – unpaid – for charities.

Through every trauma and disaster, Christina has always been there for me – putting me up in her spare room, proffering herbal tea and sensible advice. The latest being that we – by which she means me but is too tactful to say so – need to update our appearance. Hence this visit to a style advisor she has found for us.

After the dance of the seven white veils, we are duly informed that Christina is Winter – think fire and ice, she is advised. Team midnight velvet jackets with white lace collars. I like the drama of that, just add a few frilly blouses to my existing wardrobe. Sorted.

It is not to be. My ashen skin tone dictates I am not Winter but the far less thrilling Autumn. I am countenanced on no account to wear black – which at this point comprises approximately 98 per cent of my wardrobe – but to think in terms of leaves and earth tones. While Christina is given permission to wear the jewel colours of ruby, emerald and sapphire. I am steered towards rust, taupe and mustard. The colour counsellor may as well have told me to wear mould, dirt and vomit.

Fashion is often written off as trivial and inconsequential, despite the fact that the apparel and textile sector is the fourth largest industry in the world and a driving force in glossy maga-zines. I was so unaware of this, I arrived for my initial *Good*

Housekeeping interview in 1999 dressed in a Marks & Spencer skirt and a jacket from a secondhand shop. As soon as he hired me, Terry Mansfield gave me a dress allowance on top of my salary and sent me to Liberty department store where the personal shopper introduced me to designers I had never heard of – Dries Van Noten and Ann Demeulemeester – which put together with the more famous names Armani, Donna Karan and Issey Miyake created a capsule wardrobe that would pass the famous 'fashion hello' – a swift glance from top to toe with which insiders ascertain the exact provenance of every item the other is wearing, from earrings to heels.

Haute fashion isn't about wearing what suits you, or even particularly about looking nice. I have met some fashion gurus who look like a bag of washing tied in the middle. It is about 'references' – who is in, who is out, who is next. It's summed up in the Meryl Streep line in the film *The Devil Wears Prada* where she explains to Anne Hathaway the meaning behind the cheap sweater she is wearing in a specific shade of blue. My job meant I needed to pass in this arcane world but I also had to dress in a way that would see me through a day that started at 8 a.m. with the school run and finished with one of the beauty industry's champagne receptions.

As editor of *Good Housekeeping*, the engraved invitations to Fashion Week arrived on my desk every February and September, with the magic AA letters hand-written in the top right-hand corner denoting a Front Row seat. But FROW does not imply fast-track access. You still have to queue, unless you are the editor of *Vogue*, *Elle* or *Harper's Bazaar*, or one of those terrifying newspaper style mavens. London Fashion Week used to have a reputation for running late; they start on time now but it's still 20 minutes in a queue, wearing high heels and your most on-trend outfit, which includes items from the designer's previous collections. Once through the door, you realise that what looks like an upscale event in photos is often just a ware-house or marquee with tiered rows of hard benches on which the fashion world's most high-profile proponents perch precar-iously, while asserting their status. As a newby, finding it impossible to get somewhere to sit in the Front Row despite my numbered ticket, I spotted a few spaces elsewhere, in the rows behind and on the other side of the runway. They were filling up fast, so I made my way over, only to receive a sharp jab between the shoulder blades from Angela Kennedy, the doyenne fashion editor. 'Just push in,' she hissed. 'You are not staying if you don't get a seat in the Front Row. What would people think?'

She explained the rules: 'You sit in the Front Row, that is your right as editor of a glossy. As your fashion editor, I sit behind you and take notes. That's correct.' I glanced up, there were no spaces behind the spot she was busy inserting me into, but I knew that wouldn't deter her. 'And behind me,' she contin-ued. 'Our assistants. Department store and upscale boutique buyers sit on the other side of the catwalk. Never get that confused. And only students sit up in the rafters.' It was my first lesson in the strict caste system that operates in this rarified world.

I didn't dare disobey, so I pushed in and eventually learned always to do so in the middle of a bench, not the end of a row. The pushers-in frequently started a domino effect, causing the person at the end to slide off the slippery benches and to land, in all their finery, on the floor. All for a show which, however wondrous, and some certainly are, lasts a dazzling 10 or 15 minutes from the moment when black-clad flunkies remove the protective plastic from the runway to the final appearance of the 30 or so models all at once and applauding the designer who peeks out from backstage, looking absolutely exhausted. Then it's out into the street, posing for the street-style photographers – who rarely troubled me, it has to be said – air-kissing friends and rivals, and starting queueing for the next show.

Fashion only ever seemed to me to be queueing in unsuitable footwear. But clothes I loved, spending far more than my dress allowance. I had a full-size wardrobe built in my office too, where I kept my Jimmy Choo heels, Chanel handbags and a selection of jackets in primary colours for TV interviews, which were always last-minute. Dash to the studios wearing the basic black that is the default uniform of magazine editors and you look like a vampire on screen. Show up wearing a print blouse and you'll be bumped from the agenda due to the strobing. And a jacket is essential. Men wear suits on TV for a reason: jacket lapels for the mic; battery pack attached to the waistband of the trousers; phone on airplane mode, tucked in a pocket, not in a handbag which will inevitably be passed to an intern for safe – or not-so-safe – keeping. High-profile female presenters can wear cutaway tops and pretty dresses because they have dressing rooms in which to leave their personal belongings and sufficient clout for someone to gaffer-tape the battery pack for the microphone into the back of a dress. I once made the mistake of wearing a Diane Von Furstenberg dress for a Sunday morning TV news show, which meant the sound engineer had to feed a cable up under the skirt in order to be able to clip the microphone discreetly to my neckline. He was respectful and cautious fixing up the mic, but once the interview was over, in rushing to wire up the next guest he simply ripped out the wires with one sharp yank that nearly took my bra with it.

For evening events, the block colour jackets were replaced by one of my collection of opera coats: a Dries Van Noten hand-painted silk kimono, a Yohji Yamamoto floor-length bias-cut drapery of silk tweed, an emerald green Issey Miyake architectural wonder. Beautiful they were – pieces of art, really – and I could just throw them over the elegant black basics that were my uniform for the office because there was never any time to shower or change before rushing out to an evening do. For all my insistence on pampering and Time For You for the readers, there was never any Time For Me in my busy schedule. Even when I went to the party to celebrate Queen Elizabeth's Diamond Jubilee, I simply redid my make-up at my desk, half an eye on the interminable proof pages, before setting out for Buckingham Palace.

Prior to the divorce and redundancy upending my life, I was regarded as exceptionally well dressed and groomed. But even though I am sleeping better since the EMDR sessions and remembering to shower – thank goodness – I still wander around in my scruffy black leggings with unwashed hair, hence Christina deciding I needed a makeover and booking the colour counsellor. Makeovers are always the most popular sections of any magazine and the subject of TV programmes as well, as almost every woman has fantasised at some point about what it would be like to have a team of professional stylists, make-up artists and hairdressers transform her appearance. But behind the downbeat 'before' and the glamorous 'after' is a world of differing opinions and downright disagreements. What we see when we look in the mirror is rarely how others see us. We project all our hopes, dreams, misconceptions, pre-conceived ideas and self-loathing, as well as our yearning to be loved, onto our reflection. Even celebrities can suffer insecurities. I well remember one daytime TV presenter, whose agent sent over her measurements prior to a shoot – UK size 14. The size 14s duly arrived, as did the star ... who turned out to be closer to an 18. The old adage that the camera adds 10 pounds is not always true. Sometimes it does. But depending on the shape you are, the set of the shoulders, the fullness of the face, height as well, it's difficult to gauge accurately what size someone is from their image on a screen. Quite often the dresses we borrowed wouldn't do up at the back, or alternatively were so large they had to be held in place with bulldog clips.

Squeezing into a dress so small it needed to be left undone at the back wasn't on-brand for that particular day's star. She cried off all her make-up – and refused to come out of the changing room for the entire morning, despite the photographer, hair-dresser and countless assistants waiting, all on the clock, until finally a suitcase of emergency size 18s arrived by courier and peace was restored.

If years of ushering women – both celebrities and civilians – into a succession of outfits, of insisting that they have a new hair colour or cut, or that the eyeshadow they have been wearing is too bright a shade of green, has taught me anything it is this: how we dress is an unconscious dialogue between our inner selves and the outer world. The way you clothe yourself may not be intended as a reflection of your inner state – but it is how the world will perceive you and will reflect back to you in a way that can become a self-fulfilling prophesy. The most expert makeover won't change your life once the cameras stop rolling, unless you also get to grips with how you feel on the inside. Changing your appearance is not simply a question of which colours suit you best or what shape will hide a bulgy tummy or big hips. Like so much, it comes down to knowing yourself.

At *Good Housekeeping* we headlined our makeover features A Look For A Lifestyle and made a point of highlighting women who had made a difference in the world, running the shoots over two days with a night in a hotel and a trip to the theatre in between. It was expensive, but from my younger days on less well-resourced magazines, I knew that all-too-often makeover subjects were treated with rather less consideration than professional models – who at least got paid for their trouble. Once, in a rush to get everything done, we forgot to capture the 'before' photographs. So, if the day's shoot was not to be wasted – and budgets on that particular title mean that was not an option – there was nothing for it but to scrub off the artfully applied make-up and – I am ashamed to say – rub face powder into the freshly styled hair-dos to recreate the 'before' looks. That our victims – and that really is the word – were prepared to tolerate us doing that was probably because they didn't much like the way they looked in the after shots anyhow.

Turns out I can dish it out – but I can't take it! I sulk all through the Colour Consultation, mentioning those Front Row invitations, now in the past, my name deleted from the guest lists, and dropping the names of the designers I know – and you will have gathered by now I can be quite the name dropper – itemising all the expensive garments in my wardrobe. What I really want, of course, is not Christina's colour palette but her life: a role with purpose, a loving and supportive husband, two healthy grown-up children. The colour counsellor knows none of this and is understandably disconcerted by my rudeness. Christina knows me too well to rise to the bait I am trailing. She doesn't bother pointing out that, despite the terrible losses, in some ways my life has been enviable: the status, the influence, the awards. She talks soothingly, offering to let me go through her own wardrobe later and pick out any rogue autumnal shades that would suit me better than her. Eventually I calm down enough to buy a couple of T-shirts in mould and vomit which hang unworn in my wardrobe before making their way to the charity shop.

Meanwhile, I continue to wear my bobbly cashmere sweaters and threadbare leggings, looking like a down-at-heel Cruella de Vil. I may have been the queen of lifestyle magazines, but what my makeover from the colour counsellor reveals is that I don't have a lifestyle to call my own. I was a worker, an editor and a mother and a wife, too busy running from grief to know who I was underneath all the roles I played. Belatedly, I realise that if I can't accept which clothes suit the person I am now, what chance do I have of finding a life that I can bear to live?

CHAPTER 22

Cook Yourself Happy. No-Stress Suppers. On the Table in Under 30 Mins

9 May 2018: 18 months after the crash

Exiting Westbourne Park Underground station, I smell an acrid scent in the air despite the months that have passed since the Grenfell fire. The burnt-out tower, now wrapped in protective sheeting, as if in a shroud, dominates the skyline and seems to cast a malign shadow. On the night of 14 June 2017, 72 people lost their lives there and hundreds more were made homeless from the Tower itself and surrounding properties. It was the worst residential fire in Britain since the Second World War.

The morning after the fire, the women of the Al-Manaar Mosque threw open the tiny, ill-equipped kitchen in their community centre and began cooking chickens and sacks of rice to feed the displaced. Word spread and as more help was needed women came from the surroundings areas – everyone from west London yummy mummies to those who lived in the Tower, fleeing with only the clothes they stood up in. In total 14 nationalities all cooking their best-loved recipes, the dishes they had grown up with ... Comfort food in the true meaning of the words.

There is no hierarchy in the kitchen although feisty Munira Mahmud soon emerges as a natural leader and Intlak Alsaiegh as the mother-hen. None of them is a professional – most only having cooked for their families before. Each of the women prepares her favourite dish and the food is served communally at long tables; left-overs are wrapped and sent home for those who are still in hotel or bed and breakfast accommodation without cooking facilities.

The actress Meghan Markle, as she was before her marriage to Prince Harry, has been secretly visiting the kitchen for some months and realised how compromised the women were in preparing such vast quantities of food with rundown equipment and barely functioning appliances. It is Meghan who comes up with the idea of writing a cookbook of their recipes to fund a new kitchen. She approaches a publisher friend, who knowing I am at a loose end, suggests I might like to help out with what is, essentially, a dogsbody job described as simply 'writer' in the acknowledgements, which means I scamper around the kitchen, notebook in hand, tasting food and interviewing the women about the recipes as they cook. They tell me about the dishes they prepare, almost always family recipes, handed down from generation to generation. I learn about the Middle Eastern way to host a family gathering, in which everyone brings or prepares their signature dishes, which are all put on the table at once, along with some pickles, yoghurt and flatbreads. It seems a much easier way of feeding a crowd than the classic dinner party. I'll never forget in my first week at *Good Housekeeping* reading through the instructions for a Saturday night supper that began: 'Two weeks in advance …' I called the recipe writer into my office: 'If you're telling readers to start prepping for each weekend a full fortnight ahead, then we're all going to lose our minds.' I became ruthless about cutting preparation times, taking shortcuts and emphasising the difference between home-cooked and restaurant food, which is the work of several sous chefs in a near industrial setting and should never be compared with home cooking. But, with hindsight, I don't think I understood much about the importance of creating food as a bonding experience.

At the Al-Manaar kitchen I talk to women who have lost family or friends in the fire, women who are homeless in a much more meaningful sense than I had ever been, and their relatives who are visiting from the continents of Africa and Asia to help them put their lives back together.

It doesn't take long for me to realise that what is going on in this shabby community centre is something extraordinary in the world of food. Every mouthful carries the taste of heritage, love, family and community. It is a phoenix from the literal ashes story that I feel inspired to shout about – and I'm not surprised that Meghan feels the same way.

The higher I climbed in the world of magazines, the less time I had for the writing and interviewing that had drawn me to journalism in the first place. Without really registering it, I was envious of the writers I sent off to interview and now, here I am, a reporter again with my notebook and pen, working on a story that brings together two of the most talked about news events of the year.

Although she has since become a somewhat divisive figure Meghan-fever was at its peak in the run-up to her wedding to Prince Harry. Remarkably though, no paparazzi ever followed her unmarked car to the mosque. In the flesh, Meghan is tiny with lustrous thick hair. She dresses simply in jeans and a shirt but always with vertiginous heels, which still only bring her up to my shoulder. She arrives, juggling Tupperware which contains some food she has prepped at home. Then she embraces each of the women, puts on an apron, so voluminous it goes twice around her tiny waist, and gets to work, being assigned by Munira the most basic jobs like chopping vegetables and washing up. I wear trainers, because my role involves so much running around. But, still, I think, if jeans are smart enough for a soon-to-be Duchess, I can wear them for work, too, teaming them with one of my Paul Smith suit jackets. And just like that, as my new portfolio working life slots into place so does an understanding of how to dress for it.

Sometimes I go to meet Meghan at Kensington Palace, which is a rabbit warren. No grand entrance like Buckingham Palace, I arrive at a gatehouse where I show my passport, grateful that finally all my many names are aligned. While I wait to be collected by Meghan's private secretary, I sit among the piles of hat boxes and outfits in garment carriers for the royals to wear for her wedding which are arriving along with gifts of nappies and even a pram for the Duke and Duchess of Cambridge's newborn Prince Louis.

Meghan takes me into the drawing room of Nottingham Cottage where, serving black coffee and Duchy Original biscuits, she outlines her vision. 'To be able to prepare and eat food from your own culture needs to be recognised as a basic human right,' she tells me, forthrightly, going on to speak with passion about refugee camps and the value of providing displaced persons with the means to cater for themselves rather than dishing out bland slop which may have the calories needed to keep people alive but none of the social interaction and bonding elements that lovingly prepared meals can provide. As we talk, she makes her own notes in the embellished calligraphy she taught herself while I scribble away in my still serviceable shorthand.

We discuss the recipes, agreeing that the amazing rice dish that Ahlam Saeid had magicked up the other day has to be squeezed in, no matter how close we are to deadline. Ahlam has a master's degree in chemistry from her native Iraq and her recipes are always the most precise – and colourful. Green Rice – a mixture of lamb, rice, beans and herbs – will become one of the most famous recipes in the book. But beyond sharing the delicious recipes, Meghan has a bigger hope that it will spur other charities and NGOs to set up similar community kitchens.

She writes her own introduction, despite the fact that the wedding is only days away. I point out that the televised nuptials coincide with our deadline – surely, I say, she has too much to do? It's fine, she says with a shrug, she likes writing and she isn't so busy she can't fit it in. In the background, as we chat, I hear her beagle Guy yowling. 'Princess Michael's cats tease him,' she tells me.

Working on the cookbook awakened a part of me that I had never really acknowledged before. During my years as a magazine editor, I lunched with Nigella, took tea with Raymond Blanc and marvelled as Jamie Oliver juggled rolling pins while Dame Mary Berry changed her frock at a photo shoot. After the success of the 80th-anniversary issue, Prue Leith became a long-time contributing editor to *Good Housekeeping*, and we chatted regularly. But on the nights I didn't dine off canapes at events, I would go home and put a Marks & Spencer ready-meal in the microwave.

People who didn't know me very well would contrive to be invited for dinner, convinced it would be a gastronomic extravaganza. Those who knew me better were resigned to invitations that came around less frequently than the Olympics and featured the low-stress menu I had been taught by my friend Terry all those years ago: roast chicken followed – if you were lucky – by Prue Leith's chocolate mousse. And this despite the rows of cookbooks on my kitchen shelf ... Several of which I had edited and even written the introduction for.

The skill of an editor lies in the marshalling of ideas and assigning the best team to produce them. It is in the combination of the human ingredients, if you like, rather than the culinary ones, at which I excelled. I spent decades spotting trends, identifying the best cookbooks and ensuring that the recipes were comprehensible for everyday folk not expert cooks. My lack of talent at cooking was my USP. Basically, if I thought I could master a dish, it meant anyone could.

So, I was amazed when after studying geography and Chinese at university Hope changed direction announcing she wanted to train as a chef. Where did that come from? Admittedly she was two months old when I first parked her in her baby seat under the table at a restaurant – but I hadn't thought it would have such an impact. But Hope is now busy preparing Michelin-quality food for Raymond Blanc ... So I need to work out how to feed myself.

At first, I stick to the ready-meals, buying seven pre-packaged trays of chilli and pasta every week, stacking them in the fridge so I don't need to think about what to eat. I'm happy not to have to cook for a family after a long day of meetings, but my conversations with the Grenfell women and hearing Meghan defend cooking for yourself as a human right filters through my consciousness. I begin experimenting with recipes from my extensive collection of cookbooks, including those which I edited, until it becomes my new routine at six o'clock every evening – a time when previously I would have been reading proof pages or preparing to go to a lipstick launch – to turn on the radio to listen to the BBC Radio 4 news, followed by the comedy half-hour while making myself something nice for dinner. The days of a bottle of Sauvignon Blanc a night have dwindled thanks to the therapy and anti-anxiety medication, and now sparkling water does me just fine as I sit in my own kitchen, eating food I have made myself from scratch. All those years I was fighting the criticisms levelled at *Prima* and then *Good Housekeeping* for celebrating domesticity, I knew intellectually that eating properly, taking care of yourself and your home, finding creative outlets in traditional pastimes was, far from being anti-feminist, the key to good mental health. The current craze for mindfulness is simply a rebrand of taking care of yourself. I just never practised what I preached – too busy telling other women what to do! 'Cook yourself happy' was one of my most popular coverlines – it's taken me this long to really understand why.

CHAPTER 23

3 Surprising Ways to Increase Your Self-Esteem: #1 Feel Your Feet

November 2018: Two years after the crash – California

The pinto mare eyes me suspiciously from the other side of the round pen. The sun is high in a cloudless blue sky; I am on a second trip to the West Coast of the United States visiting a ranch to see how horses are being used for therapy.

'Send her away,' calls my coach. A middle-aged woman in loose jeans, a baseball cap and UV-protective shirt, she goes by the soubriquet J-Vo. I flick the halter rope at the mare who obliges by showing me her heels then galloping round the pen, snorting and kicking up sand. 'Now tell her to walk,' J-Vo instructs. 'Walk,' I say in the low, slow voice. W-a-l-k. The mare ignores me and carries on careering around the arena, throwing in the occasional buck to demonstrate her utter contempt. I'm not worried, I spent enough time around Hope's pony Rose to know how to position myself both to avoid the kicking and the biting ends. But after a while I wonder how long we can both go on like this. The pinto is a cow pony, she can carry a full-grown man on trails for a whole day; the hot sun isn't bothering her nearly as much as it bothers me. Sweat runs down my face making my sunglasses slip on my nose; sunscreen runs into my eyes, which stings.

'How are y'all doing with that,' asks J-Vo? 'Are you comfortable?'

'Um, sort of. It doesn't worry me but it's a bit boring.'

'You're never safe unless you're in your own body.'

After completing my university course with a master's degree in creative writing, I turn to my new-found interest in psychology with more study and trips, like this one to the US where I meet up again with my three life coaching amigos – Lisa, Betsy and Elizabeth – trying to match up the science with the New Age metaphors that still make me squirm.

'Can you feel your feet?' J-Vo shouts, bringing me back to earth.

'Can I what ...'

'If you can't feel your feet, you're in your head not your body. Your brain is spinning, making up stories. That's why she's taking no notice of you. You have to get down into your body.'

Of course, I can't feel my feet. All my life I have been ashamed of them. They are too big, which means they balance out my height, admittedly, but cause me to identify more with the Ugly Sisters than Cinderella. Despite not necessarily needing the height, for years I squeezed into sexy, fashionable stilettoes to make my feet appear smaller. I chose shoes that cracked my toenails, rubbed corns and callouses and made me wince with pain. Like most of the powerful women of my generation, I wore designer heels that cost as much as a weekend away, in a concession to femininity. Yes, we might have control of multi-million pound budgets, influence the public discourse and have the power of hire-and-fire over dozens of souls ... But, look at my dainty Manolos – I'm still a girl in need of protection, unable to run away when danger threatens.

Looking back, I see it as a form of foot-binding for the modern era.

I think that if I ever allowed myself to feel my feet, I might never again be able to bear the pain I have inflicted on them over the course of my life.

J-Vo gives me a short history lesson reminding me that our hunter-gatherer ancestors needed to know where their feet were. 'If your life depends on fight or flight, you need to be able to feel what is happening to the ground beneath you. We have lost that. Now when danger threatens, we go up into our heads trying to think it through, instead of down into our feet.'

However, even though we can no longer run because of our vertiginous footwear, our feet remember their job; they are loyally scouting out the lie of the land on our behalf, deciding which direction in which to flee, if necessary, hoping we'll listen to the advice they are giving.

'If you want to know what someone is really thinking,' she says. 'Don't look into their eyes, look at their feet. If that person is telling the truth, if they truly want to be with you, their feet will point towards you. If they are planning to leave, their feet will point towards the door.'

I have no idea when Mark's feet started to point towards the door, although I assume they must have. And I was too busy, too up in my head, to look down and see which way mine were facing, too.

I have never before felt my feet.

I concentrate as hard as I can on the unfamiliar act of dragging my attention down into my body. I feel the strain in my jaw as if I am chewing on iron filings, the tension in my arms as they weigh the halter rope ready to flick a warning to the mare if she comes perilously close. I feel the protective carapace around my battered and broken heart. I sink my attention through the pit of my gurgling stomach that is threatening to hurl the coffee and rolls I ate earlier. I notice that the muscles in my legs are taut, on high alert to flee, and finally, finally I feel the gritty sand of the arena underneath my trainers. I flex my toes and drop my weight down through my soles, feeling the ground secure and solid beneath me, nothing to make me stumble if I need to step quickly in any direction. My abdomen snaps to attention; now I feel balanced, solid and secure, relaxed yet alert.

I am at one with my surroundings. I take a moment to go back up to my mind to make a mental note of this breakthrough and almost miss the warm breath on my neck. The mare is standing quietly behind me, she wickers gently and lowers her head as if to say: 'What do you want me to do now?'

Well, what?

'Walk?' I suggest tentatively.

And she walks away onto the perimeter of the arena, and starts obediently pacing in an anti-clockwise direction, always keeping an eye on me.

'Stop,' I venture but even I can hear that I sound hesitant. She looks confusedly at me as if to say I am sending mixed signals. My brain starts up its chatter: you're not as good with horses as you think you are. What are you even doing here in a far country, still thinking you can be a life coach? Loser in love. Loser at work. Can't even keep your family alive.

'You will never be safe unless you are in your body,' calls J-Vo.

I am rarely in my own body; I have rarely felt safe. Oh god, this is big. Too big to think about. The mare looks at me uncertainly so I drag myself back to the present; if I can't communicate with her, she will show me her heels again.

'Feet,' I think, and force my attention downwards, down to the sand, the soil beneath, down through the rocks and the molten core of the earth.

As if by remote control, the mare halts four-square.

'Trot?'

No, too hesitant. 'Canter,' spoken from the roots of my boots. The mare settles into an easy lope, no bucks or kicks this time.

Walk.

Stop.

Come to me.

Turn.

Canter.

Within minutes we are performing a passable dressage test communicating not so much by my voice. I am not sure she even understands my English accent, and isn't the American word for canter actually 'lope'? But the connection is there informed by my body language and by a new integrity that has been formed out of the dust and sand. Who knew you could increase your self-esteem just by feeling your own feet?

December 2018: Two years and one month after the crash

I am standing outside my house in the rain, rattling the handle in frustration because it won't open. It is early evening, dark already because it's winter. Since returning from the horse-whispering trip to California, I have been working diligently on feeling my feet – but the fates have obstinately refused to go along with the new me. Now, even inanimate objects seem to be turning against me.

Home alone, as Zoe has moved back to London and Hope is with her boyfriend, I nipped out to put some rubbish in the bins – wearing my slippers, no coat – and the front door slammed shut behind me. When I tried to open it, it seemed to be stuck fast. This makes no sense, it's not locked. Luckily, my neighbours are home and able to force the door open but it jams shut again the next day.

Christina's husband comes over to have a look but can't identify the fault. I call a locksmith who changes the lock, meaning I have to distribute new keys to Hope, my neighbours and the dog-walker. But a few days later, it jams again; nothing seems to cure the problem. Some days the door works fine, other days it jams fast, trapping us inside the house or on the doorstep. I don't know which is worse. I have been training in California in how to help people organise their lives but I can't let myself in and out of my own home. Some days I lie on my bed and cry for hours at a time in sheer misery.

Despite my reputation as the doyenne of *Good Housekeeping*, I have no talent for household maintenance. I am not manually dextrous and am easily defeated by small tasks like changing the battery in a smoke alarm.

John was as hopeless as me; whenever something needed fixing around the house, he would conveniently find himself called away to report on a war – there is almost always conflict somewhere in the world. He stopped midway through painting the living room ceiling to dash off to Panama on the trail of

General Noriega. It remained half-painted until after his death, when my brothers took pity on me and finished it off.

Due to my and John's general incompetence, the Crouch End house was in poor shape by the time Mark came to value it. Books tottered in piles on the floor as there were no shelves on which to put them, while cabinet doors hung off their hinges; there was even a fireplace surround stuck to the wall with just Blu Tack. Mark didn't only relieve my loneliness, he was handy with a power drill, forever installing drying racks for the washing or rings to loop the dog leads through while I hosed their muddy paws. He even seemed to relish incomprehensible conversations with handymen about soffits and guttering. I look back at our marriage and wonder what other than sex and putting up shelves there was keeping us together? We had so little else in common. At the time, though, that seemed more than enough.

Now, I am alone, deprived not only of the sex I thought I could take for granted but unable even to go in and out of my home in the conventional manner. Luckily Hope's bedroom on the ground floor at the front of the house has French windows and we start leaving and entering the house via her bedroom. This is unsatisfactory – not least because the dogs trail muddy paw prints across her floor … And, if I'm not quick enough to stop them, they jump on her bed to dry themselves off on her white duvet cover.

I fear that the French windows in Hope's bedroom will turn on me too, locking me out of the house altogether; I am at a very low ebb.

I can't make any sense of it. Other people have front doors that open and close, so why don't I? It seems to characterise everything that is wrong with my life. Other people have husbands who stay alive – and keep their marriage vows – and children who grow to adulthood. It occurs to me there is a metaphor hidden here: just when my life is returning to some sort of order, when I can re-enter the world on my own terms, something unseen is stopping me. But why do I have a meta-phorical front door, one with a direct line to my subconscious; why can't I just have one that opens and shuts?

Eventually, I have to have the entire door and frame replaced at what seems like vast expense and inconvenience given that the house was refurbished so recently. Maybe feeling your feet on its own isn't enough – if you still can't open your front door? Maybe there's more, the two more 'surprising ways' of my banger coverline, to rebuild shattered self-esteem? I just don't yet know what they are.

CHAPTER 24

Above The Logo: Sex and the Newly Single Woman

Winter 2019: Two and a quarter years after the crash

Despite the inexplicable door incident, the gentle rhythms of these small achievable promises begin to restore my sanity and my work life re-emerges but in an entirely new direction. The *Together* cookbook topped the Amazon charts, eventually raising enough money to build a new community kitchen at the mosque, leading to other writing commissions, including collaborating on biographies for prominent people who don't have the time, or the inclination, to write their own.

Shirley Conran pops back into my life with a request for help with her various books and campaigns. She is art-school trained and worked as a textile designer until her marriage to Sir Terence Conran, founder of Habitat, ended acrimoniously. Divorced, broke, suffering from the chronic fatigue disease ME and caring for her young sons, Jasper and Sebastian, she sat down and wrote the book she wished was around to help her cope: the international best-seller *Superwoman*. And then went on to write the eighties blockbuster *Lace* and the first TV mini-series of that name as well as other top-selling novels. In spite of being a hugely successful writer herself, she asks me to help her with her memoirs as she is approaching her 90th birthday and preoccupied with what she calls her last campaign – to improve maths teaching in schools. More often though we just sit and chat, sharing a glass of cold white wine, while she tells me about her marriage to Sir Terence – and the two subsequent ex-husbands.

'People call us Superwomen,' she says, refilling our glasses. 'Everything we do, all we achieve. But remember how Superman had one weakness? It's what men are to successful women, if we're not careful – kryptonite!'

I write other books that do get published, just not under my name, and I find it satisfying to work as a 'ghost'. It matches my feelings of being insubstantial and without agency, a phantom of my former self, existing on the fringes of the life I used to have. I have nothing of my own that I want to say anyway. After years of telling the women of Britain how to live their lives, I seem to have lost my voice along with my identity. But it's pleasant to spend time with fascinating people, taking notes as they recount their life stories. I even enjoy the ventriloquism of matching my writing to the rhythms and idioms of their own voices. With interesting work to occupy me, low stress and proper food to eat, other appetites begin to awaken as well. The next line to write itself across the imaginary cover page of my life is the one I never expected to happen.

I must have nodded off as it is late afternoon when I wake. It has been snowing, which casts an eerie blue light, and the carpeting of white flakes outside muffles the noise from the nearby school run. The bed is rumpled, pillows thrown on the floor, under the duvet I am naked. The door opens and a man enters, wearing my bathrobe and bearing glasses and a bottle of Chablis, which we drink sitting up in bed.

We have been in bed all day. Like a line of ticker tape running barely noticed above the logo of the magazine of my life, romantic relationships have made a surprise reappearance. Friends had been asking when I would start dating again. One takes me out for dinner to a Sardinian restaurant and explains to me how the dating apps work – they weren't around when I was last single. 'I thought they were for millennials and Gen Z,' I say.

'We're the last of the baby boomers,' she snaps. 'We think we invented sex and we're not giving it up just because we're getting on a bit.' She is a little older than me but wearing tiny shorts that showcase her fabulous legs and yoga-toned body. And she practically thrums with sexual energy.

Over bottarga pasta, she describes to me the world of mid-life dating, of our generation having the time, energy and money for multiple flings. She tells me her twentysomething sons claim she has a busier sex life than they do, explaining that hardly anyone in our age group wants commitment, let alone marriage: 'We've all got baggage,' she shrugs airily. 'We also own our own houses, which we plan to leave to our kids, so we're not looking to complicate that with live-in relationships.

'We're just looking for a good time, for someone to go to dinner or the theatre with and then have sex. No strings.'

This is new for me. Since my teenage years I have thought of relationships as like being picked for the rounders team at school – no one wants to be last, the leftover, given a made-up job organising the kit cupboard by the PE teacher. Which was just one of the many ways it hurt when Team Johansen suddenly disbanded, not least because Mark had signed up for a new team before I even knew I was being relegated.

The dinner/theatre/sex guys aren't even that hard to find, she claims. By day they are either hard at work or, if retired, sailing the boats they bought with cashed-in life insurance or tinkering with their collection of classic cars. By night, over a glass of whisky, they swipe right on apps. I point out that older men traditionally prefer younger women – a category neither of us could feasibly fit into these days, however short her shorts. She pauses midway through a bite of tiricca pastry to pronounce: 'Young women are a liability. They want a home and babies. We are free agents.'

So, what happens when you take commitment out of the equation? It's a question for which I don't have the answer. Not for the first time, I wish I was editing a magazine that would allow me to explore the questions that life kept throwing at me. I was always braver on behalf of my readers. What would Claire do? Answer comes there none.

With scars from cancer surgery and carrying extra pounds from solaces of wine and chocolate, I had no intention of removing my clothes in front of anyone ever again. And then, this, which sort of crept up on me and was not the result of an app, just the newly old-fashioned way, of two single people who already know each other sending increasingly long and frequent texts, moving on to late night phone calls about the meaning of life and then to a rumpled bed on a winter afternoon.

He is a widower and a fellow writer, so we have a lot in common. I am overwhelmed by his musky male scent. My life has been almost entirely female-centric for more than a year and I am astonished at how this evidence of his masculinity lingers in my home.

It is glorious while it lasts. He reminds me I should feel proud of who I am. After I am awarded the MBE in The Queen's Birthday Honours list he accompanies me to various celebratory events, not remotely bothered by being in my shadow. Our relationship comes in like the tide, then after a short while ebbs away just as naturally. All my life I have only ever experienced the loss of romantic love as trauma – either through death or betrayal – so it is a revelation to discover that it can be as natural as the winter snow melting in springtime and can evolve into deep and lasting friendship.

Like the turning of the seasons, I am changing, too. Not regaining the past me but evolving into someone new. I lose my magic crystal necklace, putting it down somewhere and forgetting to pick it up, no longer needing it to summon up the courage to walk into town. But when I look back at my old life, the confidence I had – bare-faced cheek, really – going behind my bosses backs to publish scoops, badgering politicians, dictating to high-profile women what they could wear, expecting the world to bend to my whims, and generally being fairly insufferable, I can't help but wonder where she went. I don't want the old Lindsay back but a bit of that old bravado might not come amiss.

CHAPTER 25

3 Surprising Ways to Increase Your Self Esteem: #2 Be Of Service

March 2019: Nearly two and a half years after the crash – Hertfordshire

It's so cold in the barn that my breath mists on the air. Without the demands of an office to go to, I have time on my hands to try something else I have never done before: volunteering. My duties today are straightforward, just not enough to keep me warm even though I am wearing a down jacket over a sweat-shirt and T-shirt. When one of the ponies poops on the track, I grab a bucket and a small rake and walk over – I have been instructed never to run near horses – and scoop up the drop-pings which I then transfer to the muck heap. That's it. That's all I do on this one day a week, I shovel muck. And it fills my heart with joy.

When I returned from California enthused by seeing how horses can be used in therapy, Christina suggested I tag along with her to a local stables where she coaches disabled children and adults in riding. In my naivety, I imagined I would just rock up and immediately start doing good, proving that my life was still worthwhile. But I am the very lowest of the volunteering low, not yet qualified to help a child get on or to walk at their pony's head. Luckily, there is plenty of horse poo to shovel – and I can do that. I discover that I don't mind in the slightest that I am no longer in charge. I am done with making tough decisions, being responsible and having people depend on me. I feel safe here performing simple tasks.

Although I know Christina has been working for the charity Riding for the Disabled (RDA) for years, I somehow dismissed it as little more than pony rides for poorly children. Even though she had told me that the movement of the horse mimics the human gait, allowing those with restricted mobility to derive nearly all the health benefits that walking brings. It develops core stability, stretches out tight hip joints, teaches partnership and – perhaps, most importantly – builds self-esteem.

Our relationship with horses is storied dating back at least 17,000 years. For millennia, mastery of a horse meant power; the burden of carrying a heavy load became lighter, it became possible to visit other clans and tribes more than a few miles away to trade and expand the gene pool. Right up until the invention of the steam train, horses were our fastest form of land transport. As recently as the early twentieth century, wars were waged by cavalry, countries invaded astride horses' backs, and farms, even cities, built through their labour on our behalf. Yet they are a prey species constantly attuned to even the slightest hint of danger. The trust they need to show to allow us to get on their backs, which is where a predator – such as a mountain lion – might attack, is absolute. We can't dominate them by force – or not for long – even a medium-sized pony weighs half a tonne. As I intuited, aged seven years old riding old Jane on the beach, horses will only honour us with their gifts of their superior strength and speed if we are able to earn first their trust, then their respect.

Attuned as they are to minute changes in sound or body language, horses, supremely above all other species that live alongside humans, truly 'see' us – warts and all. Even as the lowliest helper, with my broom and bucket, I count myself privileged to witness the magic as these relationships grow day by day.

Although my duties are menial and unpaid it seems I can't even be let loose with a bucket and shovel until I have been trained. Quite right, too. The daily cast of animals, vulnerable children, at-risk adults, carers, coaches and volunteers could quickly descend into chaos without strict procedures in place – and that's before the free-range peacocks from the neighbouring farm decide to pay us a visit.

I obtain enhanced clearance from the Disclosure and Barring Service (DBS), chilled at the thought of how a conviction for criminal damage, let alone assault, might have made volunteering difficult, if not impossible. The next hurdle is to be trained in first aid. How hard can that be? In every office I have ever worked there were designated first-aiders, although I never volunteered to become one of them myself. I was the boss-woman, in overall charge, and far too busy. When a pregnant sub-editor fainted or one of the cooks in the GH kitchen accidentally chopped off the tip of a finger, someone other than me did the necessary and accompanied the injured to hospital; I had a magazine to get to press.

The trainer lists his impressive qualifications then issues the obligatory trigger warning about some of the issues we will deal with – injury, exsanguination, death – before noting with satisfaction: 'I come with a Good Housekeeping Seal of Approval.'

And that's what triggers me – the memory of my old life where I wore a suit and sat insulated in my corner office, fielding calls from press agents or would-be contributors to the magazine. Now I am jobless, divorced, older and about to get down on the sandy ground and practise CPR on a plastic dummy.

It's not a great start and the day gets worse as it goes on. Every imagined scenario that we rehearse – and there are dozens throughout the day – begins with a re-enactment of the scene of finding a casualty on the ground and uttering the supposedly calming words: 'Hello, John, what are you doing down there? Are you all right?'

It's a phrase that's meant to be reassuring – and I am sure to many people it is – and the name John is simply plucked out of the air as an example. But I am hurtling back to the paramedics weaving their way through the stationary cars to Peter Swift lying on the carriageway of the Southend Arterial looking as though he has fallen from the sky.

Once there I enter flashback-hell. My brain scrolls mercilessly back to the day Ellie was transferred from our local hospital to Great Ormond Street, early on a Sunday morning – less traffic they said, meaning that her condition was so precarious we were going to 'blue light' it, not even stopping at junctions or roundabouts on the journey.

Then my brain lands in that last night with John when the medics found us both sprawled on the floor of the ambulance bay – me pregnant and unable to get up – and pulled me to standing: 'Hello John, what are you doing down there? Are you all right?'

No, as it turned out.

I break out in a sweat, afraid I am going to faint, throw up or simply run from the classroom and jump in my car and drive away forever without looking back. But if I do that, I will fail the course and I won't be able to work at the stables – and what will there be in my life then? I have no job, no partner, I don't even have a child living at home anymore, Hope having officially moved in with Jamie. They have been gently getting to know each other for three years now and both share a passion for horses, which they keep at Jamie's family farm. I am delighted for her because I was so lucky to have found love with her father at a similarly young age. In some ways, Jamie reminds me of John – focused, determined, ruthlessly honest, yet deeply compassionate. But for the first time since Ellie's birth 30 years before, I have no fixed axis of a child at home around whom to build my life. So, I grit my teeth and sit through being taught how to check for blood underneath waterproof outdoor clothing and that the loss of control of the bowels or bladder might suggest a broken pelvis. We practise the Heimlich manoeuvre to save someone who is choking and learn how to use a defibrillator to restart someone's heart, for which, I am relieved to discover, an automated voice from the machine reminds you of the necessary steps – and after nine hours of this I drive home trying to blot out the slide-show in my mind.

Despite all the therapy, the EMDR, the medication and the yoga, the flashbacks are still happening. I concentrate on breathing through the moment, bringing to mind images of Hope, my mother, my unwavering band of friends; reminding myself that was the past and I live in the present. In this way I learn to allow the pictures to arise, to honour their suffering and then to fade away. It complicates my life but only in the way that the lives of the children who come to ride at the stables are complicated, probably less so. Every one of us is impaired in some way. We must make adjustments and society must make adjustments on our behalf, too. So much of the way the world is organised benefits only the physically unimpaired and mentally robust, but the call is getting louder for a more realistic society that nurtures everyone whatever their capacities. Horses are way ahead of us; without being asked, they meet us where we are, only asking that we show up as ourselves.

A week passes and an email informs me that I have passed. A certificate wings its way to me; I feel prouder than the times when I was named editor the year – it has certainly been more gruelling.

H is seven years old but small for his age. Like most of the children who come to the stables, he has multiple issues, including impaired vision. He is understandably afraid of everything. This is his first visit; he has come with the rest of his class from school but doesn't want to ride. In fact, he wants to get as far away as he can from the barn with its noise, smells and animals that he can only partially see stamping and snorting in alarming ways. But he has to wait until the minibus with his fellow pupils is ready to leave.

As no muck shovelling is currently required, I am assigned to look after H. We sit on the ground. We talk a little but are mainly silent, peaceful in each other's company. We pick up the sawdust in our hands and let it run through our fingers. We look at Angus, an elderly grey pony with a long mane and tail who is having a snooze between riders. We inhale the strange scents and sounds that horses make. After half an hour H leaves with his companions on the bus and I go back to muck shovelling.

The next week, to my surprise, H is back. He still doesn't want to ride. He still doesn't want to touch Angus. But he would quite like to sit with the pony in his line of limited sight but far enough away for safety. So that's what we do.

We do the same again the following week.

As an editor, I was known to be impatient, demanding, task-orientated, none of which bothered me because my only goal was to get thousands of words and hundreds of pictures to press every month. Now, working with children and adults for whom the basic actions most of us take for granted are arduous and not helped by clock-watching, I realise my adherence to deadlines was only ever a learned skill; targets are always conditional on the circumstances. I have no more expectations for H than I have for myself. It doesn't matter to me that we sit for hours doing nothing. All the years of rushing headlong from home to work to home again have brought me to this place where there is nothing else for me to do and nowhere else I need to be.

When the great day comes that H will consent to hold my hand while I stretch out my other arm so that I can stroke Angus's flossy mane, I am so elated that as soon as the school bus departs I go into the stable and fling my arms around the pony's neck, telling him that he is a genius.

After that breakthrough, the milestones fall fast. Or what I have now come to think of as fast. By the end of the term, H has braved the special hoist that winches him up onto Angus's back – a manoeuvre of astonishing bravery for anyone, let alone a vision-impaired child. And once up there he has allowed Angus to take a few steps, with a leader at his head and me and another helper on either side in case of wobbles. Over the long summer holiday, H catches up with other boys his age and is growing in strength and confidence.

I am not going to relate more details of the riders I meet. Their stories are their own, not for me to appropriate. Nor do they come to the stables as therapy for me – although I am amply rewarded in that respect. Instead, I will tell you about some of our equine volunteers. There's Melvin, a black and white cob who was highly anxious when he first came to us, as a result of an incident in his early life that made him lose an eye, until he discovered his special talent working with older dementia sufferers. Residents of care homes don't ride but come to us for 'tea with a pony', which involves home-made cake and, usually, Melvin, who is impeccably behaved, helping to stimulate memories of country childhoods and the days when milk and groceries were delivered by a cart pulled by horse looking very much like him. Then there's Spot, an Appaloosa, the opposite of Melvin in that he is bold, extremely intelligent and always impatient to be off. Yet I have seen him stand like a rock at the mounting block for fully 15 minutes while a rider with proprioception issues – meaning her brain doesn't give accurate feedback as to where her body is in space – sorts out the movements needed to climb on his back. Although most humans haven't heard of proprioception, Spot totally gets it, seeming to understand what's required of him. My favourite is Bill, tiny like those toys that Ellie loved – My Little Pony. His fringe, or forelock, is so long it's a wonder that he can see where he's going. Bill's specialty is hippotherapy, which involves helping medically trained therapists treat very young children, often those deprived of oxygen at birth, who use the warmth of the pony's back and the gentle rhythmic steps to enhance 'patterning' – a series of movements that improve neurological organisation. Gentle enough to be trusted with babes-in-arms, Bill is a shocking escape artist, capable of giving his minders the run-around. He knows how to untie his lead rope and remove his own headcollar, which often results in me chasing him around the yard trying to catch him in time for sessions.

H continues to ride regularly. I watch him sometimes, although he can no longer see me as he has lost his sight completely now. He controls his pony confidently with just the smallest twitch of the reins, a slight shift of his weight. On the ground H remains fearful and vulnerable, especially as his world descends into blackness. Astride Angus, he is Alexander the Great leading his army into battle.

The few short hours I spend helping at the Riding for the Disabled stables every week soon become my lifeline. Some of my fellow volunteers have long experience of working with horses, others have worked in education or healthcare. My years spent directing photoshoots, negotiating with agents and writing headlines doesn't seem to offer much in the way of transferable skills. But I do know what it is to endure ceaseless rounds of hospital appointments, to lie awake at night bargaining with God that the test results will not confirm your worst fears. And that's enough. Eventually, I progress beyond muck shovelling to side-walking, leading and even start training as a coach myself, which involves learning about all the various forms of physical and intellectual disability as well as sensory disorders like autism. It is time-consuming work but I am energised by finding a new team to belong to. After the years of business lunches, film premieres and champagne receptions, I discover there is more joy to be had in a dawn start with a hi-vis jacket and a flask of tea. One morning while my mother is staying with me, she is making breakfast as I get ready to go and teach my Friday classes. She touches my arm: 'I haven't seen you so happy in a long time,' she says.

Confidence, that holy grail of my banner coverlines, turns out to be an inside-out job. In my quest for endless new angles on promoting self-acceptance, I don't think I ever suggested being of service, of finding unpaid charitable work. I thought it was just what nicer people than me did for no obvious return. Slowly I start to understand that volunteering beats the hell out of repeating positive affirmations or finding a flattering haircut.

There are other bonuses, too. I get plenty of exercise during my days at the stables, walking miles when we take the ponies out through the woods, carrying wooden poles to create obstacle courses in the arena. Exercise, especially outdoors, is now thought to be at least as effective as drugs in treating depression and I lower my dose of mirtazapine.

The leading researcher into PTSD, Bessel van der Kolk, believes that regaining your physicality is the key to unlocking the frozen state engendered by deep trauma. He advocates tango, qigong or yoga. I have always done quite a bit of yoga but my mind still races during the asanas as I expect it would do during qigong. I tried tango lessons but my feet are now so arthritic from the years of running in heels that it's too painful to continue. Thinking back to racing the storm across the Chilean desert on cow ponies, I know that being on horseback makes me feel both peaceful and strong, the only reliable way I have for 'getting into my body'. Yet the osteoporosis caused by the cancer treatment seemed to rule out me personally getting back on a horse. But at the RDA National Championships I saw older para-riders who had profound mobility problems, getting enjoyment – and validation – from horses, which makes me wonder whether I had been too hasty in terminating my riding career.

In my imaginings, I am someone who has ridden all their life. But, of course, that isn't true at all. I am someone who's been sitting at a desk for the past 30 years, walking only as far as the waiting car which will deposit me at Claridge's, Scott's or The Ivy. I haven't really ridden on a regular basis since I was a teenager. What a time in my life to discover physicality. Bodies are vulnerable, breakable, they get sick and die. To live in your body rather than your head is to live with mortality. I wonder if I outsourced my physicality to Mark for safe-keeping? Well, look how that turned out.

I know I need more horses in my life, but how to manage that? I am not disabled enough to qualify for RDA support and reluctant to trust a riding school without specialist knowledge of my condition.

Then, quite without expecting to, I fall in love!

CHAPTER 26

The Crackerjack Factor

Summer 2019: Nearly three years after the crash

He is of mixed Argentinian and Irish heritage, with dark brown eyes and a boyish demeanor. A joker, he makes me laugh, which I don't feel as if I have done for a long time.

Destined for a life playing polo, after a season and a half he is proving not fast enough for the game; he is only five years old but has been carefully raised since birth, with no known vices other than a raging appetite for food of all kinds, and he is for sale.

We travel to Warwickshire to inspect him. Pablo is a bay, which in Native American horse legend denotes playfulness. His coat is the colour of a new penny and he has a broad white stripe – a blaze – down his nose, and three white socks. His tail is black and bushy as is his mane, from what I can see of it. He has been hogged, the mane clipped close to his neck as is usual for polo ponies, which makes him look like a schoolboy whose hair has been cut short for the beginning of term. Hope and Jamie both ride him first before pronouncing him safe for me to get on. Then Hope borrows another horse and we venture out across the fields surrounding the stables. It is evening, August, just before my birthday. And I wonder if this is going to be my present to myself? What a mad, risky gift at my age and state of health. We walk the horses side by side. Pablo is sweet and biddable. 'Trot, maybe?' asks Hope. And we go forward. Then, 'Faster?'

I am terrified of falling, but maybe, like H on Angus, like that first pony ride I took at the beach on Jane, I am also longing to find inside myself something I can't describe. Faster, I agree. And soon we are cantering side by side across a hay field.

'All good?' She cares for me so much my daughter; she won't let me fall.

'Yes,' I say, pressing my heels down into the stirrup irons.

Owning a horse at least makes sense of the fact that fate has washed me up in the countryside rather than the city that was my home for most of my adult life, but it is still expensive and time-consuming. I feel panicky about the enormity of the undertaking, not least because of the unreliability of my income from my new career as a 'ghost'. Riding is a high-risk sport and I envisage myself lying broken and helpless on the ground. As I fret over my decision, it strikes me as ironic that the best way I know to achieve mental peace is causing me so much stress.

Would I have taken this step if I was still married and had a job? When I had a job and had the money, I shared a horse called April with Christina, until my anxieties ran amok and I persuaded Hope to ride instead of me. When my osteoporosis was diagnosed, we agreed it was safest to part with April. She went to be a brood mare, producing foals we delight in visiting. It has taken more than two years and thousands of pounds spent on psychology courses – not to mention the night in a police cell – to realise that I had unwittingly strayed so far from what truly made me happy.

Pablo goes first to Jamie's farm to wind down from the pressures of polo and for Hope to start his basic training. He has been used to neck-reining for polo, changing direction according to the feeling of the rein on the side of his neck, so she teaches him to accept the more conventional snaffle, the regular metal bit in his mouth that non-polo ponies wear – and also that not everything involves a nought to 60 dash down a polo field. Six months later he arrives to begin his new life in Hertfordshire during yet another February storm that mirrors the weather on the day I took flight from my home and my marriage three years previously. Jamie drives the lorry bringing him; they are buffeted by high winds but Pablo takes it all in his stride, heading for his stable and a hay net from which he raises his head only momentarily to accept my offering of organic carrots.

That winter there are flood warnings in place across the British Isles. Everywhere is a sea of mud, all the horses on the yard are spooked by the sounds carried on the wind of creaking tree boughs and who knows what other dangers. Daily I drive through the rain, a knot of fear in my stomach, wondering why I couldn't have chosen less risky options of tango or qigong as a way of getting in touch with my physical self. But when I arrive, park up and start grooming my pony, brushing mud from his thick brown coat and untangling his tail, I feel like a teenager again, with all the capability and future dreams that entails.

I put Pablo's saddle and bride on him and cautiously take him down to the outdoor arena where the sawdust and sand underfoot will provide a hopefully soft landing should I fall off. I get on with the aid of a mounting block because I am too stiff and frail to get on from the ground. Pablo is always eager to begin, marching out at a brisk pace while, frankly, I could do with a slower start given the time it takes my tense muscles to warm up. We compromise with me directing Pablo to walk and trot in circles and straight lines, changing direction exactly at the markers arranged around the perimeter.

A couple of times Pablo shies away from the woodpigeons flying up from the fields beyond, momentarily unseating me. I clutch at his newly regrown mane to heave myself back into the saddle. At the sight of himself in the huge mirrors that line one end of the school he is amazed, skittering sideways, tossing his head and craning his neck as if convinced there must be another horse behind the glass. I keep my mobile phone in my pocket in case I fall, so I can ring for help, assuming I am conscious that is … And that I haven't landed on my phone.

Amazingly I don't fall off while riding, but one day, as I am leading Pablo in from exercise, I allow my mind to wander, ruminating on a particularly complex book I am ghosting, and while I'm distracted something spooks the horse and he spins in momentary confusion and escapes from my grip. Wrong-footed, I crash to the ground, seeing the sharp metal of his shoes flash within inches of my face. Rolling clear, I stagger painfully to standing hoping for help to arrive, but the grooms are all at lunch and I am alone. Pablo, exhilarated by his own boldness, takes off trailing his reins and kicking up his heels, bucking and farting with joy at this liberation. Luckily the yard gates are shut, which limits his choices, and it doesn't take a mastermind to work out where he is heading. I track him down, nose deep in the feed bins – too greedy to put up much of a fight when I entice him with more food back to his stable.

That evening I inspect my injuries in the bath – I have skinned knees like a child. What am I doing carrying on like this at my age? In the world of work I was the ice queen – *The Devil Wears Prada* meets Elsa from *Frozen* – known for my nerves of steel. I negotiated budgets, fired backsliders and bearded captains of industry. One morning, at a meeting at a London conference centre, the fire alarm went off triggering sprinklers which drenched me from head to foot. I dutifully followed the evacuation out on to the street then, without waiting for the roll-call, dripped along the Strand until I found a hairdressing salon that could give me a walk-in appointment. The stylist blow-dried not only my hair but my jacket too, while I repaired my smudged and streaked make-up in the mirror. Without missing a beat, I went directly to my next appointment, an interview with Prime Minister Tony Blair. An official photographer took our picture in his office at No. 10 and I have it framed on my wall. I look relaxed and business-like, the prime minister of the day is smiling at some joke I have made. Who knew what was going on beneath my professional exterior – I didn't even know myself.

Now older, weaker, spat out of the corporate world, I spend all morning the day after my stumble in a state of nervous agitation, envisaging painful death and disaster. I feel too unwell to ride, not the normal mild nausea I feel before going up to the yard but a deep existential sickness. I text the grooms and ask them to ride Pablo. I do the same the next day.

I know this can't go on; it's expensive for a start and is hardly the point of owning a horse. While I am pondering what to do, on the evening of 23 March 2020, the Prime Minister announces that the whole country is to go into lockdown due to the Covid pandemic, and the stables are closed, even to the owners of the horses – as are the Riding for the Disabled stables. I receive news that my dear friend, Father Anthony – the priest who buried John and Ellie and baptised Hope – is gravely ill in hospital, as is my former boss and mentor Terry Mansfield. Father Anthony leaves hospital after several worrying weeks but Terry Mansfield does not. It seems impossible that the boundless energy of the Barnum of magazines is no longer with us. And even more inconceivable that the man who, it was estimated, attended more than 42,000 parties in his lifetime should be committed to his maker with only a handful of mourners present, not even his beloved wife, still in hospital fighting her own ultimately unsuccessful battle with Covid.

I lose several more friends, as so many of us do, and fret over the future of others, not least my mother – of a similar age to Father Anthony and Terry Mansfield – from whom I am separated by legal restrictions and by 75 miles. I am a rule-follower and in those early weeks of the first lockdown, the rules forbid even arranging to meet up with Christina for a socially distanced dog walk. There are shortages, as we can all recall, in the few shops that are allowed to open. I buy eggs and milk from the pub next door and start baking my own bread. I hear of new couples hastily choosing to live together in these unprecedented times, fearful of being alone with no one even to bring them soup or ring an ambulance if they succumb to the virus. But, despite dating a little, romantic relationships seemed to have settled into that place above the logo on the cover page of my life: nice to have – but not a priority.

There are Zoom cocktail parties – my mother catches on quickly. I use my newly acquired baking skills to make banana bread and chocolate brownies, distributing my efforts among the neighbours. And while away whole afternoons reading Hilary Mantel's *Wolf Hall* trilogy about Thomas Cromwell. Evenings are devoted, less intellectually, watching *Tiger King* on Netflix. I am entirely solitary, a state that induced near panic when shut in a cell overnight, and discover to my surprise that, other than a totally rational anxiety about the pandemic and the rising numbers of victims, I enjoy my own company. All those years of striving to fill every waking moment: the workaholism, rushing into marriage to a man who I thought would save me from my loneliness, the existential terror when I ended up without either a husband or a job. Now there is officially nothing to do, nowhere to go. My grief comes and goes in waves, my anxiety rises and then falls away.

With more time on my hands than I have ever had before, I try extending my creativity beyond baking. A tapestry set is discarded after the first few attempts, knitting, which so many find so soothing, induces in me a frustrated rage as the ball of wool falls on the floor, unravelling as Lulu the cat pounces on it. Eventually I settle for creating simple collages from scraps of fabric snipped from old evening clothes and more of the broken jewellery that I rediscovered during the shamanic cleansing of the Canal House. They are, I know, not very good, but I discover that exercising my creativity is another way to rebuild shattered confidence.

* * *

One fine day in June 2020, I am upstairs in the kitchen eating breakfast when I hear an unfamiliar sound of the front door opening in my otherwise silent house. A burglar seems unlikely in these fearful times, so I run downstairs and find Hope standing in the hallway. 'Happy Bubble Day,' she says. Family groupings have at last been permitted to support people, like me, living alone, so she and Jamie have made this early unannounced visit. I embrace my daughter, breathing in the scent of her shampoo and then stand holding both her hands in mine – feeling her cool, dry skin and the tick of the pulse in her fingertips; the first human skin-to-skin contact I have had in three months.

We go together to place flowers on the graves – it has been bothering me that Ellie's anniversary passed while we were unable to visit. In the car, I confess that I have lost my nerve, what little nerve I ever had, for riding. Buying Pablo was a mistake at my age and state of health, I say. He has been well looked after by the grooms but now the stables have reopened to owners I am far too frightened to ride him. Yes, owning a horse was a dream but I have done that for nearly a year now. I have ticked the box and maybe that's all I needed to do, maybe it's enough? 'I think I might buy a canal boat,' I say, off-handedly. 'That would be a much more appropriate hobby for someone with fragile bones.' No matter that I don't much care for being on water – at least it won't be terrifying or put me at risk of fractures.

Hope and Jamie listen – forbearing to point out that I grew up in the Dengie, a peninsula between two rivers, and have now lived for several years on the banks of the Grand Union Canal, all without showing the slightest inclination ever to get on a boat. They agree that if Pablo is indeed too much for me then he will have to be found a new and more appropriate home. In the meantime, however, he is not to be allowed to get away with bad behaviour.

Nor, I suspect, am I.

We go together to the stables and they spend 10 minutes walking Pablo up and down past the spot where he broke away from me, which he does without incident, all the while throwing glances at me like a criminal whose solicitor has got him off on a technicality. Then they suggest that Hope rides him.

Jamie settles down in a corner of the arena to watch. I stand outside because who knows where those flying hooves will land? Hope walks Pablo, trots, rides circles and diagonals. She has to kick him on to get him to speed up and it's actually rather dull.

It's a warm day and Jamie, who has been on call overnight at the hospital, falls asleep in the sun. Hope brings Pablo to a halt, hops off and hands me the reins. 'On you get,' she says. I do so, full of trepidation. Hope sits down next to Jamie: 'Ask him for canter, really push him on,' she calls. I do. He reacts like the most laidback Dobbin imaginable.

Both Hope and Jamie fall asleep. Well, they work hard.

Eventually Jamie and Hope get back in her car and head back to the Midlands where they now live. They are supportive, but with Jamie putting in punishing hours as an A&E doctor through the pandemic and Hope in a new job developing and testing recipes for Marks & Spencer, this is all the time they can spare.

So, I plod on conscious of the dichotomy that only after I have conquered my nerves and ridden Pablo for half an hour in the arena, then put him back in his stable and given him a carrot for being a good boy, what I want to do is get back on and do it all over again – but this time without the fear. I feel like that about my life. There is so much I still want to do but I am scared I have left it too late.

Every day Pablo and I work together, building our rapport until it seems I can ask him to go faster, turn or halt just by thinking, and we move as one. I am even banned from using the reins to steer, that too comes from my legs and bum. Somehow Pablo seems to understand it all, as if he is a regular reader of *Horse & Hound*. He is, it turns out, my unlooked-for Crackerjack factor that transforms my life.

I stop taking on too many writing assignments and give myself over to horse-related pursuits, starting with stretching exercises every morning simply to remain supple enough even to swing my right leg over his back. In the afternoons, as I recover with a cup of tea and a slice of cake, my mother calls me and listens with the patience only a mother can offer just as she did when I came home from school recounting that day's lessons.

The giant oak table in the Canal House, the one that was supposed to seat 14 for dinner parties, is now cluttered with bits of saddlery that I am in the middle of cleaning or polishing. My car smells strongly of manure trodden into the mats from the soles of my boots. The utility room is strewn with washing, both my own breeches and sports bras as well as, for Pablo, saddle cloths and rugs. His brown hair clogs the washing machine, so I get down on the floor to unplug the filter which gushes filthy water everywhere. My formerly immaculate house with its orchids and fig-scented candles assumes an air of the stable yard – a barn conversion reverting to its former life as a barn.

I need a modern safety helmet, the days of velvet caps held on with elastic are long gone and have been replaced by fibreglass shells like those jockeys wear. They conform to strict and ever-changing safety standards and realising mine is out of date, I visit an equestrian boutique where the assistants spend over an hour helping me find the perfect fit, silencing me with tales of traumatic brain injury when I try to select on appearance alone. Afterwards I browse the rails thinking of buying myself some smarter riding clothes. They are unrecognisable from the wide-seated jodhpurs and all-concealing tweed jackets of my youth. I discover a wonderland of thinly disguised workout gear, all brightly coloured Lycra and sparkles. Even the black jackets worn by showjumpers are revealed to be of stretch material, tightly cut with concealed zips for an even closer fit. My months of comfort-eating and sleeping mean it's hard to find anything to fit over my bulges. The only breeches that come even close to doing up are a reasonably modest navy blue but with rose-gold stars all over one generously cut thigh. I also select a rainproof jacket with the words 'It's a passion' spelled out in diamante on the sleeve, which irritates me no end – even though it's probably true. They will have to do. But I decide to cut out the afternoon treats, simply to have the choice of more age-appropriate riding wear. When, eventually, I am able to fit into my choice of equestrian sportswear, I find myself gravitating to the autumnal shades suggested by the colour counsellor. It is so comfortable and flattering that, combined with some black pieces from my old life, it becomes the basis of my everyday dressing, too. My feet are treated to trainers and paddock boots, heels relegated to the back of the wardrobe.

My physical appearance is changing in other ways too. Ever since the chemotherapy, I have worn my fine brown hair in a short geometric crop. But I no longer have the money for six-weekly trims and to my amazement my hair is soon touching my shoulders and seems to have styled itself into a soft bob. With the increased activity and reduced cake intake, my body starts to become slender again; not the rail-thin, Botoxed look of those last years of my job and my marriage but lean and muscled. I even discover biceps from lifting the saddle onto Pablo's back.

Just before my job came to an end, I took part in a Channel 4 TV programme, *The Interview*, about hiring new testing staff for the Good Housekeeping Institute. Like all reality programmes it relied on filming hours and hours of footage to capture the unguarded moments that would be spliced together into a half-hour of entertaining TV. There were no unguarded moments from me, which made for a very dull show. I remained in character as 'the editor' for far longer than the 12-hour filming day, just as I had been doing for a quarter of a century in my real job. Eventually, I delete the recording from my TV because the freeze-frame that shows up on the planner captures the face of a woman who terrifies me. Cold, unsmiling former me looks like a skull – and not a very happy one.

CHAPTER 27

True Confession

2021: A little over four years after the crash

The Covid restrictions linger on, making socialising difficult. My magazine friends, the ones I'd hung out with since the days of egg and chips in the King's Reach Tower canteen, are all scattered to the winds by the hurricane sweeping through traditional magazines. They've gone to newspapers or PR companies, to run charities or start podcasts, the easy camaraderie we shared wrecked by the need to restart careers while paying mortgages and raising children. Other than riding and my twice-weekly sessions at the RDA stables, I am on my own a great deal in the Canal House.

Having fired up my creativity with the collages from beads and scraps of fabric, I have a go at writing a novel. That was always my plan for when I finally stepped down from being an editor and the reason I did the creative writing degree in addition to my more-than-full-time job. But nothing my imagination can dredge up seems as dramatic as my own life. Curious about my arrest, I do some online research and discover a 2009 paper by Professor Marianne Hester of the University of Bristol, which suggests that although the vast majority of perpetrators of domestic violence are men – 92 per cent – it is women who are more likely to be arrested if police are called. In Professor Hester's study, women were arrested in 3 out of 10 recorded incidents and men in only 1 out of 10. Hardly any of these women were ever charged and fewer still found guilty in court, those few that are making newspaper headlines no more than a couple of times a year. Violence by anyone is appalling, of course, but violence by females is very, very rare in all societies – so why are all these women being arrested without enough evidence to charge them? And who are they?

I read as much research as I can find but I am not a criminologist. I am an editor and the way I have tackled every social issue is with a personal account – a true confession – that long-time staple of magazines. With a sinking heart I realise the only way to flush out what is happening, why so many women are accused of crimes on scant evidence and shamed into keeping their traumatic treatment at the hands of the police secret, is by going public with my own experience. And that means admitting to the night in the cell and the reason why. I think about what John would tell me to do. I have tried so hard to live up to his faith in me, I don't want to admit to such a shameful episode.

'Write it,' is the Universal Journalist's unhesitating reply.

My close friends know, of course. Alastair, who got on the phone as soon as he woke to Hope's messages. Terry and Christina, both travelling abroad at the time and distraught at not being on hand to help. Ruby and Zoe who kept watch on Hope through the night. But when I arrived at my mother's house, my life packed in my car, just hours after being released, still in the same leggings and cashmere sweater and tainted with the smell of police disinfectant, I could not bring myself to tell my mother nor my brothers where I had spent the night. My excuse at the time was that I didn't want to upset my elderly mother, the truth being I was deeply ashamed. Not guilty; even after interrogating me for 45 minutes when I was traumatised and had no sleep, experienced officers of the law could not find any evidence against me. But ashamed of being in a situation where such an accusation could be levelled at me and believed, even temporarily. I made a formal complaint of wrongful arrest – but this was while I was excluded from my own home as well as fighting to save my career and I was incapable of articulating my case clearly. PACE regulations state that although it is legal to hold someone without charge for 24 hours, no one should be detained for more than 12 hours unless there is a very good reason. I was held for more than 16 hours. Hertfordshire and Bedfordshire Police later claimed the delay was due to my request for a duty solicitor who was not available at the time. Nor did the arresting officers take me through the At Risk checklist, which is not compulsory, but should be standard procedure in domestic incidents. If they had done so my suicidal ideation and emergency visit to the GP earlier on the day of the incident would have come to light and I would not – should never have been – locked up, even if on suicide watch via CCTV. Nor was there independent verification of how I was found, in a traumatised, nearly catatonic state. According to the official report I later received, the arresting officer had deleted the video footage from his body worn camera. The only outcome was that he was reminded of the need to retain it in future for all cases. Interesting!

The only other woman I knew of who had been through something similar was TV's *Love Island* presenter Caroline Flack. I had seen her at parties, although we never spoke. She was one of those rarities, a woman who was indeed charged with domestic violence. She vehemently denied the accusation but that didn't stop it becoming the front page of every newspaper and she was the subject of vicious online trolling. The charges were never tested in court as Caroline took her own life on the day after Valentine's Day, 2020. I recall her as slim, tanned, very pretty, eyes fixed on a faraway future she would never now experience.

There is much popular debate about mental health at the moment, but so many people and institutions remain woefully ill-informed about PTSD – as I was myself – and how the long arm of grief can stretch its icy fingers down through the years. I realise I need to tell the whole story of the perfectionism that is a little known symptom of unresolved trauma, along with the dissociation and denial which led to my incarceration for 16 hours and the possibility of reputational ruin. Although in the words of my lawyer, No Further Action meant it was as if the whole incident had never happened, I still carried a heavy burden of shame that I could have found myself in such a situation. And I was reluctant to inflict that on my elderly mother. Back and forth in my mind I went. Did I even want to publish this book anyway? I was rebuilding my life – why risk dragging up everything all over again? Just sweep it under the carpet and move on.

The spirit of John nags at me: 'If you sit on this you are covering up injustice,' he tells me. Easy for him to say!

In the end I knew, as I had known when I campaigned on flexible working for women in science, technology, engineering and mathematics (STEM) careers, and highlighting the double shift of working mothers, that if it happened to me there was a chance it had happened to other women as well. And those women might not have my resources to enable them to talk about it. And I went back to the statistical fact that right now in Britain – not in another time and place like Chile during the junta – women are being arrested on flimsy grounds that are not leading to charges being brought, let alone a court case, nor conviction. But that it can still lead to them and their children – not always adults, like Hope – losing their homes. To get this important conversation going, I need to do what I have always done and tell my own story.

And that means, first I have to tell my mother.

Even though four years have passed since my arrest, my mother is utterly devastated, imagining me locked in a cell. Tortured by what might have been. Worse, as a law-abiding octogenarian, her life-long faith in the probity of the police is irrevocably broken. Her rage at Mark undimmed since I turned up on her doorstep four years earlier is now so immense it threatens to engulf her. One of my brothers sits with her for a day while she processes it all. But then she rallies, defiant of what the neighbours might say, proud of what I am doing. Her support unconditional. 'Publish and be damned,' my mother says proudly.

CHAPTER 28

Surprising Ways to Increase Your Self-Esteem: #3 Do What Scares You

Early 2021: Four and a half years after the crash

Editing a magazine, my life was ruled by seasonality: Christmas festivities, spring cleaning, Easter bakes, summer barbecues, winter coats and so on, even down to the fact that each issue was colour-coded – not just on the cover but throughout all 250-plus pages, subliminal cues as to the mood of the month. I sent out a memo every year to all staff reminding them that after December's rich reds and gold, January's colour palette was to be a palate cleanser of silver, baby pink and ice blue. February would be dominated by the vitamin colours of yellow and green to denote the health focus in colds and flu season. March was always the pink and white of cherry blossom, a deeply feminine colour scheme to honour Mothering Sunday, while the April backdrop for the daffodils and Easter chicks was lavender and mint green. Yet even as I policed these themes, paging endlessly through the pasted-up 'dummy' of the issue checking for a stray vitamin colour in October – season of mists and mellow fruitfulness: persimmon, burgundy and bronze – I never looked up at the actual weather outside my office window, never gave it a moment's consideration. I travelled from centrally heated home to air-conditioned office my head full of the work I was engaged in, ideas to pursue, tasks to finish.

Once I went to an awards dinner in January and at some point during the evening snow started to fall. I hadn't booked a mini-cab home, so when I left at midnight I had to stand for an hour in a blizzard, wearing a cocktail dress and Jimmy Choos, trying to hail a taxi. It would never have occurred to me to check the weather forecast before setting out, or to take comfortable footwear to change into at the end of the evening. I didn't even have a coat! But then I never felt the cold either. I was so neglectful of my body that at some point I simply stopped noticing hunger, cold or fatigue – life just seemed easier that way.

Now, like a numb limb gradually coming back to life, I have started to feel everything and it is overwhelming. I discover to my horror that Hertfordshire is one of the wettest counties in southern England. Why didn't someone warn me before I moved here? Christina reminds me that she did tell me we live in a rain shadow, where the clouds dump their load of water before rising to clear the Chiltern Hills, but I had dismissed it as a poetic turn of phrase. More often than not, my soaking wet Barbour jacket and muddy boots end up draped around the house in the hopes they will dry before I venture out with the dogs or to ride Pablo the next day.

Throughout the summer months the horses are relaxed and unwilling to expend more energy than necessary. As summer mellows into autumn, we enter my favourite riding months – the crops have been harvested in the fields, leaving us with acres of arable stubble to canter across on days that start misty and cool only to burst into brilliant sunshine.

In the run-up to Christmas as the days shorten, I festoon Pablo with hi-vis leg wraps and blankets to ensure we remain visible to cars on the darkening country lanes. Christina and I wear bright yellow jackets, hers even fitted with flashing lights powered by a tiny battery.

In January, the rain turns the fields boggy, the mud so poached around the gateways that it threatens to pull off my wellington boots as I lead him up to the stable yard. It's cold and dark and black ice is a worry out on the roads, so when the temperature drops below three degrees, we stay in the arena but keep riding. It's only really snow that makes riding impossible because it clumps up inside the horses' hooves until they appear to be walking on platform shoes. We dare not even turn them out into the fields in case they trip over their snowy platforms and lame themselves, so we count the days as they stay in the stables, safe and warm, storing up energy for when they are let out.

From mid-February onwards the first daffodils and crocuses start to appear and the days get longer. There are frequent high winds that whip through the fields getting up under the horses' tails, while discarded crisp packets appear in the hedgerows flapping provocatively in the breeze. This is also when the first blades of new grass are coming through, sweet and full of natural sugars to send the blood coursing through the horses' veins after their winter hay. The mares start to come into season, giving off pheromones promising fertility and new life. Pablo, like most riding horses, was gelded at age three but he seems to have a sense of what has been denied him.

One mild March day, a couple of years after Pablo first arrived in Hertfordshire, we are walking sedately around the arena as I chat to Christina who is riding her well-behaved Portuguese mare Mafi. In an adjacent field the yearlings are enjoying the early rays of sun on their backs and frisking about. Clearly Pablo, who is still a teenager in horse years, would rather be out playing with the kids than plodding peacefully along listening to our menopausal conversation. I have not been paying attention and the first I know of his rebellious adolescent thoughts is when he spins through 180 degrees to face the opposite direction. While I am trying to gather my wits, he humps his back and jumps with all four feet off the ground. I fly up out of the saddle and by some miracle he is still underneath me when gravity brings me down again. He repeats this broncho act, bucking over and over again, until I lose a stirrup. Even so, I manage to stay on board, but my hands are flailing as I try to gather up the reins. Then thoroughly overexcited, giddy with his own naughtiness, Pablo takes flight, dashing the length of the arena, 60 metres, at a flat-out gallop. I was told he wasn't fast enough for polo but this feels very fast to me.

Despite Pablo's low-key life with me, the blood of champions courses through his veins. His half-sister, Headley Britannia, is the most successful mare in the history of the equestrian sport of eventing. I had seen her thunder into pole position around the most difficult course in the world at Badminton. She is small like him, but when she came to the giant fences, she took off like a rocket from a launch pad, clearing them with inches to spare. And at the end of the arena I'm riding in – getting closer every nanosecond – is a fence about a metre high and on the other side a muddy, rutted paddock.

Another wisp of the memory comes into my mind – the side of the lorry rearing up in front of me. I realise this is going to be yet another crash, maybe the last of my life. Pablo's genetic inheritance is compelling him to jump the fence. I am equally sure that while I might be with him on take-off we will certainly land separately. What I know – but he doesn't – is that he isn't trained for this and that landing on the rutted, muddy ground on the other side, he will almost certainly fall and break a leg, which will be fatal for him. That I will go over his shoulder and break my neck, is not in doubt either.

Perversely, now that we are going in a straight line – even if at considerable speed – I can regain my balance and my foot finds the errant stirrup. The trouble is I still have no idea how to stop. Quite literally, he has the bit between his teeth.

Riding across the Essex marshes as a teenager. I was always being carted like this but then I was young myself and I bounced. No wait, I didn't, I broke both collarbones and a leg in various falls, which was bad enough back then. Now I am old, with osteoporosis. Neither of us will survive if Pablo attempts this jump.

My thinking slows as it did in the lorry crash. Back then I couldn't avoid colliding with the lorry and that terrifying clash of metal on metal. I couldn't save Peter Swift from running out into that dual carriageway. Just as I couldn't save my family. John didn't live to see Hope born. And my darling Ellie was buried on a sunny day in June 1998, in Highgate Cemetery close to her father. All the children from her class at school attended, bringing hand-made bouquets and posies, many of them with sunflowers which they had been growing in class. The wide-open face of a sunflower, wreathed in golden petals, turning always towards the sun, seeming to sum up my beautiful gentle daughter who never saw her tenth birthday.

I couldn't save my child, so what made me think I could save my marriage or my job either. Can I save myself this time? Do I even want to? Time slows even more. Would it have been like this if I had stepped in front of the Tube train at Swiss Cottage? The fractions of seconds stretching to minutes or longer? Would I have changed my mind, regretting my actions, even as death became inevitable? And in that split second, I realise I have achieved the very thing I never dared hope for that terrible morning: out of all the pain, the trauma and grief I have salvaged a life worth saving. I want to keep living. And I want to save Pablo too. He's a young fool, a teenager, with no idea of the consequences of what he is doing. But he has placed his trust in me and I have to honour that. I have to save us both.

I stop pulling on both reins and instead pull hard on just the inside rein, changing the angle of the bit and catching him by surprise. It works! Moments away from take-off we swerve, 'motorbiking', as if on two wheels away from the fence and certain disaster. Momentarily frustrated, he attempts to go round again for another attempt but I keep hauling on the inside rein until the little horse turns reluctantly onto a circle, still thinking it's a game. Holding tight to a fistful of mane to balance myself, I make the circle smaller and smaller until he has no choice but to come back to a trot then a walk and then finally to a standstill. He is sweating profusely – as am I – and in the mirrors at the end of the arena I can see his expression which seems to say: 'I could have jumped that if you weren't such a scaredy-cat!'

Christina steers Mafi over to us to ask if I'm OK? I see the blood has drained from her face and realise how frightening it must have looked as well as felt.

I have done something to my hip in bracing for that hand-brake turn and every step he takes it feels like the bones of my sacro-iliac joint are scraping together – but I stay aboard, like Charlton Heston in the film *El Cid*, tied to his horse's saddle. After 20 agonising minutes, terrified that Pablo will repeat his stunt, I feel it is safe to assume that his memories of today will be mostly of doing my bidding rather than of that brief moment when he thought he was a showjumper.

He is still quite hot when I finally put him back in his stable, so I put a sweat rug on him and wait until he has cooled down before feeding him his dinner. Only then do I go home – no one there to put a sweat rug on me or prepare my dinner. I pop a couple of Nurofen and lie on the sofa, conscious that something has changed deep inside me.

When the doctors broke the news to me more than 20 years previously, on the morning of 11 June 1998, that their struggles to resuscitate Ellie were proving fruitless, I crumpled at the knees – I was later told – collapsing onto a sofa in the parents' sitting room at Great Ormond Street Hospital. I was covered with a blanket and encouraged by the nurses to rest quietly while Terry, who was with me, got on the phone, frantically calling Alastair and my brother Jeremy to come and help take care of me, along with Father Anthony, who was saying Mass, this being the Catholic feast day of Corpus Christi. The hospital chaplain was sent for and on arrival found me apparently asleep, on the sofa in the middle of the morning, having just received the worst news any parent can ever face. No one judged me, of course. It looked odd, but who's to say how a distraught parent will react in the midst of unbearable tragedy?

It was during my psychology studies during the covid pandemic over 20 years later that I learned that my bizarrely-timed nap – even more out of character for someone who never sleeps – was more likely to have been an extreme psychological event known as the 'collapse' reaction in the face of mortal danger. Overwhelmed by profound helplessness the body simply shuts down, exactly the way a prey animal appears to play dead when attacked by a predator. Those baby birds my brothers and I tried to nurse back to health, the mice I rescued from Lulu, died not from their injuries but from what we in our innocence simply called shock. PTSD – the lingering after-effects of trauma – doesn't exist in wild animals because faced with a predator so overwhelming that fight or flight is impossible, the prey freezes or collapses and, as a result, dies. In a savage world of kill or be killed, the collapse reaction can even be described as nature's final kindness.

Throughout history, and even now in some parts of the world, humans have faced daily terrors. And just as with the risk of lymphoedema after cancer treatment, our increased ability to survive has been accompanied by the lifelong legacy that survival brings. Only a generation ago, my suffering after the loss of a husband and child would have been cut short by my own death from breast cancer. If we suffer more PTSD now, perhaps it is not only that we have found a name for it but also that we carry on living after events that were previously unsurvivable.

For humans, what greater terror can there be than the knowledge that your child is dying and that you are powerless to save them? Apparently, I was unconscious for around 10 to 15 minutes, while all around me, on a teeming hospital ward, the doctors and nurses rushed to protect the other seriously ill children from being even more traumatised by what was happening to their dear friend. Only now does it become clear I wasn't asleep. I was so unwilling to carry on living without Ellie, my body did what it could, making valiant attempts to abandon this world, too, and accompany my beloved child on her final journey.

The leading researcher Professor van der Kolk suggests: 'Experiences that deeply and viscerally contradict the helplessness, rage, or collapse that result from trauma can help PTSD sufferers heal.' I don't think he was envisaging a runaway horse, but a form of therapy, newer even than EMDR, which has the sufferer re-enact, in a safe environment, the physical movements that they would have liked to take to save themselves. Victims of rape and sexual assault sometimes suffer collapse reactions and with this new therapy can be gently encouraged under controlled conditions to mime a physical response of fighting back. Not to be undertaken lightly, but in the right hands it has proved helpful.

When the lorry jack-knifed in front of my car, I was powerless to avoid it. The shattering impact turned my car into a time machine hurtling me back to Great Ormond Street where I could do nothing to save my child; the best medical experts in the world tried and failed. The recent disintegration of the life I had worked so hard to build; the divorce, the loss of first one then another home, the redundancy and literally being locked in a cell all night unable even to use the toilet unobserved, all reinforced that I, who had created an edifice around myself of power and control, was, in fact – and had always been – as helpless as a bird fallen out of a nest or a mouse caught in a cat's paw.

Until Pablo bolted, that is, when, terrified as I was, I realised I wasn't helpless. It was a matter of seconds, but I still had time to think through my options and choose a course of action. There was no guarantee of success. We could both have ended up in a tumble of broken bones on the other side of the fence. What I chose to do was not without consequence, as the grating in my hip reminds me, but my instinct for survival resurfaced after being dormant for so long. From not caring whether I lived or died, that most basic of human rights – free will – asserted itself. The first two ways to increase self-esteem, as my banger coverline would have it, are: (i) to get out of your head and back in your body so you know what's going on around you. And (ii) to think less about your own misery and start helping someone else, preferably through volunteering. The third, and most important, though also the most perilous, is that you have to face up to what is secretly terrifying you. You have to do what scares you most. My darkest, most hidden fear was not divorce or redundancy or even homelessness – not to understate the impact they had. Nor even the car crash itself and the subsequent steering failure. The terror that was keeping me trapped in PTSD – constantly reliving events through flash-backs – was that in the face of overwhelming peril I would freeze and become helpless, meaning that others would suffer and die due to my inability to act. But then, as I hauled on that rein – timidly at first, then with increasing confidence – I saved Pablo. And, in doing so, at last began to save myself.

Proof Marks

CHAPTER 29

My Own Seal of Approval

March 2022: Five and a half years after the crash –
Zermatt, Switzerland

Sunlight glints off the snow-covered Matterhorn, an alpine breeze whips the bride's veil around her bare shoulders. I tell her that if – at this last moment – she wants to change her mind, then she can. Forget the expense, or the embarrassment – if she has any doubts at all, we can escape. I gesture at a nearby motorised sledge, a skiddoo. 'We could steal that,' I suggest, 'And make our getaway.' And I paint a picture of us sledging, a bridal version of Thelma and Louise, down the mountain, swerving pine trees and bumping over moguls in our precipitous descent. 'I'll drive,' I say, already hitching up my pink mother-of-the-bride gown, Hope can jump on behind, the long train of her wedding dress billowing out like a spinnaker.

I have been far from the perfect mother. I was too wrapped up in my career when Hope was little and grieving for her father and sister, then marrying to escape my loneliness. Yet somehow, she has lived by her own instincts in a way I never had. Finding creative outlet in becoming an accomplished chef and turning her back on London in preference for country-dwelling with Jamie surrounded by horses and dogs. She now works as a teacher in a Birmingham comprehensive and Jamie has qualified as a doctor. Their weekends are taken up with finishing the house Jamie's father started building on the farm. It is where they will eventually make their home. Her relationship with Jamie has progressed slowly and comfortably. She has always lived 'in her own body'. My shame, as a mother, remains that it was she who came to collect me after my release from the police station instead of the other way around.

Her only small rebellion has been the logistical nightmare that she and Jamie have decided to get married in Switzerland – because along with horses, skiing is a shared passion – and that is what young people do, forge new connections and create new traditions. Somehow, nearly all the key people in our life – most of the 12 apostles in my phone – have managed to make the journey up the mountainside to a tiny Catholic church nestled 2,200 metres above sea level.

Alastair, resplendent in a kilt, has been astonishing passing skiers by playing his bagpipes in the snow. Jamie is waiting at the altar, with his best man Charlie who was Pablo's rider before I took him on. Christina is there in the church, ready to read the prayers, her husband armed with his camera to capture the bride's arrival. We have all been devastated by the recent and unexpected death of Jamie's father – but his mother Gaynor is there, too, brave in her grief and so proud of her son. There will be tears later during the traditional toasts as we remember both the bride's and groom's fathers – both named John, as it happens, as well as Ellie, who would have been maid of honour.

My niece Zoe has stepped forward into this big sister role as she has done so many times before.

Now the music changes and the bridesmaids set off down the aisle, Zoe preceded by Ruby, two of the young women who kept vigil for me and Hope that night I spent in the cells.

I turn to Hope, radiant in clouds of silk taffeta the colour of the edelweiss, her auburn hair twisted into a low chignon holding her veil in place. She carries a simple bouquet of another local flower, lily of the valley. I want her to know that I will always aspire to rescue her the way she has so often had to rescue me – and still does. Although I suspect the best I can offer is to try not to get into any more scrapes from which my daughter is compelled to save me. As she had to do as recently as yesterday.

It had been emotional, coming to this faraway place for my daughter's wedding. Ellie would be 33 now. I cannot help but monitor all the life stages she missed out on, picturing what she would be doing. Hope and I speculate sometimes. We think she would have remained as quiet and serious as she was as a child and undoubtedly as beautiful with those titian curls, porcelain skin and wide blue eyes. We agree she would still love ballet and reading, maybe working in publishing, or even writing books herself, given the way she loved making up stories for her baby sister. Hope and I agree she would have married a boy she met at uni – Edward we call him – whom Hope thinks is a bit of a drip but I defend as a nice boy. They would both be fussy eaters, we agree, as Ellie could be difficult about food and Christmas would be a nightmare. It comforts us this game but we don't play it too often, aware that we can never in our wildest imaginings capture the complexity and multitude of layers Ellie's unlived life contained. And that to dwell too long on these fantasies is to diminish the person she had the potential to be.

Would she have been here in Switzerland with the imaginary Edward, or married herself by now? Maybe there have been one of those sisterly spats when the youngest marries first? For certain, in that alternate universe, her father, John, would have been walking Hope down the aisle, not me.

And I could not help but remember the two occasions when I vowed 'til death do us part: the first time when it was literally that, the second when I was deceived, or deceived myself? Marriage is a step into the unknown so immense that a helter-skelter sleigh ride down a mountain looked momentarily like the sensible option.

The morning after arriving in the Alps, the enormity of my daughter getting married overwhelmed me; I was hit so hard by anguish that I couldn't bring myself to get out of bed. Hope was out skiing with Jamie and their friends, texting whenever she sat down on a chair lift, to see what I was doing, wondering if I had gone for a walk or shopping in the village. I replied with falsely cheerful comments that didn't fool her for a second. Intuiting that all was not right, she abandoned her companions, schussing down a black run to get back to me. She arrived in my hotel room, like a modern-day Valkyrie, shaking snow off her ski suit and bearing Swiss chocolate, which apparently is the best cure for altitude sickness – and grief – all the while reassuring me: 'You're my mum, getting married won't change that.'

Her father and I chose her name together 29 years ago, because somewhere deep down, despite his dire prognosis, we believed that hopefulness was not only all that we, as her parents, could give her, but all she – all anyone – really needs.

Even so, I could not imagine how profoundly that would be tested.

Now, in the absence of her father, I try to reassure her that however life turns out, I will always be there for her. She laughs at my suggestion of the Thelma and Louise downhill run, and, level-headed as ever, pats my hand: 'We're good mum, let's do this!'

The music changes to that Elvis Presley song about how only fools rush in. It's true, of course, we are all foolish in love, but sometimes we grow wiser as a result, even if the marriage fails. Or maybe especially if it does?

We step out slowly, my daughter supporting me, rather than the other way around, as I am teetering on the Valentino heels I last wore five and a half years ago for that birthday party. So much has happened since that I am now a different person – or maybe I have become the person I always should have been. Arm in arm with Hope, I walk down the aisle in the traditional father's role, to give away my beloved daughter to the fine young man with whom she is committing to spend her life.

Recently

It is a fine summer evening, I started the day writing. My own words now, I am no longer a 'ghost'. I still live in the Canal House with its beamed ceilings and views of the passing narrow boats. I am alone but not lonely. I could read or walk the dogs or simply sit on the terrace enjoying the evening sun. I first married when I was 25; I am more than twice that now and in the intervening years I have filled every waking hour with work, with caring for my families, battling my own ill-health and, above all, trying to stem the endless tide of grief. Now, at last, I have no one to please but myself.

The day before, I visited Pablo, now back living on the farm with Hope and Jamie. He whinnies when he sees me and trots across the field, eager for fun, then stands patiently while I groom him, grunting appreciatively as I pause occasionally to rest my head against his flank and breathe in his sweet scent. His saddle and bridle are well-oiled leather and I thread the straps through their keepers, doing up the buckles with familiar ease, my fingers finding the holes on which this tack sits most comfortably for me and for him.

He has recently turned nine and the days of broncho drama and bolting seem to have passed. In Hertfordshire we eventually became a popular combo, always happy to escort more skittish youngsters around the lanes. Pablo, fearless around cars, tractors and lorries, marching onwards like a police horse, pausing only to leer at the dogs that rush up to farm gates barking their heads off. 'Come and have a go if you think you're hard enough,' he seemed to say. We have only moved him back to Warwickshire because everything is changing yet again – a new edition of the magazine of our lives is getting ready to roll off the presses.

I lead him to the mounting block and – checking I have my phone in my pocket, because I am not a complete fool – head out down the farm track where we turn into a field that has been left fallow, a thousand acres of grassland dotted with clover and daisies. A doe with twin fawns raises her head to watch us, then unafraid but sensible ushers her youngsters away.

I never did go back to editing. Instead, I have become busy with a variety of different writing and voluntary jobs. I organise my days so I can ride and coach at RDA as well as spend time with the people who are dear to me and, in doing so, appear to have found that previously unattainable goal – a work-life balance. When I visit my mother and brothers in Essex, I drive home as usual along the Southend Arterial past the spot where the first collision happened seven years ago now. If I had died in that head-on crash with a lorry – as well I might have, people usually do die in 70 mph collisions with lorries – I would have been described at my funeral as having overcome the dual tragedies of John's and Ellie's deaths, now happily remarried and successful at my job. It would have been taken as an accurate description at the time, but it wasn't the truth. The rise of digital media was already changing the work I loved; my marriage, unknown to me, was not what I so fervently wished for. Far from facing the inevitability of change, I had blinded myself with work, designer clothes and awards ceremonies. But the deep fissure of unbearable loss was always there, running through me, ready to crack wide open if the impact was great enough.

For a while I was furious with Peter Swift for destroying the perfectly bound life I believed I had created. The police told me the name of the hospital where he was treated and I fantasised about turning up at his bedside to deliver some home truths. I set up a Google alert for his name, so I would know if he tried it again, and saw that a year after the crash he went missing, off his meds; his family put out alerts for him. I understand now that his headlong dash into the traffic that night was not about me or the lorry driver, or all those people prevented for seven hours from getting to their homes, marooned with their crying unfed babies in gridlocked cars. It was a desperate, tragic, flawed attempt to flee the pain in his own mind.

So if I couldn't blame Peter Swift, how could I blame Mark for the actions he took? I did it myself, too, in many ways. We all dissemble, prevaricate and deceive ourselves. We numb our awkward feelings with wine, with sex, or as I did with work and perpetual busyness, covering up the wreckage of my soul with every step up the career ladder. And then something happens, the demons erupt out of our sub-conscious into the real world, and our pain collides with someone else's. We don't mean to hurt them, although we do.

Mark has remarried. Hope is back in contact with him – he is after all the only father she has ever known. I am glad about that, although for a long time I found it hard to forgive him. But now just as I see the man running into the traffic in a desperate attempt to flee the torment in his mind, I see Mark confused and conflicted, smashing up our marriage in the only way he knew how. And I see myself teetering on the edge of the platform at Swiss Cottage on the brink of something violent and – worse – unsalvageable, saved by the thought of a man I never met, Peter Swift, also the catalyst for my break-down.

I no longer see that freak collision as triggering a descent into chaos but instead as the start of a miracle. I could have died, instead I was reborn. When I stepped away from the smoking ruins of my car, then my marriage and my job, I emerged – not immediately and not without pain – as someone new, ready to embark on a third act I had no idea I was capable of.

I am no longer an editor or a wife but I am a daughter, a mother and, above all, a survivor. I carry the hopes and dreams of my ancestors in my DNA. I missed out on a lot as a parent, working too long and hard, desperately compensating for the tragic losses in our lives. Now my secret prayer is that I am given the chance to make amends for that – and to be able to pass on the values I learned from my own grandmothers to a new generation.

I'm often scared, of course, because life is often scary. To feel fear is to be alive. I will continue to cry at weddings but I am no longer likely to cry at airports, confused by my own name – it has been too painfully hewn from who I am. I have finally buried my magazine avatar Claire, but in her place I have been reunited with the seven-year-old me on that long ago windswept beach who knew what would make her happy.

It is autumn now. The autumn of my life, too. I must seize the day because time is running out. Unlike so many in my family, I have survived this far against the cancer odds but I don't have forever; nobody does.

Pablo, however, is getting bored with this introspection. He lives in real time, in the present always, and this glorious golden field of wild flowers is offering itself to us as a wide-open vista. Like Jane, the pony on the beach at Walton-on-the-Naze, I chose to remain bridled because that was all I knew. It wasn't my choice to kick over the traces; it was done for me. But in extricating myself from the tangle, I discovered for the first time in my life what it is to be unbridled – and unbound.

Pablo, the Crackerjack factor, stamps his feet – it's time to go. My weight is evenly supported in the stirrups, my muscles relaxed yet poised to make any necessary adjustments to my balance. Down the reins the electricity of communication fizzes between horse and human in a dialogue that has been going on for 17,000 years. I feel strong and free, more so than at any other time in my life.

I give the horse his head and he stretches forward into a canter, then feeling my encouragement accelerates into a flat-out gallop. I crouch over his neck, like my great-grandfather, Cuffo the jockey, forgotten muscles in my back and legs straining to hold my position, every nerve-ending alive. The lowering sun paints the hedgerows red and orange in the purest golden light and the drumming of hooves underneath me merges with my heartbeat until in one thunderous crescendo there is no separation between us. This creature, stronger, faster than a human could ever be, offers me not only his strength and speed but also his playfulness, asking nothing in return except that I pay attention.

And to think, I once believed that happiness came perfect bound, when it turns out that saddle-stitched is so much the better way to live.

The next morning

A new emotion has been washing over me lately, making me feel secure, even content – a word I haven't had much call for in my life. I have been happy, very happy at times, joyful, ecstatic even. I have known tragedy – more than many – but I do not deny I have known bliss as well. Perhaps as much as anyone has a right to. What I don't remember experiencing very often, if at all, is this warm hug of 'contentment', all the more surprising because I have weaned myself off the antidepressants. I find it disconcerting at first, because it makes me feel vulnerable, so much so that a half-heard strand of music can start tears in my eyes, as it aligns my senses with my surroundings.

There are kingfishers nesting nearby on the canal, the ancient Greeks believed them to be foretellers of epic love. So tiny and quick, they are nearly impossible to spot if you look directly for them. But if you relax your eyes, stay quiet and simply allow yourself to be, then sometimes they appear, in a blinding flash of iridescent blue, almost too beautiful to be real. I have seen quite a few lately, and now making breakfast I spot one from my kitchen window. As I go out onto the terrace for a closer look, my phone rings and I answer quickly as it is Hope, who is nine months pregnant, although when I saw her yesterday there wasn't any sign that the birth was imminent.

No decision to create a family is ever taken lightly. Parenthood is a risky, fragile, and frankly terrifying choice for anyone to make, yet for the whole of history humans have laid down their hearts to ensure the survival of the next generation.

The reason is summed up in the one word that has under-pinned my entire life even – or especially – when it has seemed most absent, engaged in a pursuit of perfection that nearly destroyed me. It is the name I gave to the child born without a living father.

29 January 1993, 30 years ago

A tiny internal rupture, it feels like a click, wakes me in the small hours of the morning. I am five months widowed, 39 weeks pregnant and alone in the house but for Ellie, age four, who is fast asleep in her bed with the pink duvet cover.

In the fugue state in which I have been since John died, I get up to go to the bathroom where I stand watching as if from a place outside myself as gallons of dirty brown water gush from between my legs onto the floor. I have been to enough ante-natal classes to know that my waters have broken and the colour means that the baby is in distress, but somehow I can't connect that with what is happening. This baby will be born dead, of course; life can't come from death. It is the small hours, not yet light outside. I decide the best course of action will be to run a bath.

I lie in the warm water until it eventually goes cold and some guardian angel persuades me to heave my elephantine body out of the bath and ring Terry, which I have to do on the landline, there being no mobiles back then. As soon as the bath is full again with clean, fresh water I get back in, feeling as disconnected as if I were watching a scene in a movie.

Terry thunders up the stairs, finds me in the bath and starts pulling at my arm, slick with water. 'We need to go to the hospital,' she says.

I refuse, because I know they will tell me my baby is dead and I want to delay that moment for as long as possible.

Terry goes into my bedroom to ring Nanny Su to look after Ellie as well as a doctor friend on-call that night at a distant hospital. He tells her to hold the phone at the extent of its cord, whereupon he shouts down the line at me: 'Get out of the bath and get in Terry's car now – or I am calling an ambulance!'

We speed through the night-time streets, Terry doing 60 mph down the Marylebone Road, all the while noting the gaps when I can't speak for pain – contractions, she guesses – timing them via the dashboard clock of her car. Thirty seconds apart then 20 seconds apart. She swerves her car into the ambulance bay of St Mary's, Paddington in exactly the way I did that night just a few months previously when I drove John to the Hammersmith for the final time.

As happened that night, paramedics run out. They put me in a wheelchair, pushing me at a run, down corridors and into a lift, Terry shouting over the noise of my screams that my waters have broken and the contractions have been coming very fast.

When someone dies, the number of people in the room suddenly and terribly decreases by one. The birth of a baby is like that video in reverse, the number of souls increases not decreases – if they are alive that is. I am not ready for any of this. I know how closely entwined are the beginnings of life and its end and I have no idea if I am the one giving birth or the one dying.

There is no time for the pain relief to take effect. I am barely into the hospital gown and hoisted onto the bed when there is a baby's cry. So not a stillbirth. The number of souls in the room has increased by one and John's second daughter is very much alive and kicking. She weighs nearly nine pounds and has red hair like her father and sister. Terry hasn't even had the chance to take off her coat before a baby is thrust into her arms. 'Have you decided what you are going to call her?' the nurse asks me.

29 September 2023: Six years and 11 months after the crash

Hope's voice on the phone sounds tired, as if she has been awake all night, but there is also something new, that I haven't heard before. I assume she's gone into hospital. Perhaps she is calling while pacing the corridors, timing contractions? But she sounds too calm; in her voice there is a timbre that reaches through time to her own birth and beyond to the ancestors who yet still live within us.

'Turn on your phone camera, Mum,' she says. 'There's someone who's been in quite the hurry to meet you.'

Further Reading

Beck, Martha: *Steering By Starlight* (Piatkus Books, 2008)

Kolk, Bessel, van der: *The Body Keeps the Score: Brain, Mind and Body in the Healing of Trauma* (Penguin, 2015)

Hester, Professor Marianne: Who Does What To Whom? Gender And Domestic Violence Perpetrators (University of Bristol in association with the Northern Rock Foundation, 2009)

Prather, Aric A: *The Sleep Prescription* (Penguin Life, 2022)

Randall, David: *Universal Journalist* (Pluto Press, 1996)

Asking for Help

If you are experiencing suicidal thoughts, please tell someone. In the UK, you can call The Samaritans on 116 123 at any time, 365 days of the year. Or find them online at:

www.samaritans.org

Acknowledgements

During the writing of this memoir, I have reflected on such resilience as I possess and where it comes from. What I know for sure is that it is rooted in the unconditional and loving support of my family and friends.

My beloved mother Sheila Nicholson; my brothers Jeremy Nicholson and Hugh Nicholson; my cousin Dr Susan Baker and her daughter Zoe Sharp represent the gold standard. Along with my dear friends: Alastair Campbell, Susan Edwards, Carmel Fitzsimons, Christina Grieve, Fiona Millar and Terry Tavner; these were the first names I put in my new phone when my life imploded. I have also leaned on the wisdom and compassion of: Marion Hunter, Siobhan Kenny, the Rev Anthony Maggs CRL, Liz Murphy, Angie Litvinoff, the Rev George Pitcher, and Baroness (Gail) Rebuck. I owe them and their families an enormous debt of gratitude.

The years I spent working in magazines were a daily source of happiness and fulfilment for me. I am grateful to the past and present staff of *Good Housekeeping* and of Hearst UK, including but not limited to: Denny Barnes, Karen Barnes, Eve Cameron, Ella Dove, Celia Duncan, Helen Hart, Michelle

Hather, Aggie MacKenzie, Farrah Storr and Ray Walsh. Louise Court kept me on track with our Monday morning 'production meetings', while Liz Murphy reminded me of print processes and practices in newspapers as well as magazines – any errors are mine alone. The inimitable June Walton was my co-conspirator in so many magazine adventures.

There is a view that you can't make new friends later in life but in Dr Betsy McLeod, Elizabeth Merrill and Lisa O'Sullivan, I have been privileged to discover soul-mates, who shored me up during some very dark days. I also thank Bev Barnes and our group of Beautiful Souls not least for the term 'sistering' which, in carpentry – I learned – is when a new strong beam is attached to an older, weaker beam to restore its structural integrity – and that seems apt!

I am indebted to the legend that is Gillian Stern for cheerleading this memoir and to Nicci Gerrard who has long kept the faith. Julia Bell, course director of creative writing at Birkbeck, London University, advised the class of 2018 to find our writing tribe. I was lucky enough to find mine with Allison Williams, Dinty Moore and the writers of RYB Tuscany 2021 (especially Tower girls Jessica Ribera and Elita Suratman and photographer Constance Owens). The queen of memoir Cathy Rentzenbrink has been an unfailing supporter and is consistently generous with her wisdom. Another writing group, The Memoir Makers, grew out of a course Cathy led and I am grateful to all these busy writers for the time they took to read the manuscript in whole or in part, providing thoughtful feedback.

The charity Riding for the Disabled was a lifeline for me and I am particularly grateful to Hertfordshire County Coach Margaret Keith and East Region Chair Suzanne Brown for their support, along with all the riders, staff and volunteers of Gaddesden Place RDA. Should you wish to know more, or to buy a handful of oats as a treat for our hard-working ponies, then you can find all the details at www.gaddesdenplacerda.org.uk

Mary Kelly offers a loving home-from-home to Belle, Scarlet and Lulu when I am working or away on my travels while Penny Birch Jones and the team at Platinum Dressage provided a safe and welcoming environment for me to get to know Pablo. Stephen Purdew of Champneys and Tony Diamond helped me maintain such physical fitness as I can lay claim to.

There are so many other family and friends who supported me, some are mentioned by name in the text, others not – for reasons of length or because quiet, empathic support, while crucial, does not move along the narrative. There will also be those whose words and actions were of immense value to me but whom I have over-looked or forgotten due to the extreme emotions I was experiencing. To them, I also offer my thanks.

I consider it the greatest good fortune to be represented by Rory Scarfe of the Blair Partnership, who somehow has an uncanny ability to read my mind.

Sarah Emsley of HarperCollins championed *Perfect Bound* from the outset and together with Imogen Gordon Clark has held my hand throughout what has been a deeply personal and emotional project. I am also indebted to copy editor Nicky Gyopari and to Ellie Game who designed the beautiful cover.

Those we have loved never really die. My beloved husband John Merritt and our daughter Eleanor Merritt live on in my heart and I feel their presence and guidance every day. During the timescale of this book, we also said goodbye to Baroness (Tessa) Jowell, Dr Steve Le Comber, Ellen Levine, Terry

Mansfield, John Potter and Maggie Rae. May they all rest in peace.

The printing presses of life keep rolling and I feel extremely blessed to be connected through Hope to Jamie Potter and Dr Gaynor Potter. I relish the new family bonds we are creating. Cora Eleanor Potter is, rightly, the light of my life and I can only aspire to emulate the example handed to me by my own grandmothers.

But above and beyond all and everything, there is one person whose love, support and constancy I value above all else. Hope Potter, you are, and have so often been, my reason for living. Your father and I named you well.

Thank you!